Penny Kemp has been active in Green Politics for ten years. She was candidate for Maidstone, Kent, in the General Election of 1987 and candidate for Kent East in the European election of 1989, where she scored 19 per cent of the vote; Member of the Green Party Council from 1986 to 1989; Convenor of the Media Committee for the Green Party Council from 1987 to 1988; and one of the three co-chairs of the UK Green Party from 1988 to 1989. She is a freelance writer and teacher and has written articles for local papers and national magazines. She was contributor to *The Sanitary Protection Scandal*, published in 1989, and to *Under the Rainbow* (with Hilary Wainwright, Ken Livingstone, Frieder Otto Wolf and others) to be published. Together with Pierre Junquin and Frieder Otto Wolf, she is one of the contributors to *For a Green Alternative in Europe*, which is to be published in Britain in 1991 and translated into several languages.

Derek Wall has been active in Green Politics since 1979. He was Member of the Ecology Party Council on the Elections Committee from 1983 to 1984; Organizer of the University of London Green Group from 1983 to 1986; candidate for Bath against Chris Patten, MP, in the General Election of 1987; and candidate for Bristol in the European Election of 1989. He is also one of the three European Speakers of the party who present the green case to the media in the run-up to the Euro-elections and has recently been re-elected to the Green Party Council. He is a lecturer in economics and contributes regularly to local papers and national magazines. He has written *Getting There – Towards a Green Society*, published in 1990.

Penny Kemp and Derek Wall

A Green Manifesto for the 1990s

Penguin Books

PENGUIN BOOKS

Published by the Penguin Group
Penguin Books Ltd, 27 Wrights Lane, London W8 5TZ, England
Viking Penguin, a division of Penguin Books USA Inc.
375 Hudson Street, New York, New York 10014, USA
Penguin Books Australia Ltd, Ringwood, Victoria, Australia
Penguin Books Canada Ltd, 2801 John Street, Markham, Ontario, Canada L3R 1B4
Penguin Books (NZ) Ltd, 182–190 Wairau Road, Auckland 10, New Zealand

Penguin Books Ltd, Registered Offices: Harmondsworth, Middlesex, England

First published 1990
10 9 8 7 6 5 4 3 2 1

Printed and bound on recycled paper
in England by
Clays Ltd, St Ives plc
Filmset in 10/12 pt Monotype Sabon

For Tracy Annabel and Cora Nadine

To Francis Ona: keep up the good work. When you have
won, can we come down and have a chat about things?

To Green revolutionaries from Papua to Paris,
Portsmouth to Portland: keep going!

How to be green? Many people have asked us this important question. It's really very simple and requires no expert knowledge or complex skills. Here's the answer.

Consume less. Share more. Enjoy life.

CONTENTS

Acknowledgements

Many people have encouraged us; a few have thwarted us; and a few thought it an impossible task. But without the excellent research work done by many organizations this book would have been difficult to put together.

For helping us with research our thanks go to Peter Tatchell, Steve Cowan, Nina Baker, John Morrissey, Duncan MacDuffie, Mark Kinzley, David Taylor, Brig Oubridge, Ann Darnborough, Ben Whitwell, Richard Lawson, Chris Rose, Liz Sheppard, John Gribbin, Angela Henderson, Doug Holly, Charter 88, Shelter, Child Poverty Action Group and Peter Barnett. As always, Ian Coates helped to develop our ideas and gently pushed us into new areas.

New Internationalist kindly let us use material, and we owe a considerable intellectual debt to those who have put forward policy to the 'Green Party Manifesto for a Sustainable Society', from Dr Peter Allen onwards. Ted Trainer, Allen Roberts and Murray Bookchin also deserve thanks; without their efforts our thinking and that of other Greens would be considerably diminished.

We thank all those who have read early drafts, especially Ron Bailey, who put lots of work into the chapters on democracy and social justice and the conclusion; our parents; Richard Lawson; the animal rights policy working group, including Tina Pye, Allen Stevens and others; Chris Turner; Pete Taylor; David Taylor; Angela Henderson; Joyce Millington; David Batchelor; our sympathetic editor, Ravi Mirchandani, for his encouragement and help with putting the project together; David Icke for his ideas.

We both share houses with others, are members of local Green parties and have friends and family who have supported us and put up with our foibles while we were writing this book. We thank East Bristol Green Party (Pete, Sam, Calvin, Bob, Dianne, Hilary and Martin and the rest) for putting up with absences from activity and for 'getting it done' with an enthusiasm that puts others to shame;

Sheena Anderson for putting up with the bass on Ska records; and, of course, the Specials, Buzzcocks, X-Ray Spex and the other exponents of loud, raucous and somewhat old music that is needed to jolt the brain into productive activity; Maidstone Green Party (Sue, Keith, Kizzy, Steve, Jan, Jim, Chris and the others who have encouraged and been extremely patient); and, finally, the 2.5 million people who had enough faith in the Green Party to register a vote because without them this book would not have been commissioned.

P.K.
D.W.
March 1990

1 GREEN ROOTS

Green politics is radical in the sense that, to solve any problem, one must go to its roots. To be effective and get to the roots of the ecological crisis Green has to be political. Greens (with a capital G) believe in a new kind of politics of harmony and justice that demands an end to poverty, the introduction of ecological economics, a revitalized and transformed National Health Service (NHS), disarmament, real democracy and much else besides. The substitution of green rhetoric for green policies will not work despite the fact that everything and everyone has seemingly gone green. The membership of groups such as Greenpeace and Friends of the Earth has rocketed. Publishers issue handfuls of new books about the environment. Those giants of consumerism and waste, the out-of-town supermarkets, compete to produce the most ecological forms of washing powder and sell the greatest quantity of free-range eggs. National newspapers that formerly backed Mrs Thatcher with hardly a murmur of criticism now give the Greens a sympathetic hearing. Everybody has changed colour a shade or two. Trade unions campaign against the dumping of PCBs and strike against nuclear power. The monarchy plays its role, with Prince Charles pushing for humane architecture and beginning to convert his vast Duchy of Cornwall estates to organic agriculture. More of us than ever before recycle our paper and cook with additive-free tins of beans. Today even the politicians say that they are green.

Conservatives claim to be true 'friends of the Earth'. Mrs Thatcher picks up litter; Chris Patten pushes his 'Green Bill'; and young Conservatives up and down Britain no doubt do their bit. Maggie's turquoise tendency sees green politics as synonymous with conservation, heritage and English values but can live with leaky atomic submarines, cracked nuclear power stations, new motorways and a thriving arms-export industry. Sadly, although there are genuine environmentalists within the ranks of the Conservative party, Mrs

Thatcher, the only political leader in living memory who refuses to board a train, is not among them; her revolution has been for commerce, not the countryside. The Green Party's commitment to ending poverty and increasing local democracy gains little sympathy in No. 10 Downing Street. Eco-Thatcherism is a concept that rings hollow after a decade of increasing environmental degradation, declining water quality and support for nuclear technology. While marketing advisers suggest that the present government must become 'greener' in appearance to retain electoral support, the Cabinet remains motivated by the needs of capital rather than those of the planet.

Labour claims to be even greener while retaining a commitment to nuclear weapons, increased economic growth and a traditional enthusiasm for the 'white-hot heat of the technological revolution'. The Democrats, in their previous Liberal incarnation, could at least honestly claim to be the greenest of the ungreen, as they were the one party to criticize economic growth and firmly reject nuclear power, but the arrival of the SDP and renewed support for Trident and NATO have robbed former Liberals of those early eco-credentials. Yet while Paddy Ashdown rejected the real Greens as 'Calvinists' and 'eco-Fascists', thereby recycling all the clichés about medievalism and the politics of the palaeolithic cave dweller, other Democrats were far more positive. Green Democrats put a motion to their conference congratulating the Green Party on their strong showing in the Euro-elections, going on to note, 'Our Green Democrat members, especially those who formed the Liberal Ecology Group in the Seventies, have never regarded the Greens, then the Ecology Party, as irrelevant, illiberal and unrealistic. We reject unwarranted and dismissive statements from our leading policy theorists in that vein.'

But few attack the Greens outright. Most politicians recognize the real concerns underlying the popularity of the Green Party, which make any assault upon them appear to be a dismissal of worries about pollution, food adulteration and the destruction of nature. Instead of rejecting ecology, they have tried to become greener than the Greens. The Greens, by taking money away from industry via consumer boycotts and votes away from the conventional parties at election time, have managed to lever ecological concerns on to the agenda. Green politics cannot simply be tacked on to old-fashioned ideologies. The likes of Mrs Thatcher and Neil Kinnock cannot just apply paint and gain the green vote. Green politics is not a transitory phenomenon, a protest vote or Euro-flash in the pan; it is a mass movement with strong practical and intellectual roots. And the Greens are growing not just in Britain but right across the world.

Many see green politics as an instant invention of the late 1980s, but political action on ecology can be traced back to 1974, when René Dumont, a professor of agronomy, stood on behalf of 100 local groups as their candidate for the French presidency. Although Dumont received only a small percentage of the vote, French ecologists grew from strength to strength, electing hundreds of councillors in a period when the then UK Ecology Party still numbered its members in tens rather than thousands. Other Greens were active in the radical PSU, or Socialist Unity Party, while in the late 1970s ecologists, feminists, regionalists, supporters of non-violent direct action and others stood in local elections under the joint banner of *Front Autogestionnaire*. In 1980 another presidential candidate, Brice Lalonde, polled over 1 million votes and was the first political ecologist to be on the receiving end of international attention. Sadly, such early success was short-lived: the Greens split into a number of factional groups that often competed electorally; the Mitterrand government continued to support the expansion of the country's domestic nuclear-power programme (one of the largest in the world) and the retention of an independent nuclear-weapons capability; the charismatic and politically impatient Lalonde first joined a Social Democratic list before finally defending nuclear tests in the Pacific as a socialist minister. The Greens forgot much of their earlier sophistication, becoming probably the least imaginative and least successful green party in Western Europe. Despite internal problems, including financial troubles and an unfavourable climate of opinion, most French Greens managed to unite around a single candidate and did respectably in the 1988 presidential elections. Gains were also made in the following spring's municipal elections, when Jeans-Loris Vial became the first Green councillor in Paris. Greens did particularly well in Brittany, where widespread fear of sea and river pollution from factory farming and industry paralleled such concern in Britain. More stable as a party than ever before, and with nearly 11 per cent of the votes in the 1989 European elections, the success of Les Verts seems likely to continue.

Although West Germany's Die Grünen entered the electoral arena six years after Dumont's pioneering effort, they were the first to make green politics really succeed. Despite well-publicized splits between 'realos' (who favour an alliance with the Social Democrats) and 'fundis' or fundamentalists (who don't), conservatives and radicals, 'alternative' and 'conventional' leftists, and other obscure fissions, they have played a far more important role in the propagation of alternative politics than any other green party. State funding of political parties in Germany has enabled them to mount successful political, ecological and social campaigns; consequently, they are the richest green party in the world. With large numbers of members elected to all levels of government, it seems that they will be a permanent feature of the German political scene. With a cooling of the dispute between 'realos' and the 'fundis' it is likely that they will govern the country as a part of a red–green coalition at some point in the near future.

There are many accounts of the German Greens, and it would be impossible to record their history in detail here, but it is worth noting that they were the first ecological party fully to take on board wider political concerns that showed that environmental salvation, if it were to be effected, had to go hand in hand with nuclear disarmament, social justice and an end to Third World poverty. Their programme (and that of the green movement worldwide) is best summarized in a four-part agreement that united former conservatives such as Herbert Gruhl (originally a Christian Democrat representative who crossed the floor to create the world's first parliamentary Green Party, albeit with one member only), leftists and ex-members of the Free Democrats and SPD, committing the Greens to 'ecology, social justice, decentralization and non-violence'. Interestingly, rather than being founded as a national party with a single office in Bonn and centrally supervised membership lists, the German Greens have evolved from dozens of regional, city-based and even local alternative factions and parties. These, with such evocative titles as the *bunte Liste* ('colourful or green lists'), *Grün-Alternative-Liste* or *Grüne Aktion Zukunft* ('green action for the future party'), have, along with groups opposed to nuclear power and broad-based citizens' initiatives of all kinds, gradually coalesced into an effective political force without losing the elements of local diversity. The Greens have constantly done well in elections, electing their first group of parliamentarians after the 1983 general election and maintaining an elected presence in virtually all of the West German *Länder*. Die Grünen, although volatile, have managed to link immigrants, farmers worried by threats to their land, former conservatives, libertarian leftists, peace people and a variety of other activists more successfully than any other ecological party in Europe.

The Greens have also been successful in neighbouring Austria, where an eco-socialist grandmother, Frieda Meissener-Blau, entered the electoral contest on their behalf, fighting the 1986 presidency primarily to prevent protest votes from going to a neo-Fascist fringe candidate by default. Since then Greens have been elected in most of the Austrian provinces, and the party has campaigned strongly on behalf of minority groups and against the re-emergence of the far right. With eight members in the present parliament, the Greens have maintained constant pressure on the governing grand coalition of conservatives and social democrats and have proposed many pieces of eco-legislation, some of which (including demands for environmental damage to be allowed for while calculating economic growth) have been accepted.

The movement has always been strong in Belgium, cooperating across the cultural divide that separates Flemish and French speakers. Agalev, the Flemish speakers' party, derives from a Christian group that emphasized life-style change. Both Agalev and its French sister party, Ecolo, have had representatives returned to the national parliament since the early 1980s. Former investigative journalist and Green Member of the European Parliament (MEP) Paul Staess provided much of the evidence against the nuclear industry in the Euratom scandal over the misappropriation of high-level radioactive waste. Paul Staess was also arrested by the British police outside the Queen Elizabeth Conference Hall for taking part in a Greenpeace action against the dumping of British waste in the North Sea, which has blighted Belgian shores. He was instrumental in stopping the half-baked scheme to build toxic-waste islands in the North Sea, a plan approved at the time by both the Belgian and the British government. Other Green actions have included a mass cycle ride to the Belgian parliament by newly elected representatives.

Greens in neighbouring Luxembourg have split disastrously along personality lines. Wherever Greens have perversely put their trust in strong leaders (France, Luxembourg and New Zealand) they have swiftly come to grief.

While the Dutch Green Party is tiny and received a mere 0.2 per cent of votes in the 1988 general election, the Green Left coalition, which comprises a number of radical, left and Christian groups, has been far more successful at picking up votes and seats in recent elections. Given the amount of flood damage that any rise in sea level would do, concern about green issues in general and the greenhouse effect in particular runs high among the Dutch electorate. The pre-election coalition of Liberals and Christian Democrats was the first government in the world to fall over an ecological issue (funding for pollution controls and conservation taxes). The incoming government, and virtually all the parties bar the right-wing Liberals and neo-Fascistic Centrum, are committed to sweeping environmental reforms to combat the dangers of global warming. As early as 1979 the Radical Party, which had evolved from the Christian Democrats on a programme of sustainable economics and disarmament, held a place in the European-wide coordination of green and radical parties. Together with the dynamic Pacifist Socialist Party, Evangelical Christians (not of the Billy Graham variety) and, most controversially, the Dutch Communists, a Green/Rainbow alliance won several seats in the European Parliament in the 1984 and 1989 European elections. This grouping, which has shown that it is possible for both radical Protestant and radical Catholic parties to work with reds and greens, is now recognized by the European Coordination of Greens as the official Dutch group. Smaller numbers of Greens have remained independent, and local green groups and parties are active throughout the country.

In Finland the Greens have put much of their energy into defending and extending the rights of disabled people, putting forward a wheelchair-bound candidate as one of their first political representatives. In neighbouring Sweden twenty-one Green representatives were elected to the National Parliament in 1988. In Norway and Denmark the small green parties that do exist have been far less prominent, given the support of politicians such as Norwegian premier Brundtland for ecological transformation. The Danish Greens have campaigned with great effect for organic farmers.

The Irish Green Alliance surprised everyone by electing a deputy in the Dublin Central constituency in the 1989 general election, while a strong and swiftly growing group of activists, which has links both with the Republic and with Britain, compromises the Northern Irish Green Party. The Greens in Eire picked up 61,041 votes in the Euro-elections, gaining 3.8 per cent of the vote by comparison with Sinn Fein's 2.3 per cent. In the North the vote was far lower but still ahead of that for the Workers' Party, which has seats in Dublin, and two Labour candidates.

In the Latin countries green politics has been slower to get started, but it has begun to play a prominent role in Spain and Italy. Spanish eco-regionalists coexist uneasily with a national Madrid-based party, together bravely opposing bull-fighting with graphic poster campaigns. Both groups have fallen into dispute with radical Basques, who have tried to push the Greens into supporting their armed and often bloody struggle for regional autonomy. Despite their rejection of such ungreen violence most Greens in the country see themselves as supporters of a Basque, Catalonian or Andalusian party rather than a Spanish one.

Green politics in Italy is also diverse and extremely difficult to get to grips with. After the 1989 European elections four different political factions joined the Green group in Strasbourg. The oldest, the Democratic Proletariat (DP), originated in the 1970s as a fusion of two older left parties and has combined a socialist agenda with green concerns. A second left grouping, the Rainbow List, which hoped to link DP, the Greens and other left/alternative parties, also gained elected MEPs. At the same time the official Green Party List saw elected members. Finally an anti-prohibition candidate, elected on a platform that advocated legalizing cannabis and removing restrictions on the sale of alcohol and cigarettes, became part of the group. Members of the Pythonesque Radical Party, whose candidates have included post-Marxist and fugitive Professor Tony Negri, striptease artist La Cicciolina and former British Liberal leader David Steel and who left the original coordination of green and radical parties (founded in 1980) because other Green MEPs found them 'too chaotic to work with', are again cooperating on some issues with the Euro-parliamentary grouping. Matters are perhaps even more confused in the arena of strictly domestic Italian politics, where just about every party, from the Communists to the Christian Democrats, has filled its parliamentary ranks with environmentalists in response to the rise of the Greens. Whether such diversity and eco-pluralism will ultimately turn out for the best and lead to a re-orientation of the Italian political spectrum on an ecological basis or will merely divide Greens against each other is an open question. What is certain is the strength of green politics in Italy. Having originated as a loose network rather than an ecology party with national pretensions, as in Britain or France, the

Italian Greens came together for the 1987 general election to elect thirteen deputies. The vote in Rome doubled to 7 per cent in October 1989, putting local Greens into fourth place above the ailing neo-Fascist MSI. Hundreds of Greens have been elected on a local level and, despite a relatively late start, have shown that the potential of green politics in southern Europe is just as strong as in Britain or Germany.

There is green political activity of some sort in virtually every part of Europe, although green consciousness has yet to penetrate Albania, the last bastion of Stalinism, or the whale-hunting Faröe Islands. Green politics, although a rather white and Eurocentric phenomenon at first sight, has grown on a global basis. There are Greens on every continent, in the urban jungles of the newly industrialized countries, among Indian peasants and even above the Arctic Circle in Sweden and Canada. The Greens are everywhere.

If Europe is the home of parliamentary eco-politics, Australia can claim to be the intellectual centre of the movement. Australian writers and activists have put most thought into developing a coherent and effective alternative. In the late 1970s an unusually politicized and effective Friends of the Earth produced the first – and for many years the only – detailed guide to green strategy under the title 'Changing the Cogs'. Ted Trainer has produced perhaps the most devastating critique of the ecological crisis and the present economic system, arguing that we have to set limits on human greed or face extinction as a species. Boris Frankel, coming from an eco-socialist perspective, has subjected the ideas of green visionaries like Gorz and Bahro to critical but constructive scrutiny, showing how the foundations of a green economy might be built. Alan Roberts, in his book *The Self-managing Environment*, examines the roots of the ecological crisis to show that greed and over-consumption are often forms of compensation within a system that neither gives us much control over our work nor allows us to develop as creative, fulfilled human beings; he condemns both capitalism and state-run economies as innately flawed.

Green politics in Australia also has a very practical side. Links between trade unionists and Greens have been strong since the Builders' Labourers' Federation, led by Jack Mundy, introduced the concept of 'green bans', whereby workers took action not just to improve pay and conditions but in defence of the natural environment.

In short, the builders refused to work on new developments that ate into areas of wilderness and beauty that local communities wanted to conserve, and Mundy was arguing, a decade before the British Trades Union Congress came to similar conclusions: 'In a modern society, trade unions must broaden their vision and horizons and become involved in wide-ranging social, political and environmental activities ... Not only has the trade-union movement the right to intervene, it has the responsibility to do so.' Greens in the United Tasmania Party, the first Australasian green party founded to fight the destruction of the rainforests in a fashion complementary to Mundy's activity in New South Wales, came within 200 votes of electing an MP in 1972. Both the Tasmanian Party and the activities of green trade unionists were severely curtailed by opposition from state and federal government, the trade-union hierarchy and business interests.

Australian Greens have had to cope with the kind of opposition normally associated more with the pre-*glasnost* Soviet bloc than with a supposed democracy. The now world-famous green bans linked trade unionists with 'middle-class' environmentalists. This unlikely alliance began in 1971, when a group of women banded together to fight to save the last remaining bushland on the Parramatta river, and the union backed them. Mundy described it as 'an alliance between the enlightened middle class from Hunters Hill and the enlightened working class from the NSW Builders' Labourers' Federation joined in common environmental struggle'. After attempts by the New South Wales government to break the power of the green bans failed, Jack Mundy said, 'If I had accepted only some of the bribes offered to me during the four years of the green bans [1971–5], I would be a multimillionaire today. It shot home to me the corrupt nature of late industrial capitalism in general and the widespread nature of corruption in New South Wales in particular.'

Years later a greenish Sydney City Council, including Jack Mundy as a member, pursued his philosophy of opposing destructive development so successfully that it was sacked by the state government. A left Labour Prime Minister, Gough Whitlam, opposed to nuclear weapons and committed to Aboriginal land rights, was unseated in 1975 after a series of *Spycatcher*-type machinations, only to be followed by later Labour administrations committed to the retention of all things nuclear and only lukewarm to Aborigine demands. Members of the governing Labour Party hinted in 1987 that they would exert more pressure on the rainforests if the Greens dared to field candidates against them in the coming general election. Such manoeuvres are linked with the oppression, and often the genocidal extermination, of the Aborigines, showing that those who have stood in the way of 'progress' have traditionally been given a very hard time.

Despite the tough nature of Australian politics the Greens are gathering strength and creeping into positions of influence. After the dissolution of the United Tasmania Party a campaign of opposition to the destruction of the rainforests, based on a robust strategy of direct action (with celebrities like David Bellamy and deep ecologist John Seed chaining themselves to trees), led to the formation of a new Tasmanian Green Party, which won enough seats in 1989 to force the state Labour Party into coalition government and into halting the damage.

Green politics in New Zealand, despite a gentler political system, has been far less successful. In 1973 ecologists who based their principles on the ideas propagated by the UK magazine the *Ecologist* founded the Values Party on a programme entitled 'A Blueprint for New Zealand'. The party grew fast only to collapse equally swiftly. Personality squabbles and leadership controversies, the growth of Social Credit (an SDP-like grouping that siphoned off votes), a strongly anti-nuclear Labour government and a failure to make the links between ecological politics and social movements all contributed to this failure. The party, now refounded as Green Alternative and with stronger links with the native Maori population, still exists; it will be interesting to see whether it can regain support on the basis of the strength of its Australian neighbours and the world-wide explosion of interest in Green politics.

The path to green growth has also been somewhat twisting in North America, although from Mexico to northern Canada there are Greens working actively for change. Like Australia, North America has been a centre for green political thought; writers such as Kirkpatrick Sale and Murray Bookchin have argued cogently for a green alternative. But, given Democrat/Republican dominance over the democratic process and the millions of dollars needed to fight any kind of effective electoral campaign even on a local level, the Greens have firmly rejected the idea of a single USA-wide party and have kept out of presidential contests. United by the journal *Synthesis*, local groups coordinate national activities and common policy. Cells known as 'committees of correspondence' are based on groups of the same name that conspired to defeat the British in the 1776 War of Independence. US Greens are particularly keen to learn from the failure of the left to build a socialist party in the early part of this century. They put a premium on democracy and have been inspired by the anarchist Murray Bookchin, who believes that they should recreate the direct democracy of post-independence New England, where townsfolk would gather to make decisions at large public meetings rather than trusting elected representatives and bureaucrats. Bookchin, who places himself within the left Green network, likes to use the term 'social ecology' to indicate his displeasure with the deep ecologists, whom he criticizes in brilliant but not always helpful polemic.

The deep ecologists – while not necessarily antagonistic to Bookchin's approach, which combines ecology with campaigns against social deprivation, racism and inequality – argue that ecological politics is about protecting the planet rather than helping people. Deep ecologists, who regard humanity as just one species among many, reject human activities if they harm other creatures. By opposing 'less enlightened' ecologists as anthropocentric (i.e. human-centred) they have caused immense controversy. One deep ecology group, Earth First!, espouses dramatic direct action, which includes the sabotage of vehicles posed to destroy wilderness and the hammering of huge metal pins into trees threatened by the chainsaw. Less savoury elements of Earth First! ideology include extreme neo-Malthusian praise for diseases like AIDS, for famine and for other maladies that reduce human numbers (but, presumably, don't kill the editors of deep ecology newsletters). Deep ecologists argue that Greens should beware leftists who are determined to use ecology as a vehicle for their own goals rather than being prepared to learn from ecology. They emphasize that there is a difference between genuine love for the planet and the approach of 'shallow ecologists' who are concerned merely with the conservation of resources as a form of rational economic management for human gain. There is also evidence that deep ecologists have been infiltrated by both the CIA and far-right groups that, while supporting the culling of Third World populations, are less interested in looking after nature.

Most Greens in North America take on board elements from both deep and social ecology, arguing that while the natural world should not be subjected to the whims of just one species, social and economic pressures on that species have to be tackled if the destruction of the natural world is to stop. Bookchin himself has argued, 'the movement must realize that the idea of dominating nature ... stems from the domination of humans by humans' (*Green Synthesis*, No. 28, September 1988, p. 12). Another activist in the same issue of the magazine argues, 'This useless bickering between social ecologists and deep ecologists must stop,' claiming that the two forms of domination are equally significant.

The green movement has been influential in the Soviet Union and the Eastern Bloc, with green representatives elected from the Baltic states, a significant green party in Estonia and a strong post-Chernobyl anti-nuclear movement in the Ukraine. One fifth of the population of Lithuania signed a petition against the building of a new nuclear power station, and parliamentarians in Moscow, like politicians in Britain, clamour to be greener than their colleagues. According to the *Economist* (4 November 1989), 'Green feelings now run as deep, and are as politically challenging, as anywhere in the world.' The Soviet Union suffers from a range of problems that fuel such feelings: industry produces 60 million tonnes of atmospheric pollution each year; nearly one third of the population of Leningrad suffers from respiratory diseases; 175 million people live in areas of acute environmental damage, according to the head of biology at the Academy of Sciences.

The worst scandal is that of the fast disappearing Aral Sea in Uzbekistan, an Asian republic whose 'internationalist duty' was to produce cotton. The same issue of the *Economist* reported:

Once the world's fourth biggest lake, it has lost over half of its water in the past twenty years. The last fish died in 1983; fishing villages lie abandoned 40 miles from the receding coast; large ships lie beached on the giant salt flats that were once the seabed ... Every year 75,000 tonnes of salt and dust are picked up by the winds from the dry seabed of the Aral and blown over the cotton fields. It will require billions of roubles merely to prevent the fields becoming deserts by the end of the century – by which time the Aral will be a series of salty puddles.

The extinction of the Aral is likely to make the climate of Central Asia hotter and drier, exacerbating the greenhouse effect. Already this crisis of nature kills Soviet citizens: two thirds of those living in the Kara-Kalpak republic suffer from liver disorders, typhoid and cancer of the oesophagus. Many children die within one year of birth. The importance of green politics is self-evident to millions of people who cannot get unpolluted water and are forced to drink what is essentially dilute pesticide solution – and all because of a grandiose, and unsuccessful, scheme for cotton.

There are five main green groups that operate throughout the vast country. The largest of these is the Social-Ecological Union (SEU), with 200 branches under its umbrella, which believes that 'ecological problems can be solved only through political change'. A more strictly environmentalist organization, the Ecological Union, broke from the SEU in 1988, while the Ecological Society of the Soviet Union is linked to the right-wing nationalist movement Pamyat, and the ill-named All-Union Movement of Greens is supported by the Communist Party's Youth Wing. An Ecological Foundation wants to set up an ecological bank, using payments from polluters to clean up toxic waste and promote alternative energy. Numerous local groups campaign and mount Greenpeace-style actions against environmental damage. Most of the popular fronts that exist in every Soviet republic, from Leningrad in the West to Vladivostock in the Siberian east, which press for political, cultural and economic autonomy, began as green lobbies. It is interesting that the Greens' greatest concerns after the environment are democracy, decentralization and regional autonomy, whether in British Columbia, Moldavia or Ireland.

Green politics in East Germany, with its strong links between peace, ecology and Church activism, has paralleled that in the West. Members of New Forum, the group that was instrumental in freeing the East from domination, are close to Die Grünen. Throughout the 1980s, and well before the changes that swept in democracy and demolished the Iron Curtain, many Green activists in the East managed to move westward and have supported Die Grünen. The East German Green Party actively opposes reunification, favouring a confederation of provinces from Saxony to the Saar, and is keen to work with Greens in the West, Czechoslovakia and Poland.

Even before the upheavals that have transformed Eastern Europe Hungarian ecologists, nicknamed the 'Blues' (as in Blue Danube), successfully campaigned against the construction of a huge dam, financed in part by Austria, which would have destroyed vast areas of forest. They too are developing into a green political party now that Eastern Europe is opening up its doors to democracy. In Poland, perhaps the primary source of acid rain and certainly the most polluted country in Europe, environmental concerns are very much on the population's mind, and the Green movement is growing fast. The small non-political ecology club of Kraków, which drew in a number of scientists, has now evolved into a fully fledged green party and has the backing of Greens right across Europe.

Bulgaria's Ecoglasnost group sparked off a revolution during an international congress. Three meetings were held, each attracting over 1,000 people, and more than 9,000 signatures were collected in support of a petition against the damming of the Mesta river, which would destroy nature reserves and raise the water table around the country's second largest city, Plovdiv. The government's response was to arrest thirty-five members of the organization and attack Mike Power, a UK journalist trying to take photographs. As a result of international pressure and considerable embarrassment over the affair, Bulgarian officials admitted that they had gone too far and even sent a spokes- man to discuss the dam project at one of Ecoglasnost's public meetings (*New Scientist*, 4 November 1989). The organization has since been granted legal status as Bulgaria's first non-governmental organiz- ation and is playing a major role in the post-Stalinist state. A Green Party, founded in December 1989 with a starting membership of 1,000 and fifteen branches, is now thriving. A year ago it would have seemed just a dream.

All the Eastern bloc countries have managed to establish green parties, including Czechoslovakia, where Lubos Benniak, a journalist with the popular *Mlady Svet* or 'Young World' newspaper, noted, 'Air pollution, more than the existence of the Iron Curtain, brought about the revolution.' In Romania environmental concerns were also important in bringing people on to the streets, Ceauşescu's plans to demolish thousands of traditional villages and rehouse their popu- lations in concrete agricultural collectives fuelled the explosion of popular feeling that blew his power away. Ceauşescu, no lover of nature, was famed for his bloody hunting trips, during which *apparatchiks* would often drug animals to make them easier targets for his rather shaky aim. Neglect on the part of Communist authorities has also led to the destruction of the Danube delta, once home to thousands of pelicans and formerly the greatest wetland in Eastern

Europe, now severely contaminated with mercury and radioactive waste. Following the revolution an appeal signed by 5,000 people has led to the formation of an effective green movement, the Miscarea Ecological (ME), which the actor Ion Carmitu (a member of the interim National Salvation government) intends to transform into a fully fledged political party.

Despite liberalization the growth of green politics behind what used to be the Iron Curtain will not be easy, though economic reforms that reduce the power of the central planners and give local councils a say will help, both by banishing gigantic and dangerous projects such as new hyper-dams and nuclear power stations and by letting people control industry more directly. Modernization may help Soviet industry's smokestacks belch a little more cleanly, but political change will prompt contradictory demands for a clean environment and Western-style consumerism. Ecological movements, while they are spreading through Eastern Europe, are in a very difficult and delicate position. On the one hand pollution problems are particularly severe because of a run-away nuclear power programme and little control of industrial emissions; on the other, individuals in the East want more factories and more growth so as to emulate the perceived opulence of Western consumer society. While *glasnost* has provided an opportunity for Greens to organize out in the open, they may find such contradictions difficult to reconcile.

One way in which the West has managed to bridge the gap between growth and conservation is to export the production of the most highly pollutant goods to newly industrializing countries like Singapore, Taiwan and Brazil. According to Martiner-Alier, a dissident economist from Chile, the Third World has most to gain from a green revolution that would reallocate resources currently used to fuel First World greed to the Third World, where they might be used to meet real needs.

The knot of deep versus social ecology can be cut by Third World Greens such as the Chipko movement in India, which recognizes that colonialism and post-independence equivalents have exploited both the environment and indigenous people and that social justice has to go hand in hand with ecological concern. Third World peoples are on the frontline and suffer most from the destruction of the environment that is caused, more often than not, by the First World. Consequently green movements in the less developed countries are growing fast.

The Consumers' Association of Penang opposes Malaysia's destruction of the environment, while Mrs Thatcher, as a 'friend of the Earth', has been keen to sell the Malaysian government military equipment that helps it to quash rebellion among those who oppose the logging of their rainforest homes.

In north India the Chipko movement protects trees by literally hugging them to prevent the onslaught of the developers' chainsaws and resulting soil erosion, floods and geological instability. Further south, in Karnataka, a group of penniless fishermen banded together during the 1989 general election campaign that unseated Rajiv Gandhi to field the ageing author Shivaram Karanth as India's first Green candidate. Although he was 89 and spent the election campaign receiving medical treatment at an American hospital, he gained 10 per cent of the vote.

In Brazil a strong Green Party works in cooperation with the left-wing Workers' Party to protect the rainforests and to aid the poor. Brazilian trade unionists do not necessarily see a contradiction between their jobs and the conservation of the rainforests and have been at the forefront of ecological campaigns to protect the Amazon. Chico Mendes, a member of the Workers' Party and green supporter, organized a union of forest people, comprising both rubber tappers and forest-dwelling Indians, to show that the forest could meet their economic needs and, far from standing in the way of 'progress', guarantee the prosperity of both groups. But multinational companies, military-backed governments and large owners of land are more likely to use lead than logic to win their side of the argument. Chico Mendes was assassinated in December 1988 by a member of the landowners' union who wanted to clear and ranch the forests. Members of the Brazilian Green party fear that the military would step in if they achieved electoral success.

In Nicaragua the Sandinistas have argued that their revolution against the Somoza regime has been not just a blow for the people but an event that 'the whole of natural creation cried out for', firmly linking popular struggle with ecological concerns, programmes for soil conservation, national rainforest parks and chemical-free agriculture.

Greens and ecological reformers are beaten up, tortured and killed for their beliefs in some of the poorest and most oppressed countries of the world. The natural wealth of their countries is ripped out, leaving them and the environment poorer, local elites more powerful and we in the wealthier countries smugger than ever with our king-size prawns, out-of-season strawberries from Kenya and mahogany toilet seats from rainforest woods. While there is no contradiction between environmental protection and real development, Greens and their allies face difficult tactical choices. Can Greens remain non-violent under the threat of torture and starvation or does armed struggle, even in defence of justice, lead inevitably to an accelerating cycle of violent chaos? Greens have yet to develop a strategy for liberating the most oppressed and often forget that those with power, wealth and, above all, ownership of the land are unlikely to give it back to the poor or to Mother Nature.

Friends of the Earth in Surrey or Sheffield rarely connect their worries with those of working-class families devastated by the pollution of industrial production, landless peasants starving while their landlords send cash crops to Western tables and indigenous groups under threat of genocide. This said, Greens are active in even the poorest countries, and many liberation movements, including the Eritreans and the Nicaraguans, are beginning to take more of their ideology from ecologists than from old-style socialists.

The overtly green Bougainville Revolutionary Army (BRA) is the most dramatic sign that ecological politics is being integrated with the struggles of the poor. Based on a lush, forested island to the north of Papua New Guinea, its objective is to close down the vast copper mine opened up by a subsidiary of Rio Tinto Zinc, which has devastated the land and displaced local people. BRA's founder, an ex-surveyor employed by the mining company, is asking for $11.5 billion to be paid to the island by RTZ and for local, decentralized self-rule. He now has a price of $200,000 dollars on his head and is hiding in one of the remaining areas of rainforest. By blowing up pylons the self-styled army has stopped copper extraction and put both the Papuan and the Australian government very much on the defensive.

The BRA's violent tactics may put it beyond the ecological pale, but green politics certainly has a wide geographical range. It also has clear intellectual roots, and these need to be examined to clarify what green politics is, rather than what those outside the movement (including journalists and advertising consultants) would have it become.

The first element of green politics can be found in the science of ecology and in a vision of the almost inevitable destruction of our planet by ourselves. The first Greens were not peasants, workers or political activists (nor, for that matter, concerned Conservative house-wives) but scientists forced into building a political movement by fear of their own data. Green politics is above all the politics of survival. It is about not simply the conservation of natural beauty or the preserva-tion of amenities but the combating of dangers that could devastate the planet and perhaps destroy its higher forms of life. As early as 1948 people argued that it would be impossible to maintain ever-increasing economic growth without causing ecological damage. Such concerns crystallized into the 'Limits to Growth' report, which noted that exponential growth was leading to the exhaustion of mineral resources, over-population, pollution and the removal of natural habitats necessary to maintain the planet's life-support system. Not all of the report was accurate, but for many it was just too terrifying to be ignored; while it could not predict the future, it certainly identified a highly destructive trend. It showed that environmental problems were rooted in economic activity and that, if they were to be solved, political change was necessary. Ecology parties were born of the inability of conventional politics to take on environmental con-cerns because they were so wedded to the logic of more and more.

A second root of green politics is social concern, comprising not only the issue of survival but also democracy, justice and freedom from oppression, not just the liberation of nature from excessive human demands but also the liberation of humanity. This concern extends the analysis of the ecologists by showing that ecological politics also needs to understand how economic pressures and the nature of the international financial system perpetuate the cycle of destruction. It draws on a tradition of aberrant and repressed radicals, including the Diggers (so called because they occupied and dug land left fallow by large landowners, while the populace had none, before being slaughtered by Cromwellian troops) and the Owenites (fol-lowers not of David but of William, a reformed industrialist who wanted to set up communities and let workers organize their factories in the nineteenth century), as well as ecological eccentrics such as William Morris and Oscar Wilde, who both argued for socialism with a human and ecological face, Edward Carpenter and perhaps even William Beckford, yet another eccentric who used the wealth created by his forefathers from sugar and exploiting slaves, among other enterprises, to plant a quarter of a million trees around Bath. Such colourful figures argued that there is no contradiction between social justice and the appreciation of natural beauty, while more recent thinkers, such as the late Raymond Williams, have argued that socialism need not be based on violence, centralized state control or hostility to nature. By emphasizing such ideas green politics has put the concerns of some of the most marginal and hidden traditions at the centre of political debate. Those promoting green ideas in the past – the Maoris, the American Indians and other native people who lived in harmony with the planet – have, time after time, been left out of the history books by their victorious oppressors. The Russian Greens, an early twentieth-century league of libertarian peasants, struggled against both the Tsars and the Bolsheviks but have vanished from Soviet chronicles of the Revolution. The alternative movement born of Dubček's Prague Spring and the Parisian students' unrest of 1968 has also been an important complementary strain of green politics.

A third element of green politics is spirituality. While there are Green Christians of all types, Buddhists, Hindus, Muslims and, of course, pagans, all Greens understand that we cannot live by bread (or consumer durables) alone. Greens understand the truth that if human life is defined in purely economic terms, it will be unsatisfactory. Green politics has grown up to counter a conventional wisdom that increasingly sees human beings as economic ends, a politics that measures progress in terms of things rather than feelings. Greens believe that none of us can really be happy, however well fed, clothed and sheltered, without a spiritual outlet, good creative work and the opportunity to be close to nature.

The Green movement is very much a women's movement, and ecofeminists such as Susan Griffin argue that patriarchy and male domination are root causes of environmental catastrophe and that only when men take up their share of domestic work, especially the work of bringing up children, will we be able to achieve a fundamental change. Despite the conservative views of some early ecologists, Greens are committed to sexual emancipation. The UK Green Party strongly supports gay and lesbian liberation. As we have seen, green politics has also attracted supporters of Third World liberation, and aid agencies have increasingly come to take on an ecological orientation.

While many green interests coincide with those of the left, there is division over animal rights. Green concern for nature is framed in

terms not only of preserving natural resources for future generations
but also of nature's own rights. Greens do not believe that the
exploitation of the natural world and other species is right, even if it
brings benefits to humanity. In particular Greens are appalled by
factory farming and vivisection. All Greens argue that we in the West
eat too much meat and obtain it in an unnecessarily cruel and
wasteful way. The majority of Green Party members advocate vegetarianism and veganism as ways of restoring the balance between humanity and nature, improving human health and helping the Third
World. Many members of the Green Party in the UK actively support
the movement for animal liberation. Although they reject violence
against other humans or animals, Greens see nothing wrong with
liberating animals from the clutches of vivisectors or factory farmers.
The Spanish Green Party has caused uproar by opposing bull fighting,
while Japanese members of the Green Earth Federation have argued
that their country's tradition as a whaling nation must end. Being
green may be about trying to live more gently, but it is not about
ignoring pain and suffering because that is electorally expedient or
makes for a quiet life. However controversial it may seem to some,
Green politics equals animal liberation.

Greens are also decentralists who wish to dismantle bureaucracy and
demolish conventional power structures, arguing that for both political
and pragmatic reasons society needs to become more democratic and
locally based. Centralization, which forces people to travel increasingly
long distances to work and community facilities, is a massive waste of
energy, but decentralization is about more than fuel-saving. Greens
believe in empowerment, in breaking up concentrations of financial or
political control. Greens do not feel that it is enough simply to elect
councillors or MPs who will green society; ecological change will come
about only with popular involvement, and people will get involved only
if they have a real say. Greens look at the way in which radical
movements have ended up taking power and controlling the state, only
to be corrupted by it and to form new elites. Although it will be far from
easy to take power, giving it away and creating real decentralization will
be even more difficult. As we have seen, many Greens are regionalists.
From the Spanish eco-regionalists and the ecologically inspired popular
fronts of the Soviet Republics to the bio-regionalists in Vermont and
British Columbia and the ecologists in Central America, all value a
regional identity and the creation of small states rather than large ones.

Greens are critical of big technology as well as big government, although they are far from simplistically anti-science. Ecological advance can come via technology (after all, it would be difficult to build a bike without the relatively sophisticated machines necessary to produce ball bearings and brake wire), but it is not enough to put our faith purely in technology or to forget its side effects. Greens believe that ever-increasing technical prowess can lead to greater capacity to hurt individuals and destroy nature. The more powerful we become as a species, the more dangerous we are to the other inhabitants of planet Earth. Technology needs to be scaled down to human needs and to be balanced with ecological principles. A greener society will demand advances in scientific knowledge, but technological fixes are no solution to problems such as poverty and pollution, which have social causes.

Above everything else, Greens are holistic; they aim to bring together interacting themes and to avoid providing simplistic solutions to complex human problems. The different individuals, groups and strands of thought in green politics, while giving rise to tensions, are generally creative rather than divisive, though there is a danger that groups may regard all the world's problems as symptoms of a single malady for which they have the only cure. For example, it is not enough to attribute all ills to the profit motive, as the Marxist left often tries to, forgetting the issues of patriarchy and the human dominance of nature, which would occur even without capitalism. Nor do New Age groups, which see personal change as the sole way forward, often selling spirituality as a newly packaged religion for the middle classes, have the answer. Green politics is pluralistic.

Combining the insights of both spiritual and political mentors, Greens must beware those who would hijack ecology for their own uses. Some manufacturers see green as merely a new way of promoting greed, a means of selling more washing powder. Many on the right would like to use ecology to promote racism and preserve patterns of inequality, justifying their attitudes by claiming that they are necessary to protect nature. Perhaps even more dangerous than those who use ecology to promote their own politics, often quite unecological, are those who want to depoliticize ecological issues. In fact, nearly everyone tries to wash the colour out of green politics, depoliticizing it so that green becomes little more than a concern for hedges. Yet if we love trees, we have to love people as well and to look at the economic, social and psychological reasons why both are under threat.

2 THE GREENS IN BRITAIN

Ecology as a science was invented by Ernst Heinrich Haeckel in 1869, but its roots can be traced back through William Morris, John Ruskin, Prince Peter Kropotkin, the seventeenth-century Levellers, William Cobbett and even classical writers. It is impossible to do such thinkers justice in a book of this length or to acknowledge adequately their contribution to the development of green politics.

In *The Hope of a New World* Archbishop William Temple wrote in 1940, 'The treatment of the Earth by man the exploiter is not only imprudent but sacrilegious. We are not likely to correct the hideous mistakes in this realm unless we can recover the mystical sense of our one-ness with nature. I labour this precisely because many people think it fantastic. I think it is fundamental to sanity.'

In the early 1960s scientists were so concerned about the destruction of the environment by the activities of the human species that they seriously considered running as a political party under the banner 'Movement for Survival'. However, as they were scientists, not political animals, they contented themselves with messages of concern, which were later picked up by various green parties around the world.

It was Rachel Carson who launched the new ecological age when she shook society with the publication of *The Silent Spring* in 1963. Until then most people had felt that the Earth was large enough to cope with all the forms of pollution that humans were creating. No thought had been given to increasing industrialization and consumption. Rachel Carson showed that the eco-systems of the planet could no longer be relied on to break down or disperse the pesticides and poisons that technology was producing.

In April 1968 the scientific community began to undertake serious research into the effects of technological progress. Thirty eminent scientists and economists met in Rome to discuss the mounting ecological problems of the planet. The group was headed by Dr Aurelio

Peccei, an Italian industrialist, and out of it grew the Club of Rome, which set itself the ambitious task of examining the problems facing humanity. The following were felt to be the most urgent:

poverty in the midst of plenty
the degradation of the environment
loss of faith in institutions
uncontrolled urban spread
insecurity of employment
the alienation of youth
the rejection of traditional values
inflation and other monetary and economic imbalances.

The Club of Rome set up a project to assess the predicament of humankind and engaged the Massachusetts Institute of Technology, which produced the now famous document 'Limits to Growth' in 1972.

At the same time, in the United Kingdom, Edward Goldsmith of the *Ecologist* magazine established a team to examine the same issues. Its conclusions were published in January 1972 under the title 'A Blueprint for Survival', which contained this assertion:

The principal conditions of a stable society − one that to all intents and purposes can be sustained indefinitely while giving optimum satisfaction to its members − are:
1. minimum disruption of ecological processes,
2. maximum conservation of materials and energy,
3. a population in which recruitment equals loss,
4. a social system in which the individual can enjoy, rather than feel restricted by, the first three conditions.

In June of that year the United Nations held in Stockholm a conference based on the findings of Barbara Ward and René Dubos, who had written *Only One Earth* (Penguin, 1972), which endorsed the reports of the Institute and of the *Ecologist*.

British political ecologists were given their initial impetus not by a scientific report but by a soft-porn magazine, *Playboy*, for which Paul Ehrlich had written an article on the destruction of the rainforests. Tony and Leslie Whittaker, solicitors in Coventry, gathered a few friends together to discuss the article and the worsening global crisis. In February 1973 a small political party called People was born.

The Whittakers took the four statements of 'A Blueprint for Survival' as the basis of their political party, and the newly formed People placed an advertisement in the *Coventry Evening Telegraph* announcing its existence and asking for candidates to stand in forthcoming elections. More than fifty people attended the inaugural meeting, which was held in the Midlands.

Edward Goldsmith was one of the founding members of People. Under the influence of his work the party's early literature showed it to be talking boldly. People leaflets indicated the party's clear intention to field 600 candidates at the next election and asked, 'Can we any longer rely on politicians who repeatedly fail to recognize root causes of unrest and disillusion – who place false idols before the electorate and hold out untenable promises to secure re-election?' The *Guardian* took up the story on 6 December 1973 and reported both the birth of People and the fact that forty local groups had been set up around the country. When questioned about its ambitious plans for the election Clive Lord, a group leader and still an active member, replied sceptically, 'No matter how serious the fire, it is no use turning the hosepipe on to it until you have connected the water.'

In any event five candidates stood in the February 1974 general election, plus two affiliated candidates – one independent and one People and Agrarian Party member. They obtained an average of 1.8 per cent of the vote, the highest proportion in Coventry North West, where they gained 3.9 per cent.

The party held its first national conference in June 1974 at Coventry, where its manifesto, 'A Manifesto for Survival', was adopted. The twenty-six-page document was a truly radical one, promoting not only environmentalism but also detailed policies ranging from MPs' salaries to foreign affairs. For instance, it stated, '[The People Party] will have careful regard to the level of remuneration of Members of Parliament compared with that of the average wage earner . . . [The People Party] considers that Parliament should have no other employment connection, since through increased contact with their constituencies, Members will retain a better understanding of economic, social and associated problems.'

That year Britain was in deep political crisis, facing the three-day week and the miners' strike, and the country went to the polls for a second time. Four constituencies were contested by People in October, when its share of the vote fell to 0.7 per cent.

The party's 'Manifesto for a Sustainable Society' was drafted by Peter Allen and adopted after 362 amendments had been put to the 1975 conference. This continually updated document still serves the party today.

Differences over the direction of the party led several of its more active members to leave and join the various pressure groups that were springing up. At the same time People changed its name to the Ecology Party. In the years 1974–6 the party engaged in little national activity, but local groups continued to flourish. The national arena was occupied by independent pressure groups such as Friends of the Earth, Greenpeace and the anti-nuclear organizations that regarded their role as non-party-political. The one exception, the Campaign for Nuclear Disarmament, supported not People or the Ecology Party but the Labour Party. Today many members of CND regret that early partnership, as they have seen Labour modify its politics in order to gain electoral advantage. (Whether this strategy will work is, of course, another matter.) Labour had formed its own internal environmental group, the Socialist Environmental and Resources Association (SERA), in 1973, and the Liberals' Ecology Group emerged in 1977.

By April 1977 the Ecology Party's newsletter reported a membership of 200 and an annual income of approximately £600. Even so, seventeen candidates stood in the May election, and over 5,000 people voted for ecology, with Cornish candidates attracting a massive 17 per cent of the vote. At the 1977 Birmingham conference the constitution of the Ecology Party was formalized, and Jonathon Tyler, an ex-member of the Labour Party, and Sally Willington from Cornwall, both drafters of the constitution, were elected chair and national secretary respectively.

By 1978 there were approximately 650 members of the Ecology Party, and after much heated debate at the annual conference the decision was taken to field fifty-three candidates at the 1979 general election. (This reflected the fact that a political party is eligible for party political broadcasts if it contests fifty seats or more.)

Ecology documents show that the National Executive had been talking to the Liberal Party about the possibility of trading seats in the south-west. Meetings were held with Lord Beaumont, who offered help with the Ecology Party's election campaign, and with Tony

Beamish from Liberal Party headquarters, who wished to discuss election pacts. Other documents indicate that Michael Steed, with David Steel's authorization, had been in contact with Ecology Party chair Jonathon Tyler. In the chair's report to the 1978 Ecology Party conference it is clear that the initiative came from the Liberal Party, worried that eco-intervention in seats such as David Penhaligon's Truro or John Pardoe's North Cornwall would lose it MPs. The public disclosure of Jeremy Thorpe's impending trial must have further disturbed the Liberal leadership, though nothing came of such talks. The formation in October 1978 of the Green Alliance, a group of people who were active in the environmental field, no doubt worried both the Ecology Party and the Liberals, as it had indicated its intention to field candidates in parliamentary elections. In the event, however, following discussions in which Ecology Party members made clear their feelings about pacts with other parties, none was pursued. Ironically for a party gripped by election fever, the editorial written by Peter Frings in the first issue of its newspaper, *Econews*, which appeared in March 1979, asked: 'What do we ultimately hope to achieve by playing the parliamentary game? Is the objective to form a "government of ecologists", a notion stated in party literature, and cherished by many prominent members? . . . The first act of a truly ecological government would be to dissolve itself . . . The Ecology Party stands for participatory democracy – what other kind of democracy is there?'

By this time Jonathon Porritt, then an English teacher at a comprehensive school in Shepherd's Bush in London, had risen to the position of the Ecology Party's vice-chair and was the main instigator of the party's 1979 general election manifesto entitled 'The Real Alternative'. Along with other members, notably Jonathon Tyler and David Fleming, he raised the party's profile and rewrote its literature in a more accessible style. The manifesto proposed six fundamental changes:

A move towards a sustainable way of life, conserving the Earth's capital, learning to rely mainly on those resources which can be renewed or recycled.

A move towards a stable economy, ensuring basic material security and prosperity for all.

A move towards economic self-sufficiency in terms of the basic necessities of life, particularly food and energy.

A move towards a decentralized way of life, so that people become more responsible for themselves and for others.

A move towards seeing things in the long term rather than settling for convenient short-term measures.

A move towards a society which places less emphasis on material values, and more on personal development and achievement.

The manifesto ends by saying:

If there is an answer, then it lies in our own hands, working together in our own communities. We need the kind of political system that lets us all get stuck in, fully committed, fully involved in the decisions that concern us. Either we go on as before, indifferently supporting policies that in the long term will quite literally cost us the Earth. Or we consider the real alternative, of an ecological, sustainable future – even though at the moment it may seem an alternative fraught with difficulties.

Fifty-three candidates, nineteen of them in the south-west, stood in the 1979 general election, polling an average 1.5 per cent of the vote. Jonathon Porritt, standing in St Marylebone, obtained 2.8 per cent of the vote, along with Guy Woodford in Worcestershire. In all, 39,918 votes were cast for the Ecology Party. In media terms it was a huge success, and membership of the party climbed to over 5,000.

Sustaining this success brought new problems to the Ecology Party mainly in the shape of administration and finance. The young party could not cope with the influx of inquiries, and the decision to stand three candidates in the June European elections almost bankrupted the party. Jonathon Porritt, Teddy Goldsmith and Mike Benfield stood, Porritt gaining over 4 per cent of the vote. By 1981 membership was beginning to drop, and at the end of 1982 it had fallen to about 2,500. Membership has been rather fluid, but there has always been a substantial number of activists whose commitment to green politics has never been in doubt.

More important in the long run, however, this period saw links forged with other green parties on the Continent, a process that has strengthened the role of the international green movement. In 1981 Brice Lalonde polled over 1 million votes in the French presidential

election under the green alliance banner 'Aujourd'hui Ecologie'. Lalonde accepted an invitation to speak at the UK Ecology Party conference at Malvern in 1981 after National Party Council member Sara
Parkin had written enthusiastically of him in the party magazine
Eco-Bulletin. (Parkin was later to change her mind, attacking Lalonde
after he accepted the post of Secretary of State for the Environment
in Michel Rocard's socialist government.) The conference confirmed
the party's commitment to strong social reform with policy motions
on land, health and Northern Ireland. An Ecology Party summer
gathering at Glastonbury attracted over 1,200 people, including
Die Grünen's Gertrud Schilling, and discussion ranged from international feminism to whether the Ecology Party should hold a
selective boycott at the next general election, not opposing Labour
or other unilateralist candidates.

By 1983 Greens in other European countries had been elected to
national parliaments, and optimism about the impending general
election in the UK ran high. Membership was growing again. Jonathon
Porritt was seen as a highly articulate spokesperson, and the national
media began to wonder whether the Greens could obtain a seat. Sadly,
in the event the party was squeezed out by a variety of factors: the formation of the Alliance, an electoral agreement between the Liberal
Party and the Social Democratic Party; the Falklands War; and the UK
electoral system. The disappointing result was an average vote of 1.0
per cent, less than had been achieved in 1979. The first-past-the-post
electoral system in the United Kingdom proved to be a major block
for any new political party, including the Alliance, which gained only
twenty-three seats, although it had received 25.4 per cent of the vote.

Despite the poor showing in the 1983 general election, the party
fielded seventeen candidates in the 1984 European elections, gaining
on average over 2 per cent of the vote. Broadcasting rules meant that
they could not obtain a party election broadcast despite an application
to the High Court. Mr Justice Taylor gave the Ecology Party leave to
go ahead with its application against the broadcasting companies, and
although they could possibly have overturned the rulings of the
Election Broadcast Committee (which, incidentally, meets in secret),
lack of time prevented the action from reaching a conclusion. Significantly, Porritt, although still an influential member of the party,
subsequently left Party Council in 1984 to take up the directorship of
Friends of the Earth. In 1985 the party changed its name from the

Ecology Party to the Green Party. This caused heated debate at the autumn conference, but the arguments were overcome by the success of the Continental Greens.

The party was growing once again, and its organization was being questioned by some of its more vociferous members. The Green Party has a commitment to decentralization that is enshrined in its constitution. The Green Party Conference is the supreme body of the party, and a Party Council is elected to implement the will of conference and to administer party business between conferences. A conference is held in the spring; in the autumn there is the Annual General Meeting, at which new members to the Green Party Council (GPC) are elected. GPC is composed of twenty-six members, fifteen of whom are elected by area, four by postal ballot of the whole membership and four from the conference floor. Three elected councillors or Members of Parliament are elected by an electoral college. To keep the party democratic, no member may serve for more than three consecutive years. At the first GPC of each year three co-chairs, a party secretary and various other officers and convenors of committees are elected. By adopting these methods of election and procedures the Green Party ensures that power does not accumulate in one person and that the public can identify with policies, not personalities.

Organizing in a green way is not always easy, but the party could not function if it imitated the models of hierarchy, leadership and bureaucracy that it seeks to displace. The Social Democrats, with their charismatic leader and media favour, have virtually disappeared, while the Greens have gained millions of votes without having to play the usual games of marketing and personality cult so despised by the British electorate. Although in conventional terms the green way of organizing may seem unnecessarily unwieldy and media-hostile, the reasons behind it are sound. It prevents power from being concentrated in the hands of the few; it allows local branches the freedom to organize effectively; and it has proved successful in electing Greens world-wide. Doing Green politics in a Green way has on occasions proved too challenging for some members. In 1986 Jonathon Tyler and Paul Ekins, ex co-chairs of GPC, brought to conference a set of constitutional amendments that they believed would streamline the party administration and make it more efficient. When the motion was lost Ekins called for the formation of a covert pressure group known as Maingreen, which would eventually take control of GPC.

If this strategy failed, Ekins hinted, a new Main green Party might be set up; he aimed to establish 'a national green political grouping, with sound organization, mainstream image and effective leadership either by changing the Green Party into such a grouping or by becoming such a grouping itself'. Papers were circulated only to those people thought to be sympathetic, and a meeting was called to discuss strategy.

Ekins and Tyler were deeply concerned that members of the party who had 'opted out of the formal economy' were gaining strength. An alleged group of anarchists/decentralists who 'simply do not accept the mainstream party-political objectives of the organization of which they are members and exercise undue influence at Conference because our customs allow them to do so despite their patent lack of a constituency' were also singled out. The party was accused of collective incompetence and weaknesses that would prevent it from becoming an important national political force.

Another area of concern was that of image and leadership. The Maingreeners were terrified of Sid Rawle, a prominent Green Party member who lived in Tepeé Valley, Wales, and had been identified by the *Daily Mail* as 'self-styled King of the Hippies' and possible party leader. Tyler, who had tabled a motion to become effective leader in 1979, was concerned by Sid's unusual lifestyle and polygamous relationships.

One of the then co-chairs, Jo Robins (now Fox-Graham), who received the papers, was aghast at their proposals. She contacted the other two co-chairs, and they agreed that the papers sought to subvert party structures in a way that was secretive and undemocratic. An emergency meeting of the GPC on the same day that Ekins and Tyler proposed their Maingreen meeting, 10 May 1986, condemned the secrecy of the Maingreen proposals and recommended that the papers should be available to all members. It was customary for meetings to be open in the Green Party (any member has the right to attend), and the co-chairs felt that all members of the party had a right to see, and judge for themselves, the Maingreen papers. Thanks to Jo Fox-Graham, the democratic procedures within the party were preserved, and the party was able to put the Maingreen episode behind it.

Between 1983 and 1987 the party concentrated on local elections and extra-parliamentary activity. Members were instrumental in orchestrating successful campaigns of civil disobedience to prevent nuclear-waste dumping. The campaign to stop the general election deposit from being raised from £150 to £1,000 resulted in evidence from the Greens being heard by a House of Commons committee, and eventually the deposit was raised to £500 with a threshold of 5 per cent of the vote.

The Campaign for Real Democracy (CARD) instigated by the Ecology Party, advocating proportional representation and a Freedom of Information Act, continues today. A Green Magna Carta was signed in 1988 by members of the GPC at Runnymede, and copies were sent to all 650 MPs at Westminster. The party also supported the miners' strike and called for non-violent resistance during this particularly bitter struggle. Party members gave evidence to the Sizewell nuclear power station inquiry as well as supporting the peace camps at Molesworth and Greenham Common. John Marjoram, later to become a Green Party councillor in Stroud, helped set up Green CND, which put pressure on National CND to become more radical.

The Other Economic Summit (TOES) was also established as an independent organization, and TOES helped the Green Party to form desperately needed economic policies. TOES is still in operation today, having held a successful conference in Paris in the summer of 1989.

The 1987 general election was contested by 133 candidates, who polled an average of 1.4 per cent of the vote, slightly up on 1983. All mainstream politicians had played significantly for the green vote, which led the highly influential pressure group Friends of the Earth to say, 'Whatever the result of this election, we can at least be reasonably confident that the next batch of MPs will be more sympathetic to the environment cause, and more committed to some concerned programme of action.' By this time both Jonathon Tyler and Paul Ekins had resigned from the party. Ekins had been one of the organizers of Tactical Voting '87, a scheme to try to oust the Tories in 100 marginal constituencies. Inevitably, it caused some friction where Green Party candidates were standing, as Ekins openly advocated voting for the candidate most likely to beat the Tories. That year also saw the formation of the Association of Socialist Greens, a group of long-standing Green Party members, including many who had held positions on the GPC, that argued that social issues had to be linked far more strongly with ecological ones.

Another initiative was the formation of Green Voice, an organization to promote dialogue between radical Liberals and Greens. At one point it seemed possible that the MP Simon Hughes, then a unilateralist, could become the Greens' first Member of Parliament. Tim Cooper, co-chair of the GPC, and Simon Hughes, MP, addressed a meeting in London at which Hughes stated publicly that he would be prepared to stand on a Liberal Green ticket. The talks broke down because of the official merger of the SDP and Liberals; Hughes decided that he could serve in the newly merged party.

The years 1988 and 1989 saw three women co-chairs of GPC: Janet Alty, Liz Crosbie and Penny Kemp. Little did the three realize that they would preside over the turning point in green politics. Despite some personality conflicts and arguments over ways of working, the three managed to spearhead the party's most successful electoral campaign to date. Much of the credit must go to Liz Crosbie for organizing the party election broadcast that was to revolutionize political advertising. The Green Party was fortunate that Crosbie, an advertising executive, was able to secure the talents of David Bailey for no fee.

David Icke joined the Green Party in 1987 and quickly rose to the position of Party Speaker. As prospective parliamentary candidate for the Isle of Wight and a well-known TV sports commentator, he was well placed to be a public face for the Greens. Sara Parkin, now one of the three co-secretaries of the European Greens, made her début on *Question Time*, to be dubbed 'Queen of the Greens' by Robin Day. Both Icke and Parkin were later to deny that they wished to become the Green leader.

The 1989 local elections provided a clue to which way the wind was blowing. The 646 Green Party candidates scored an average 11 per cent of the vote and in places gained over 30 per cent, but neither the media or other political parties recognized the change of mood. The European elections in the same year brought the Green Party's major breakthrough. Achieving 15 per cent of the vote (the highest ever obtained by any green party in a major election) ensured media attention. The size of the green vote showed the concern of the British electorate with the state of the planet. On every day leading up to the election there seemed to be another environmental disaster in the national papers. The death of thousands of seals off the British coast, the state of our water systems, listeria and salmonella all played their part in contributing to the Greens' success. Even the national newspaper

Today took a green editorial line and urged its readers to 'have a flutter' on the Greens. The highly imaginative party election broadcast directed by David Bailey had an effect, and the brave decision to field a candidate in every constituency, despite the huge financial risk, paid dividends.

However, with the Green Party in the spotlight, some of the more disreputable tabloids began to delight in misrepresenting its policies. Headlines such as 'No foreign holidays – Greens would ban air travel' and 'Did you know what you voted for? They would take your car away' appeared. Peter Brooke, Tory Party chairman, produced a broadsheet that sought to discredit the Green Party, accusing it of hiding its policies behind 'a cloak of superficial environmentalism . . . many people were tricked into supporting them'. Edwina Currie claimed the Greens were 'like an American religious sect turning their backs on the modern world . . . if they seriously believe we are all willing to go to work on a horse, they have another think coming'. Christopher Monckton in the *Evening Standard* stated, 'They [Greens] would replace the Prime Minister with anarchist soviets', while Paddy Ashdown compared the Greens with neo-Fascists. Jeremy Seabrook, Green Party member, retorted, 'The Greens have renewed social hope and offered a way through the immobilism of the past decade, so it's not surprising other parties will stop at nothing to stifle their politics.'

An investigation revealed that most voters were well aware of controversial green policies concerning unilateralism, social justice and the less developed countries. The arrogance of the other political parties in suggesting that the voters did not understand the Greens only goes to underline what little respect our elected Members of Parliament have for the people of this country and their capacity to make informed electoral decisions.

Success also created internal strains. Many Greens were shell-shocked by what the *Economist* magazine was to describe as the greatest increase in any party's share of the vote in British electoral history. The result led Chris Rose, UK Election Co-ordinator, to say 'Bloody hell, now things are going to get really tough.' Difficulties in adjusting to their new-found political 'stardom' made some members of GPC question the direction and role of the party. A vocal minority wanted to remodel the Greens along the lines of the traditional parties, and there was talk of a national leader, a Shadow Cabinet, streamlined organization and a manifesto based on marketable, electorally safe, non-controversial policy. Some pushed for an approach of pure environmentalism and the discarding of the economic and social ideas that had moulded eco-politics in the 1980s. Others emphasized that it was the very fact that the Greens were not like the mainstream parties that had brought them to the forefront. A strategy of pushing the line of neither right nor left but *ahead*, in order to continue forging a radically different ideology from that of conventional mainstream politics, won the day among party conference-goers. That continued success depends upon the ability to present to the electorate the need for a new ecological paradigm and radical restructuring of society on decentralist lines remains the broad consensus of the party.

During this time membership doubled to over 15,000 with inquiries running at over 100 a day. Green Party HQ, comprising three tiny offices under a banking school in Balham, four paid employees and many, many volunteers, was stretched to its limit. For every new member two journalists would appear to conduct interviews and find out more about the political event of the decade: the unpredicted triumph of the Greens. The 1989 autumn conference attracted 500 journalists, much to the amusement of long-standing members used to token representatives from the *Guardian* and *The Times*. Electoral success across Europe also led to a stronger green group in the European Parliament, giving Euro-Greens a powerful voice. Because of the bizarre workings of the UK electoral system, despite gaining the highest green vote in Europe Britain failed to return a single eco-MP to Strasbourg. A demonstration was organized on the opening day of the Parliament with the help of sister parties on the Continent.

The European Greens decided that UK Greens should be represented and they now have a Member, although she can't vote in the main Parliament. Jean Lambert, an ex-co-chair and long-standing member, has been chosen on a rotational basis.

In 1989 the Scottish Green Party voted by three to one to go independent and to federate with the British Greens, and the Welsh Green Party began a dialogue with Plaid Cymru, with which they share a number of objectives. Brig Oubridge, a previous co-chair of the UK Green Party and member of the Welsh Executive, was to give a platform speech at the Plaid Cymru conference (mostly in Welsh), at which he welcomed the moves for closer cooperation between Plaid and the Welsh Green Party. Derek Wall made a successful tour of Northern Ireland during his term as European Speaker, and moves are afoot to put the Northern Ireland Green Party on some sort of consistent basis. Until now Northern Ireland's green politics has been a rather hit-and-miss affair, with few members and little direction. Wall was able to show that green politics offers hope to both loyalists and republicans in the province.

It is true to say that there has been a drop in support from the Green Party since the European election, and we have seen the party fall back in the polls. However, the number of new local parties is encouraging, and plans are well under way for the next round of local elections in 1990. All local green parties are autonomous, and many are busy writing their own local manifestos, believing that decentralization is the key to winning seats at a local level.

Journalists irritated by their failure to spot a trend (*Newsnight* didn't even have green on its computer-drawn bar charts and had to use grey to record the green vote on Euro-election night) have eagerly sought the typical green voter. Long-standing ecologists from all strands of the political spectrum have been keen to find out who the new Green voter is as well. The rise of the Green Party has been paralleled by a huge growth in the wider green movement. There are now over 4 million members of ever-growing environmental organizations, ranging from local preservation societies and 'Save the Tiger Orchid' to that multinational corporation of ecological concern, Greenpeace. Such environmentalists are almost inevitably potential green voters. The party has also attracted those from a more radical background who believe that sweeping lifestyle changes and a new green consciousness are necessary elements of any political party worth supporting at the polls. Peace activists dismayed by Labour's shift on nuclear weapons have also been attracted in large numbers by the party's unmitigated stand on the arms trade and nuclear weapons. Although CND makes no secret that its largest political membership is that of the Labour Party, in recent months it has expressed the view that it would like a closer working relationship with the Greens. A Mori poll conducted after the elections showed that the electorate believed the Greens to be not only the party of the environment but also more caring and more concerned about the needy than any of their political rivals. Forty per cent of the electorate would consider voting green, and support for ecological change grows every day.

A recent survey conducted among members and supporters showed that Green Party members and activists are generally educated beyond the age of 16, are members of other radical and environmental groups and read the *Guardian* newspaper. They have fewer consumer goods than most but own more computers. They tend to earn either high incomes or none at all. A surprising number are members of the clergy and teaching or medical professions. Others came from a wide diversity of backgrounds, from the anarchist tradition to Conservative, although many have described themselves as political virgins. The survey showed that members of ethnic minorities are under-represented in the Green Party.

Nearly 40 per cent of Green Party members had either belonged to, or voted for, the Labour Party. However, when we look at the voting patterns in the European elections the Green Party, somewhat surprisingly, did best of all in the Tory south. Nick Bagnall, candidate in West Sussex, scored a massive 24 per cent of the vote. At first glance it would seem that the basis of its support came from disaffected Liberals as the Social Democrat vote collapsed, but a closer examination shows a recycling of votes, as SDP supporters tended to vote Labour and committed unilateralists who may previously have voted Labour went green.

Although Mrs Thatcher appears to have assumed a green mantle, many Tory voters were not convinced by her then Minister of the Environment, Nicholas Ridley. There is no doubt that many Tories, sick of green rhetoric and media attention paid to all matters green, decided to place a protest vote. However, the poll shows that approximately half of those that voted green in the European elections will continue to do so, so each of the mainstream political parties now has something to fear from the Greens. Each is setting about capturing the green vote.

Jonathon Porritt, in a dynamic speech to the 1989 Green Party conference at Wolverhampton, described the coming months thus: 'These are heady days for the Green Party, exhilarating but dangerous at the same time. Though all political parties are distinctly vulnerable to bouts of hyperbole and glutinous grandiloquence, particularly during the party conference season, I think it fair to describe the next few months as a veritable watershed for the Green Party.'

Kenneth Baker, Tory Party chair, was later to describe the Greens as a party that wanted to stop the people of Britain having children, to make them garage their cars and to turn them into environmentally friendly peasants.

Read the rest of this book and judge for yourself the accuracy of Mr Baker's analysis of green politics.

The *Global 2000* report stated in 1982, 'If present trends continue, the world in 2000 will be more crowded, more polluted, less stable ecologically and more vulnerable to disruption.' The next millennium, discussed in the report, is a few short years away, yet governments still fail to act on its proposals and ignore its conclusions. The environmental crisis is real and growing; green politics is very much the politics of survival. From the oceans to the skies a crisis is looming and with it, at long last, the realization, even on the part of economists and politicians, that our very existence is at threat. Green concern has increased among both Government and Opposition parties but more through green voters than through scientific evidence.

Scientific reports backed by hard evidence are one thing. The evidence of our eyes is something else. Have you talked about the weather lately? The last few years have seen changes of global weather patterns that twenty years ago we would not have imagined. Britain suffered hurricanes in 1987 and 1990, with the loss of over 15 million trees. Hurricanes Gilbert and Hugo caused horrific damage and death; whole towns and cities had to be rebuilt, Bangladesh saw its worst flooding in living memory: over 3,000 people died. Citizens died in Greece because of the searing heat, and in December 1987 Arizona experienced snow at Christmas for the first time. In 1989 Ethiopia had on its hands another famine that could cause 4 million deaths. Droughts occurred in China and the Soviet Union as well as in Africa. The USA suffered crop failure because of the heat, and experts think that a 17 per cent loss of grain yield is possible over the next forty years. The consequences of this could be disastrous because over 100 countries around the world depend upon the USA for their food supply. All of us could add other examples to this list of climatic catastrophe.

Scientists agree that we cannot afford to wait another forty or fifty years before taking action. If we wait for conclusive evidence of changing weather patterns, we will have waited too long.

It may sound simplistic to state that our own health, that of our children and even that of the economy depend upon the health of our planet, but it is true. If we try to dominate nature or ignore the environment, we will destroy ourselves. We cannot sustain the waste and destruction of present industrial society into the future. A recent television programme showed a North American Indian asking rhetorically, 'Tell me, what are the objectives of your industrial society? Can you perpetuate it for the next 6,000 years?' Politicians, bureaucrats and economists have no answer. Until the arrival of the Greens they didn't even pose the question.

Nature has never been static. Species have come and gone. There have been extinction and evolution. But today a more frightening scenario presents itself. Humanity has demonstrated its capacity to violate life on a massive scale. Referring both to the greenhouse effect and to the practice of biotechnology, which redesigns life for narrow human ends, Bill McKibben goes as far as to talk of 'the end of nature'. Rampant industrialism by so-called developed nations has shown itself capable of producing catastrophes equal to those natural phenomena that nature increasingly demonstrates. From the manufacture of poisons to the prospect of the nuclear winter, we are capable of destroying all life as we know it. Not content with the degradation of the land and the oceans, we disturb the delicate balance of the skies. In the last hundred years more damage has been done by the activities of the human species than by the combined efforts of all generations before us.

Often when we talk of desertification, rainforest destruction and ozone depletion they seem so distant that we are unable to make the connections between them and our daily lives. Pollution is different. We can see it, and its implications are easily understood. 'Pollution knows no boundaries' was the opening remark of many a speech made by Tory MEP Christopher Jackson during the 1989 European election campaign. Yet however much turquoise rhetoric comes out of the mouths of Conservative MPs, it is at variance with their actions. Global pollution is increasing; projected figures of carbon-dioxide emissions are shown in the table opposite. Nearly 6 billion tonnes of carbon dioxide were released into the atmosphere in 1987, 10 per cent more than in 1983. If we link this with the 12 million hectares of

Actual and projected annual emission of carbon dioxide
(millions of tonnes)

Area	1986(%)		2030%		Average annual growth
United States	1,299	(23)	3,257	(18)	2.1
Soviet Union	1,030	(18)	2,940	(16)	2.1
Western Europe	621	(11)	1,218	(7)	1.5
Less-developed countries	1,452	(26)	5,891	(32)	3.2
Japan	260	(5)	419	(2)	1.1
South-East Asia	146	(3)	532	(3)	3.0
World total	5,575	(100)	18,184	(100)	2.7

Notes: Figures in parentheses indicate percentage of world share. China is included as a 'less developed country'.
Source: MITI, Japan.

forests we cut down each year, it is impossible to believe that we are not on a course of deliberate ecocide.

The statement by Nicholas Ridley that Britain leads the world in environmental protection is laughable to anyone who has strolled along Britain's shores. Long- and short-outfall pipes bring raw sewage back to our beaches. A local green party in Essex collected sanitary towels, condoms, faeces, hypodermic needles and other unsavouries from their local beach and, in protest, dumped them at the Ministry of Environment's door. Dean, 9 years old, fell into the sea from a canoe in Southend and ended up paralysed. Out of sixty-eight beaches in the south-east only six managed to comply with EEC directives about the quality of bathing water. This sorry state of affairs is repeated around the country. Even Blackpool's golden sands have been condemned as unfit.

Water is an issue we all understand. The composition of the human body is 70 per cent water, and without pure water we cannot exist. Clean water should be our birthright, but we have been let down badly. The chance of getting pure water from our tap is negligible. A survey into tap water conducted jointly by Friends of the Earth (FOE) and the *Observer* found that over 2 million people were at risk from high levels of lead; that a further 2 million drink water contaminated by aluminium; that another 1.7 million drink water that breaches EEC regulations for nitrates. FOE further identified

298 water supplies that exceeded maximum permitted levels for pesticides. Geoffrey Lean, environmental correspondent for the *Observer*, introduced the survey on water pollution thus:

> Right at the beginning of this sweltering summer, a special festival was put on in Hyde Park to celebrate the quality of Britain's food and farming. The Queen turned up to open it, ministers attended, everyone was in a self-congratulatory mood. But sceptical pigs stole the show.
>
> Trucked in from around the country, trapped in London traffic jams in the hot sun, the pigs arrived at the festival desperate for a drink. But when presented with water from the capital's taps they stubbornly refused to touch it. 'These animals were very hot, you could see them wilting,' said Dr Tony Andrews, the chief vet at the festival. 'We were dousing them with water, but they would not drink.' Eventually they had to be brought pure water from Harrod's private artesian well. (*Observer* supplement, 6 August 1989.)

Nicholas Ridley, speaking of the above incident, said, 'I'm not sure that I am prepared to accept the pigs as the ultimate judges of water quality. Maybe they would have preferred wine.'

Successive governments' neglect of our water systems means that to bring drinking and bathing water quality up to minimum EEC standards would cost approximately £39 billion. 'Liquid Costs', an environmental report on water written by John Bowers and Cathy O'Donnell of Leeds University, concludes that only 30 per cent of the £18.6 billion of government money earmarked for capital spending by the ten new water companies will be used on environmental improvements. The remainder is needed for government neglect. If EEC standards are to be complied with, water bills for consumers will have to soar. Under the government's privatization scheme, the report concludes, river pollution will become worse because the government has relaxed the controls on sewage discharge to make ownership of shares in the industry more attractive. This report was suppressed until the Water Privatization Bill was on the statute book.

While the Thatcher government has made noises about the level of pollution and damage to the eco-system, it has been busy cutting funding in those very areas seeking to promote a better understanding of the biosphere. Governmental spending on environmental research was £161.2 million for the year 1988–89, contrasted with a defence budget of £19,215 million. Spending by the energy-efficiency office was slashed by £6 million in the year 1987–88 from a high of £24.5 million in 1986. The Select Committee on Energy in July 1989 said, 'The government's cutting of the Energy Efficiency Office's budget shows misplaced complacency . . . it indicates a misjudgement both of the evidence and the analysis of this issue.'

Her Majesty's Inspectorate of Pollution set up in April 1987, supposedly at the heart of the government's commitment to all things 'green', has been a dismal failure. The director, Brian Ponsford, who committed suicide in December 1989, had written a damning report of the Inspectorate's activities. Lack of money and staff and low morale had meant that monitoring undertaken by the Inspectorate was woefully inadequate. Britain had thirty-two full-time anti-pollution police, while Holland had 1,000 staff and the United States Environmental Protection Agency 20,000 staff for air pollution alone. In his report Ponsford highlighted the Inspectorate's inability, through lack of staff, fully to take part even in national emergency exercises. The privatization of the electricity industry means maximizing profit by maximizing consumption rather than by promoting energy conservation, which is essential if we are to combat the greenhouse effect and to preserve fossil fuels for future generations. If this or any other previous administration had poured the money used for research into the nuclear industry into the promotion of energy conservation and alternative renewable energy resources, we would today be well on the way to having a safe, clean renewable energy supply.

Britain is one of the largest importers of other people's toxic waste and plans to build more incinerators. In 1986 it disposed of an estimated 1,580,000 tonnes of toxic waste, and 1988 saw the importation of over 100,000 tonnes of dangerous waste on the grounds that the UK has the advanced technology to deal with it. The truth is that British laws are more relaxed than those of the country's counterparts and that profit is more important than either health or safety.

However, when faced with public pressure, angry environmentalists and tightening controls, some companies have sought to export their hazardous cargoes to less developed countries where standards are not as strict. More than a hundred shiploads of highly poisonous waste has been sent to places such as Brazil, Mexico, Venezuela and

West Africa. The ship, the *Karin B*, tried to land in Nigeria with 4,000 tonnes of highly toxic chemical waste, including PCBs and dioxins whose containers were leaking. Nigeria refused to handle the waste, and the *Karin B* toured the high seas looking for a port that would accept its lethal cargo. When it appeared that Britain might take in the waste, public outcry ensued and government officials quickly changed conditions for entry. Eventually the ship returned to Italy, the producer of the waste.

The high cost of toxic-waste disposal in industrialized countries (approximately £750 per tonne, compared with £20 per tonne in Africa) make the Third World an attractive dump. When developing countries pressed the industrialized countries to stop dumping waste on their territories, the West refused to agree. Indeed, the United States objected to a clause in the UN Environment Programme that required exported waste to be handled just as safely in the receiving country as in the exporting country. This led Greenpeace delegate Kevin Stairs to say, 'The Basle Convention was not drafted in the spirit of compromise. The demands of developing countries for protection from the international waste trade have been largely ignored. Industrialized countries had the power to stop waste exports to the Third World; instead they opted to legalize them.'

It makes no global sense at all to transport toxic waste over long distances, so that the chance of accident during transportation becomes greater. Greens say that it is far better and more sensible to transport the technology capable of dealing with toxic substances until we are in a position not to produce the dangerous chemicals in the first place. In the case of countries that are unable to pay for such expertise the technology should be exported free of charge. It is this sort of action that would do much to promote international cooperation to combat global pollution.

British Nuclear Fuels Limited (BNFL) actively seeks contracts for reprocessing nuclear waste from abroad and maintains that these are vital for its business and Britain's balance of payments. At present most spent fuel from abroad and the UK goes to Sellafield, where it is stored under water to await reprocessing and the extraction of plutonium. The spent rods inevitably corrode and contaminate the water with radiation. In 1988 Penny Kemp, in a radio interview with a spokesperson from BNFL, accused the nuclear industry of putting profit before the safety of people. The conversation went something like this:

PK: Do you not think it morally wrong to import dangerous substances from abroad, like nuclear waste, which poses a threat to the health of people?

BNFL: It is not right to call it nuclear waste. It is spent fuel, a valuable commodity, and by your continued insinuations you are ruining a multi-million-pound industry, which profits the people of this country.

PK: You are therefore prepared to put profit before the health and safety of the people.

This is the organization of which Lord Marshall, then chairman of CEGB, wrote in a draft letter to the then UK Energy Secretary, Peter Walker, 'We are under attack from environmentalists and our critics for storing Magnox fuel in water. The attack is difficult to answer because it is basically correct . . .' BNFL was reported recently to have told workers to stop fathering children because of the risk of cancer.

The practice of using our seas as international dumping grounds must be stopped. HRH The Prince Charles said, when opening the North Sea Conference in 1987, that the North Sea is 'not a bottomless pit for all our waste and it makes no sense to test it to destruction'. Britain was a willing signatory to an agreement to stop dumping toxic materials harmful to the marine environment in the North Sea by December 1989. Well into 1990 the Thatcher government is shown to be full of broken promises and confirms Britain's reputation as the 'dirty man of Europe'. Britain is the only North Sea state to continue polluting the seas in this way.

An international monitoring commission must have powers to deal with pollution, whether it be on land or sea or in the air, and any penalties must be severe enough to ensure that it is not financially worth while to pollute. Too often it is cheaper to pay fines than invest in alternatives. In 1987 reported incidents of river pollution in Britain numbered 23,253, of which 1,402 were categorized as 'serious'. Yet only 288 prosecutions were made, and many of those convicted were given conditonal discharges or small fines. Considering that the river authorities themselves were responsible for over one fifth of these incidents, it is no surprise that industrial polluters fail to take the new Green Bill seriously. The National Rivers Authority, under the chairmanship of Lord Crickhowell, has said that it will be much tougher with polluters when it takes over enforcement of the law. Lord

Crickhowell told the House of Lords 'The water authorities and the Department of the Environment had formed cosy, incestuous relationships that have inhibited effective action.' The Green Party waits to see whether the National Rivers Authority will have any bite.

Acid rain is another sphere in which Britain consistently fails to meet international standards. By heightening chimney stacks we solved the dreadful smog pollution of the 1950s, but we managed to disperse sulphur dioxide across Europe. The Swedes were the first to present evidence of acid-rain pollution to a United Nations conference in 1972. Around 100 million tonnes of sulphur dioxide are released annually, giving rise to pollution on a massive scale. In Sweden alone over 20,000 lakes have been affected: fish stocks have been wiped out, and the water has become unfit for human consumption. Lakes and forests in Scotland, Germany, Austria, Poland and Czechoslovakia have suffered likewise. Nor is acid rain confined to Europe; the United States has its share. In Cologne, Germany, the authors witnessed at first hand the results of acid rain on the sculptures surrounding the cathedral. 'This is *your* acid rain that ruins our buildings,' German MEP Frieder Otto Wolf told us angrily.

Yet as long ago as 1880 the effects of smoke pollution were known, and apparatus was invented for removing sulphur dioxide from smoke. Sadly, like so many ecological inventions, it was not thought to be 'appropriate', and a century later we are still not prepared to use desulphurization equipment because it is said to be too 'costly'. The cost of the innumerable trees killed by sulphur, the buildings that are eroded, the fish that are slaughtered and the wildlife that is driven from its natural habitats has never been fully calculated. Sulphur dioxide pollution can be stopped: we have the technology but lack the political will. Not only can its pollution be stopped but sulphur can be put to positive use. At the Wilhelmshaven power station in Germany nine-tenths of the sulphur is removed from flue gases and used in the production of gypsum. The cost of all this? An increase of 10 per cent in the generation of electricity, which could easily be offset by energy conservation.

John Gribbin, physicist and author of *Hole in the Sky*, states that ozone is a pale-blue gas that is poisonous to animal and plant life even in small concentrations. It is formed in the summer, when hydrocarbons and nitrogen oxides from cars react with sunlight. The summer of 1989, one of the hottest on record in Britain, saw the concentration of ozone exceeding World Health Organization (WHO) recommended levels. In Devon in May of that year figures released by the Department of the Environment recorded ozone levels exceeding 100 parts per billion for as much as twenty hours. The WHO recommends limits of up to 102 parts per billion for one hour and between 51 and 61.2 parts per billion for eight hours.

However, up in the stratosphere ozone is essential for the well-being of human life, as it protects us from the harmful effects of solar radiation. We have all heard of the hole in the ozone layer, but it is worth repeating the extent of the damage already done. The hole is now the size of the United States and the height of Mount Everest, Destruction of the ozone layer causes skin cancer and cataracts and blights food crops. Humans are destroying it by their use of chlorofluorocarbons (CFCs), gases that are found in aerosols, packaging, furniture foam and fluids in refrigerators. Public pressure has gone a long way to block CFCs in aerosols. It is worth noting that it has been the green pressure groups, notably Friends of the Earth, that have done much to make the public aware of the dangers. The government, as usual, dragged its feet despite its many claims to the contrary. Even after headlines such as 'Thatcher crusade to clean up cars and fridges – Britain leads Ozone Battle' and a major conference hosted by Britain in March 1989, companies are still free to export aerosols containing CFCs.

There has been much talk by government about the necessity of international cooperation but little action. Signatories to the Montreal Protocol, an international agreement, merely undertake to reduce production of CFCs by 50 per cent in three stages by 1999. Although we should be thankful that thirty-three countries ratified the Montreal agreement, the terms need to be looked at carefully. By 1990 production of CFCs is to be frozen by the signatories at 1986 levels. In 1994 it is to be reduced by 20 per cent and, later still, by 30 per cent. There is a catch, however. The Montreal Protocol allows the production and export of CFCs to developing countries – ostensibly to stop them manufacturing their own. This raises the permitted level to 110 per cent of that allowed in 1986 by 1990, with a reduction to 65 per cent of that level by 1999. The damage we have already done to the ozone layer will be with us, and our children and grandchildren, throughout the twenty-first and twenty-second centuries.

Global warming is the most serious environmental problem we

face. As the Toronto conference 'The Changing Atmosphere', held in June 1988, concluded:

> Humanity is conducting an enormous, unintended, globally pervasive experiment whose ultimate consequences could be second only to a global nuclear war. The Earth's atmosphere is being changed at an unprecedented rate by pollutants resulting from human activities, inefficient and wasteful fossil use and the effects of rapid population growth in many regions. These changes represent a major threat to international security and are already having harmful consequences over many parts of the globe.

The EEC Environmental Commission, headed by Stanley Clinton Davies, has produced a document entitled 'The Greenhouse Effect and the Community' in which it has shown that global warming will have far-reaching consequences, from the relocation of populations in low-lying areas to a serious effect on agriculture. Sea-level rises could have disastrous consequences, as three-quarters of the world's population lives near the coast. Sixteen million people live in the Nile delta, and most of the Netherlands is reclaimed land. In September 1989 British scientists discovered that the Arctic icesheet had thinned by one third in the previous ten years. Sea-level rises of 5–7 metres would mean that half the state of Florida could disappear. The EEC Environmental Commission suggests some measures to combat sea-level rises: sea walls and flood barriers; national flood-insurance programmes; the construction of reservoirs (to combat increased salinity); the abandonment of developed regions in low-lying areas; the relocation of populations away from vulnerable sites; and the protection of coastal eco-systems.

There is not a single area of our lives that global warming does not threaten.

From an agricultural point of view global warming could mean more frequent famines and endemic diseases that require moderate temperatures to survive, which would change the length of potential growing seasons. Some experts believe that the recent regional extremes we have seen are more than just climatic fluctuations.

The World Resources Institute has considered four scenarios, from 'do nothing' and 'high growth' to voluntary emission-reduction policies, and their impact on global warming.

1. Base-case scenario
- Business as usual – the inertial model of growth and change in the world energy industry.
- No policies to slow carbon-dioxide emissions.
- Minimal stimulus to improve end-use efficiency.
- Modest stimulus for synthetic fuels development.
- Minimal stimulus for development of solar energy systems.
- No policy to limit tropical deforestation or to encourage reforestation.
- Minimal environmental costs included in price of energy.

2. High-emissions scenario
- Accelerated growth in energy use encouraged.
- No policies to slow carbon-dioxide emissions.
- No stimulus to improve end-use efficiency.
- Modest stimulus for increased use of coal.
- Strong stimulus for synthetic fuels development.
- No stimulus for development of solar-energy systems.
- Rapid deforestation and conversion of marginal lands to agriculture.
- Token environmental costs included in the price of energy.

3. Modest-policy scenario
- Strong stimulus for improved end-use efficiency.
- Modest stimulus for solar energy.
- Substantial efforts at tropical reforestation and ecosystem protection; intensive rather than extensive agriculture encouraged.
- Substantial environmental costs imposed on energy prices to discourage solid-fuel use and to encourage fuel-switching.

4. Slow build-up scenario
- Strong emphasis placed on improving energy efficiency.
- Rapid introduction of solar energy encouraged.
- Major global commitment to reforestation and ecosystem protection.
- High environmental costs imposed on energy prices to discourage solid-fuel use and encourage fuel-switching.

The high-emissions scenario (number 2), based on accelerated growth in energy, rapid deforestation and the conversion of marginal lands to agriculture, could commit us to a 14° degree increase in global warming by the year 2075. The implications of this are too frightening to contemplate – the loss, for example, of all low-lying areas, including the whole of south-east England. The Thames flood barrier would be under water. We would see not only the melting of the large icesheets of Antarctica and mountain glaciers but also a decrease in the amount of water available for human consumption. The salinity of estuaries and coastal aquifers would be drastic for marine ecosystems, resulting in a significant decline in natural diversity. Some scientists believe that the human species could not survive beyond the twenty-second century under these conditions.

The slow-build-up scenario (number 4), on the other hand, commits us to a maximum of three degrees' warming by the year 2075 and is the only scenario that would show a reduction of carbon-dioxide emissions by the same year.

As we have shown, scientific evidence confirms that global warming is no longer a theory. It is a reality. We are committed to a certain amount, although no one can predict with certainty what that level will be. Of one thing we can be sure, however: the challenge to humanity to safeguard the planet for future generations is very real, and only a genuine commitment to global cooperation will produce results. Green parties all over the world are facing up to the policy challenge of moving from runaway growth to an environmentally stable system. The issue is greater than political change. Our personal behaviour will determine what sort of future our children will have, for what the industrialized world does in the next fifty years will have far-reaching consequences for all humanity.

If we take the World Resources Institute's slow-build-up scenario as the only possible route for survival, how do we start? We need to look at three levels: the personal, the national and international. The Green Party does not isolate the greenhouse effect as a single problem with a single solution. All Green Party policies must be taken as a whole, for they are inextricably linked. In our quest for a sustainable society based on conserving natural resources rather than increased consumption, we must convince the electorate that we are concerned not with lowering standards of living but with improving quality of life for all.

During the European elections the Green Party talked of a 'conserver' economy, one that measures success in terms of using less energy and fewer raw materials and producing less waste. It stated that restoration, repair and recycling should be entered on the benefit side of government accounts rather than on the cost side, as at present. A conserver society is one that has learned the lessons of Chernobyl, Seveso and Bhopal and indulges in no activities that pollute either itself or its neighbours. In Chapter 12 you will find the Green programme on decentralization and devolvement of power: Greens recognize that local communities often know what is best for their own environment. That does not mean, of course, that we can dispense with the need for national and international cooperation and planning. What we must do is to understand the damage and destruction the present nation state causes in the name of self-interest. Government has a responsibility to lead the way in protecting the environment.

The Green Party's policies are divided into long-term aims and short-term aims. Quite simply, the Green Party's long-term aim on pollution is to eliminate it. Greens point out that pollution cannot be accepted on the grounds that it is uneconomical to prevent it. It is this very attitude, shown throughout this chapter, that has brought about much of the environmental degradation we face today. If it is uneconomical to produce goods by pollution-free methods, then we should cease to produce them. If responsibility for eliminating pollution were placed on those that caused it in the first place, industry would quickly find less polluting methods of manufacture.

Every political party has to look at the current situation and act accordingly. Therefore the Green Party's short-term aims include strong legislation to give an Inspectorate of Pollution the powers and the finance that are necessary to achieve its purpose and the keeping of strict records on pollution control, be it by industry or government; such records would be open for public inspection. New legislation would impose heavy fines on polluters and would ensure that industry paid the full cost of removal and disposal facilities provided by local authorities. Any new chemicals developed would be rigorously tested (though not on animals), and the use of no new chemical would be allowed until it had met strict criteria regarding its necessity and how it might affect the health of people.

For example, dioxin, a deadly poison more commonly known for its use in the Vietnam war as the defoliant Agent Orange, has been reponsible for birth defects and is associated with cancer. The Women's Environmental Network has done much work to show that there are residues of dioxin in bleached white paper such as that used for disposable nappies, coffee filters and milk cartons. (Paper is bleached with the aid of chlorine, a by-product of this process being dioxin, and the advertising industry has spent millions of pounds convincing us that 'pure white' is safe, clean and necessary to enhance the quality of life.) The Women's Environmental Network has researched and produced a book, *The Sanitary Protection Scandal*, in which it argues convincingly that the chlorine-bleaching process is not only dangerous but totally unnecessary. It is at present running a campaign to stop manufacturers using chlorine bleaching for paper. Once in the environment, dioxin, a man-made chemical, is impossible to eradicate.

Pesticides are another example. DDT, discovered in the 1940s and believed by its inventor to be 'too good to be true' because of its ability to kill insects, soon lived up to its name. The truth was that not only did it eradicate pests but it killed wild life as well. In 1958 Clear Lake in California was treated with DDT in order to eliminate gnats. One thousand pairs of fish-eating grebes were reduced to just twenty-five. In Britain it was concluded that DDT was responsible for the reduction of the peregrine falcon population and other birds of prey. Worse was to come with the discovery that DDT lodges in the fatty tissues of living organisms and that as it moves up the food chain, the ratio of DDT to body weight increases. DDT was eventually banned in the United States in 1972 and in the United Kingdom in 1984. However, it is still manufactured and used in the Third World.

These chemicals, deemed too dangerous to use in the First World, are apparently 'safe' for use in less developed countries, where, it has been estimated, each year over 10,000 people die from poisoning by chemicals banned in the country of export, and a further 750,000 become seriously ill. Even if chemicals are not officially banned in the First World, exporters often provide no instructions about how to use them. Generally labels are printed in English, and protective clothing is unavailable. Are we prepared to take so little responsiblity for our actions that we sanction the unnecessary deaths of 10,000 people a year? The answer appears to be an unqualified yes.

Consider this. In a recent debate a representative of the chemical industry was asked whether the industry felt any responsibility for the misuse of pesticides exported abroad that often cause hardship and suffering to those unfortunate enough to have to handle them. His reply suggested that companies don't compel customers to buy their products and that in a free market people have free choice. What he did not elaborate on was the fact that these chemicals are often returned to the First World by virtue of having been sprayed on cash crops deemed for export.

Of course, there is no point in talking about pollution control unless we also talk about the use of resources and recognize that primary raw materials are either in finite supply or subject to sufficient external limitations to make growth in production unrealistic. It is important to point out here that the Green Party is not anti-technology; it is in favour of *appropriate* technology. Any technology that devises new ways to improve the quality of goods and minimizes waste is welcome. A Green government would introduce what is described as an 'amortization tax' – that is, a tax on consumer goods that discourages built-in obsolescence and is reduced as the useful life of an article increases. Legislation to extend the length of guarantees on goods and to ensure the supply of spare parts would provide manufacturers with incentives to produce goods of high quality.

Again, if we look at the slow-build-up scenario that the World Resources Institute posits as the only sane way to combat the greenhouse effect, it is evident that we need a massive commitment to reforestation. At present, an area the size of the United Kingdom is destroyed each year. At present rates, by the end of the century over 500 million hectares of forest will be permanently lost. The consequences of rainforest destruction are catastrophic. Rainfall patterns become erratic; global warming increases; soil erosion increases; floods become more commonplace; and natural eco-systems are interfered with, which in the long run will have serious consequences for us all. We are all partly responsible for rainforest destruction: the hamburger, the yuppie teak table, the mahogany loo seat – all play their part in helping to destroy the rainforest. Recently rock stars and other well-heeled celebrities have taken to buying large areas of rainforest to protect them. Worthy this may be, but it is hardly the complete answer. Instead we need united global action. The United Nations Environmental Programme should promote agroforestry and reinforce the prevention and fighting of forest fires. Proper monitoring systems must be implemented, and developing countries must be given financial assistance to enable them to manage their forests on a sustainable basis. Adequate funding must be given for the establishment and management of fuel-wood plantations in the tropics.

The United Nations Environmental Programme must be given more teeth. Earlier on we showed that agreements like the Montreal Protocol, while not perfect, can lead to international action and cooperation. We must have international agreement on the future protection of the atmosphere. The United Nations must make the dissemination of information a primary goal and emphasize the benefits to be gained by large-scale energy-saving policies. The Villach Conference, which took place in Austria in 1985, made the following observation:

> Many important economic and social decisions are being made today on long-term projects – major water-resource management activities such as irrigation and hydro-power, drought relief, agricultural and land use, structural designs and coastal engineering projects and energy planning – all based on the assumption that past climate data, without modification, are a reliable guide to the future. This is no longer a good assumption, since the increasing concentrations of greenhouse gases are expected to cause a significant warming of the global climate in the next century.

The European Community has recognized that any global policy must involve the less developed countries and must work towards sustainable development. It is the industrialized nations of the world that have caused the greenhouse effect, and it is their primary responsibility to repair the damage. However, it has to be remembered that global warming is inextricably linked with problems of development and Third World debt. The rich nations can get to grips with environmental problems only by actively helping the less developed countries. We must find ways to reprocess the debt and give aid for suitable energy schemes in order that the wholesale destruction of the rainforests is not inevitable. We can exploit appropriate technology to help with solar power schemes and agricultural problems; we can point out the errors of our kind of development and encourage the Third World to look for alternative models. We must demonstrate positively that we are prepared to rethink our lifestyle in the West, remembering that actions always speak louder than words.

So what can be done on a personal level to halt the environmental degradation of our planet? One thing that is common to all modern societies, whether they be capitalist or socialist, is the feeling of individuals that they are powerless to act. Yet we have shown the tremendous power of the consumer with regard to ozone depletion. Green consumers have become a powerful lobby. *The Green Consumer Guide*, written by John Elkington and Julia Hailes, demonstrates the power of the individual to influence the market. The next step is to question the very notion of our own consumerism. Is what I buy really necessary, and do my purchases waste resources or damage the environment? Do the goods I buy harm the less developed countries? Can I buy locally, thus reducing transport costs? And, most important of all, am I prepared to assume personal responsibility for the state of the planet? Recognizing the links between ourselves and the planet is the first step.

Perhaps the most important action we can take is to use less energy. As we have shown earlier in this chapter, global warming is perhaps the greatest threat to continuing life on this planet. And one of the biggest contributors to global warming is the amount of energy we use, whether it be by driving cars or by generating electricity. If we used energy efficiently, we could reduce carbon dioxide emissions by some 127 million tonnes each year.

We can each plant a tree, eat less meat, demand food free from poisonous chemicals, reject unnecessary packaging and buy cruelty-free produce. We can join and support environmental groups such as Friends of the Earth and Greenpeace. We can complain about pollution, and we can lobby MPs and local councillors. We can try to lead lives that are in harmony with our environment rather than in competition with it.

Global arms spending of $1 million every thirty-five seconds needs to be seen for the madness it really is. The money currently spent on defence should be spent on making the world a healthier place. The idea that militarism or global capitalism will cure the planet's ills is a delusion.

Production based on profit rather than on need does not lead to higher standards of living for all; it benefits the rich minority and greatly increases the chances of total ecological collapse. In other chapters we have shown the immense power of the multi-nationals to control national economies and bypass national laws on environmental control.

Only when governments understand the seriousness of the global crisis rather than waiting for yet more proof will the green vision be realized. Only when politicians take concrete steps to reduce global warming instead of pandering to the whims of industrialists and financiers will we be able to say that a sustainable future is possible. Economic activity is a root cause of ecological crisis. To solve our environmental problems we must also transform our economy. A green model would be based not on the nightmare of continual material expansion and waste but on sustainability, cooperation, justice and respect for nature. Although change is never easy and often uncomfortable, the green route is the only one that would lead to both ecological and economic sanity.

In short, we need a different kind of growth.

4 INDUSTRIAL DISARMAMENT

Criticism of growth is regarded as unacceptable. To be against expansion is the ultimate heresy in a society that sees money as its god, econometricians as its high priests, advertising executives as its clergy and pieces of plastic as icons. Yet tackling growth is vital. Environmental problems cannot be banned, filtered, legislated against or taxed out of existence; they demand that we change our economic thinking in a way that is fundamental.

The logic of all other political parties is one of more and more, of politics as the pursuit of economics, economics as the creation of more things. Even the term 'sustainable growth' has been stolen to mean the substantial exploitation of the Earth rather than as a way of meeting human needs while maintaining ecological balance. However else they may disagree, political parties (other than the Greens) unite around one policy, an ever-increasing Gross National Product (GNP). But GNP cannot continue to soar skywards without creating the kind of instability that will bring it and all of us crashing back to the ground with disastrous results.

There are dozens of reasons why the economy cannot expand for ever, but one of the most fundamental challenges comes from the greenhouse effect. Since palaeolithic times we have lit fires and burned wood to cause CO_2 and particle emission. Some argue that coal was used in Britain as early as the Bronze Age. After just a century or so of industrialization and little more than forty years of high-growth consumerism in half the globe, we have drastically increased the percentage of carbon dioxide in the atmosphere. Economic growth will be limited by the greenhouse effect because we cannot continue to burn large quantities of coal, oil or natural gas without causing global warming.

Even if we ignore the greenhouse effect, it is clear that increasing the consumption of fossil fuels as a means by which to produce increasing quantities of goods will have potentially ecocidal effects.

Energy demand puts direct pressure on the Earth's eco-systems, key to the global life-support system. It is not just that oil and coal will some day run out (although this is another limit to growth) but that as they become scarcer they will become more expensive in both economic and environmental terms. The more distant fossil fuels are from 'civilized society', the greater the network of roads necessary to get drilling equipment to the site of an energy reserve, the deeper the mine, the larger the quantity of tailings (refuse). For the Earth to sustain life, it needs a diversity of habitats. In particular, the oceans and the tropical forests are vital to the maintenance of the basic biochemical cycles that are essential to life. The more coal and oil we take out of the ground, the more such cycles are in danger of disruption. (Alaska has suffered from a major oil-tanker accident; the Carajás mountains in Brazil are the site of a multi-billion-dollar development that will destroy further rainforest). The more the world's economy grows, the greater will be the rewards of developing new reserves of energy whatever the consequences.

Mrs Thatcher proclaims that nuclear power is the only solution to the greenhouse effect, deftly plucking us from the fire and into the radioactive frying pan. Nuclear power produces a tiny percentage of our energy. Only a minority of countries have nuclear power stations and in all but France and the countries of Eastern Europe nuclear power generates only a fraction of the energy required (in Britain, despite Mrs Thatcher's advocacy, a mere 7 per cent). To meet even 20 per cent of present energy needs nuclear power production would have to be increased massively.

Nuclear power is no bridge over the barriers to growth. Every stage of the atomic cycle, from mining the uranium to transportation and reprocessing, from the operation of the Chernobyls and Harrisburgs of this world to the unsolved problem of what to do with ever-growing quantities of waste, is fraught with difficulties. Every stage is a source of cancer-creating radiation and rocketing costs. Quite simply, nuclear power is too dangerous and too expensive to meet even the tiniest fraction of present energy needs, let alone replace fossil fuels in an expanding global economy. The USA hasn't seen the construction of a new nuclear power station since the 1976 Three Mile Island accident. Austria, Sweden and a host of European countries are phasing out their nuclear power programmes, while even

France and the USSR are seriously questioning their commitment to this source of poisoned power. The accidents that 'could not happen', from minor leaks to the Chernobyl fire, cancer blackspots at Sizewell, Dounreay and Sellafield, the proliferation of nuclear weapons via energy production – these and many other considerations make the risk of nuclear power unacceptable. It is inconceivable that a nuclear power programme that met 50 per cent (or even 100 per cent as Mrs Thatcher might wish) of our global energy demand instead of 0.5 per cent, multiplied in turn by exponentially increasing economic growth rates, could do so without causing apocalyptic damage. Even if we learned to live with a high radiation environment, such a programme would absorb all of the world's known and predicted reserves of uranium within a few short years – hardly a sound basis for sustainable economic activity, as is claimed by its supporters.

Fast-breeder reactors, which produce plutonium and can generate up to seventy times more energy than conventional power plants, may be seen as another nuclear way forward. But breeders are difficult and dangerous sources of energy, as they operate at very high temperatures, use highly volatile sodium as a cooling agent and contain 4–5 tonnes of plutonium. It is difficult to see how tens of thousands of reactors could operate without contributing to the risk of meltdown or the proliferation of nuclear weapons, which need just a few kilograms of plutonium to be effective.

Fusion is heralded as a new source of electricity too cheap to be metered, just as fission used to be, but it is both technically a distant prospect and has its own risks. Although the risks of catastrophic meltdown or explosive nuclear reaction would not apply, fusion would produce large quantities of waste. Ted Trainer, in his book *Abandon Affluence!*, notes:

> There would also be a considerable problem of disposing of old reactors. Their life may be much shorter than that of fission reactors; twenty years has been mentioned. Neutron bombardment in the reactor would induce radioactivity in some materials that have very long lives. The niobium which is necessary to contain corrosive lithium has a radioactive half-life of 29,000 years. Permanent waste storage would be needed for these substances. If we had 15,000 reactors, each with a life of twenty years and each containing 150 tonnes of radioactive materials,

then each year 112,500 tonnes of material would have to be
buried permanently and safely. This is more than twice the
quantity of fission reactors. (Page 74)

Lord Marshall, the former chair of the Central Electricity Generating
Board (CEGB), an enthusiastic exponent of the nuclear dream,
stated, 'The chance of it [fusion] being commercial is zero.'

Even if energy could be produced safely, without the risk of cancers
or the emission of carbon dioxide, continual growth would remain
problematic. Western consumerism creates havoc on a global scale.
Peasants in Africa, Asia and South America are pushed off their
tenancies because it is more profitable to produce coffee, tea or soya
for us than to use the land to feed them. Our demands force the
poorest people on to hillsides and other types of marginal land, where
desperate attempts at cultivation cause soil erosion or destroy areas of
wood or natural grassland. Market forces transmit destruction right
across the planet. Rainforests are seen as uneconomic and burned to
make way for short-lived cattle pastures to supply North American
burgers before degrading into desert or being transformed into groves
of eucalyptus, in one case for the production of toilet rolls.

As our economies grow, so the waste mounts up. After just a few
decades of consumerism we are already running out of rubbish dumps,
and toxic waste is increasingly being exported to the Third World,
destroying the health of local peoples as well as assaulting the natural
environment vital to the well-being of all of us. Nor is the First World
immune: New York City once offered a local council in Cheshire $1
million to dump its rubbish in the Manchester Ship Canal!

Much has been made of the decline of traditional 'dirty' industry,
which produces cumbersome capital and resource-expensive items,
but silicon can be just as dirty as smoke stacks. Information technology is by no means clean technology. Silicon Valley in California
has had its pollution scares. A computer-components factory in Thai-
land caused so much damage that the local population burned it to the
ground.

During the twentieth century thousands of new chemical compounds, with unknown or toxic side effects, have entered the environment. The excessive use of antibiotics in factory farming is having
repercussions. Pesticides have created more virulent pests. Biotechnology, seen by both 'green' socialists such as Ken Livingstone and

'green' capitalists such as John Elkington as an environmentally accept-able solution to our problems, is potentially very dangerous. While new 'bugs' may be used to suck oil from otherwise uneconomic wells, transform rubbish into feed for farm animals, stop ground frost from decimating Californian strawberry crops and perform other miracles, they have the potential to do cataclysmic harm. The splitting and splicing of genes will undoubtedly resemble science's attempts to split and splice molecules into lucrative new compounds – penicillin as well as thalidomide, plastic as well as plutonium, deadly new illnesses, mal-engineered pests that wipe out wheat fields or cause planes to crash. The most useful by-products of biotechnology might, in the wrong context, do real harm: bugs that degrade synthetic rubbish would be deadly on the loose, degrading telephone wires, aircraft engines, the components of kidney machines. ICI, in its 1988 annual report entitled 'Making the World a Better Place', proudly announced that 'the seeds business works on methods of giving nature an added nudge towards greater efficiency ... Plants can be given capabilities which they otherwise would not have.' The idea of Frankenstein-like financiers and industrialists inventing and claiming ownership over entirely new species is both frightening and immoral.

'Development', in the form of concrete and of monoculture, threatens to turn the whole planet into a biological desert. Cities are expanding at an alarming rate. Inter-tidal zones are being polluted as mangrove gives way to marina. Over-consumption is leading to soil erosion and desertification, which in turn cause famine and exert pressure on formerly fertile areas. We are pulling out the plugs of the system that keeps us alive. Every indicator is showing red: species diversity, water quality, weather patterns, the number of refugees. There is even growing evidence that some earthquakes are caused in part by human actions. We are unravelling nature like an old jumper.

While we need to develop eco-friendly technology, legislate against poisonous chemicals, remove additives from food and create incentives for energy conservation, all such measures remain peripheral to the main cause of our troubles – an ever-expanding economy. Quite simply, the economy cannot grow for ever and has probably already grown too large to be supported by the natural wealth and natural systems of planet Earth. Even if the present system of global apartheid persists, whereby a powerful elite in the north lives off the cheap food, cheap labour and cheap raw materials supplied by a suffering south, it is difficult to see how such over-consumption can be maintained, let alone allowed to grow further or exported to the poorest. As Brig Oubridge, a former co-chair of Green Party Council, puts it: 'By any sober analysis conventional politicians and economists are apologists for the most excessive system of all-consuming greed in human history'.

Greens, rejecting the industrial growth proposed by just about everybody else, believe that we need industrial disarmament. Opposition to institutionalized greed defines our politics more than any other single factor. We need to use less, rationing the content of the larder today and allowing it to be replenished naturally, instead of gorging ourselves today and leaving our children to starve tomorrow. An ecological economy would conserve, rather than consume, resources for the future. Non-renewable resources such as metals would be used as sparingly as possible and replaced with renewables wherever possible. The substitution of high-performance ceramics for steel components is one particularly exciting example of eco-friendly technology. Potentially renewable resources, from rainforests to the living soil, would be used in a sustainable manner rather than ripped apart for short-term profit. Nuclear power would be phased out and non-polluting energy sources used to replace the burning of fossil fuels. The provision of local services, an expansion in social capital, including libraries, schools and community centres, plus investment in new systems of public transport would all reduce resource use. In essence, a green economy would recycle all its elements so as to maintain prosperity on a long-term basis.

Despite being derided as dreamers, the Greens are the only political party to have mapped out a path to a society that is sustainable into the future, and its policies are described in its *Manifesto for a Sustainable Society* (MFSS). The old-fashioned parties almost totally ignored ecology until the late 1980s, although warning signs have been clear since the late 1960s. Only the Greens have looked at the economic roots of our ecological problem and found ways of achieving ecological sustainability without damaging economic stability. The Green Party believes, however, that sustainability must be linked with social justice. It is no good saving energy while at the same time increasing the number of pensioners dying from hypothermia, or reducing petrol consumption by isolating one-parent families on sprawling housing estates far away from the doctor, the school and the shops. Economic justice is explored in detail in subsequent chapters, but it should go without saying that ending poverty is as important to solving our problems as removing pollution.

Generating energy in an ecologically sound way is vital. At present 90 per cent of our energy requirements are supplied by fossil fuels – petrol for cars, coal and oil to fire power stations, gas for domestic heating. Nuclear power, which provides the balance, is unlikely to increase because of its cost, which is prohibitive even to a government as pro-nuclear as Mrs Thatcher's. Alternative sources of energy, principally in the form of hydro-electricity, supply a mere 3 per cent of the total. The equivalent of 325 million tonnes of coal each year is needed to provide for the 56 million people in the UK; a comprehensive conservation plan could cut our consumption to a fraction of this volume without discomfort. We use the equivalent of 6 tonnes of coal per person per year: we could get by on just two. A Friends of the Earth energy report concluded that we could save up to 50 per cent of our energy requirements simply by promoting energy conservation. Instead the Thatcher government has taken steps to reduce funds for those bodies whose job it was to implement energy-efficient schemes. Green Party policy emphasizes the importance of the so-called 'fifth fuel', that of conservation. But even if energy consumption were markedly reduced, we would still need to produce energy, though without irreparably damaging nature and at a cost that we could afford.

Renewable sources of energy are unlimited in a way that coal, oil or uranium can never match and, for the most part, can be produced with zero pollution. The energy of the sun, wind and waves could be harnessed to meet a large chunk of our energy needs. Electricity produced from waves could, without any new technological innovations, provide 10 per cent of present energy needs (30 per cent of the total, given proper conservation). Geothermal energy, produced from the heat of 'hot rocks' deep below the surface of the Earth, could provide 1 per cent of needs by the year 2000 (3 per cent in an ecological society). Wind farms are already planned by the CEGB and may provide another 10 per cent (again, 30 per cent if energy were used sparingly). The gains could be higher. The official 'Strategic Review of Renewable Energy', produced by the government as long ago as 1982, argued that fully developed renewables could meet all of our energy needs even without allowing for conservation, and it estimated that, if necessary, offshore wind generation could supply 50 per cent of all needs and wave energy 25 per cent. Less ambitious commentators admit that even at current prices much of our energy could be generated economically by renewable resources. Electricity produced by wind turbines, at a production cost of 2.5–3.2 pence per kilowatt hour, compares almost exactly with coal at 2.5–3 pence per kilowatt hour. Small wind generators can be installed on roofs for £300, and the price would fall if scrap materials were recycled. Solar power could provide energy as well, both via photo-electric cells (which, although expensive, are falling in price) and through designing buildings to catch the heat of the sun by means of what is known as passive solar design. Wave power generation would cost little to establish initially (though large barrages would probably become necessary) and would also push up energy production appreciably.

The delight of alternative energy production is the large number of sources that, in combination, offer energy production that is both economically and ecologically acceptable. The drawbacks are years of neglect, underfunding and lack of serious investment or research. Greens would phase out nuclear power within four years and progressively reduce energy production from fossil fuels. Over the years governments of all shades have been grossly irresponsible about planning for when oil reserves run out. The greenhouse effect now makes the need for energy efficiency and alternative sources of production extremely urgent.

Some alternative energy sources actually reduce the quantity of greenhouse gases that reach the upper atmosphere. Biogas generation produces energy by burning methane given off by human or animal waste, rubbish or decaying vegetation. Methane is a far more potent gas than the carbon dioxide that it breaks down to on burning, and if we could burn off methane in large enough quantities the greenhouse effect would be eased considerably. There is another good reason for burning methane productively: the Inspectorate of Pollution has warned that many landfill sites that are used to dispose of our rubbish carry 'a significant risk of accidental explosion' because of the gas. Several explosions have already occurred, and the risk increases daily, yet if tapped for fuel, such dumps could generate 3 million tonnes of methane and make a significant contribution to our energy needs. Given the political will, methane generation could turn both rubbish and sewage into a beneficial resource rather than a cost.

Energy can also be 'grown'. Crops such as sunflowers, sugarbeet, belts of fast-growing trees and many other biological sources of energy can be planted and harvested for conversion to alcohol fuel. Alcohol can easily be substituted for oil. During the Second World War, when petrol was rationed, enterprising people used industrial spirits to get around. Alcohol is an extremely clean fuel and has few of the carcinogenic and polluting by-products that are associated with burning petrol. Although when burning it releases carbon dioxide this would not necessarily be a problem if new fuel crops were grown to absorb the CO_2 from the atmosphere in the kind of sustainable forms of production advocated by the Greens. Alcohol, alas, is not the solution to our problems. The romantic dream of growing all our power and producing other by-products for export and social activity is far from realistic as alcohol is an expensive energy source and likely to remain so. Further, in developing countries such as Brazil the production of ethanol for cars has displaced food crops for the hungry. Alcohol will have a role in an integrated green energy strategy, especially when the wind drops or the sun hides behind clouds. Sadly, producing your own energy by this method is illegal in Britain today!

Energy crops can be used in other ways, and biological sources known as biomass already make up a significant part of global energy production. Wood can be produced and burned on a sustainable basis using traditional practices like coppicing. Straw is used to power Lord Montagu's Hampshire estate at Beaulieu, and many farmers are now finding it a convenient source of energy.

This chapter is not a technical report, and although it would be possible to examine exotic and ecological sources of energy for another ten or twenty pages, the most important point to be made is that power can be produced by sustainable, non-polluting methods. Our ability to meet energy needs without destroying our environment or wrecking the economy depends on the proper funding of the sources of energy discussed above. The Green Party, it goes without saying, would divert the billions of pounds now invested in the technical cul-de-sac of atomic energy into renewable sources. Central to its energy policy is the creation of new District Energy Authorities, which would 'implement a long-term rational energy policy well suited to the District and based on using such local energy resources as were available' (*MFSS*, EN 200).

Greens would also strive to reduce energy consumption. Energy conservation can be achieved without pain. Practical steps have already been taken by some local authorities (although, admittedly, only a minority) to meet housing needs while cutting energy bills. Fifteen low-energy terraced houses built in Cheetham, Manchester, in 1981 combined floor, wall and loft insulation with separate temperature controls for each room to cut energy use to one third of the UK average, although higher internal temperatures were achieved than on neighbouring housing estates. The measures paid for themselves in just two and half years and are now being introduced into all new local authority building in Manchester.

Very few houses are now being built by local authorities because of the government's distaste for council housing. The Green Party would like to see the money acquired from council house sales reinvested in conservation homes in order to reduce both energy consumption and homelessness. (Under present legislation this would be illegal for Green Party-controlled local authorities.) More ambitious alterations than those used in Cheetham could cut energy consumption further: windows could be used to increase the amount of daylight so as to harness energy from the sun's rays; ventilation systems, rather than open windows, could keep air fresh in winter; other waste heat could be recycled. Some new office blocks use no extra heating, gaining all the warmth needed in well-insulated and well-designed buildings from the heat given out by photocopiers, coffee machines and office workers!

It would be possible to reduce energy bills for commercial and home heating to a mere 5–10 per cent of current costs, but this would demand the rebuilding of most of Britain to conservation standards, a task that would be both physically and economically impossible. Instead we should design for conservation and fund a massive campaign of insulation for existing housing stock.

Greens argue that the increasing use of gadgets like electric carving knives, power-assisted toothbrushes and automatic tin openers creates unnecessary waste and that such devices could be phased out without causing the able-bodied any real inconvenience. It is tragic that so much research is devoted to trivial electrical goods when the majority of our disabled citizens lack the tools they need to lead independent lives. An electric wheelchair gives genuine freedom rather than the illusory freedom so many of us think we have when we purchase quite useless products. Even the appliances that we do need can be made to run on less power. A typical fridge uses 270 kilowatt hours of electricity a year, yet the best-designed models on sale in the European Community use just 70 kw hours (well below a green two-thirds energy-conservation target). Although energy-efficient fridges cost £40 more than standard models (at 1989 prices), they save £11 a year in electricity. Better motors and seals would reduce the energy demand of a wide variety of appliances. A green energy policy would promise to make all energy-efficient goods cheaper. The Stop Hinckley Expansion campaign, giving evidence to the inquiry into the construction of a third nuclear power station in Somerset, showed that the introduction of low-energy light bulbs into every British home would reduce energy demand by the equivalent of two pressurized water reactors. The present government, despite its supposed greenness, has no plans to introduce labelling for energy-saving products. Consumers must be given the information to make energy-efficient choices.

The car has been the advertiser's dream. Speed, strength, success with women, wealth, superiority – these are just some of the images that surround the car. The mean machine has become a status symbol for most young men. We give our cars names. We cherish them. We race them. We make love in them. Our world is structured around them. Cars are killing machines that cause more fatal accidents than any other mechanical device known to Western civilization. Cars kill more people in Northern Ireland than the armed conflict. Directly and indirectly, motor-vehicle fatalities account for more deaths per annum than war. There are over 5,000 deaths and 70,000 serious injuries a year on British roads alone.

Not only do we kill with cars but we are slowly killing our planet because of them. About 30 million cars are manufactured every year, and each one contributes to the massive 6,000 million tonnes of carbon dioxide that we pour into the atmosphere annually. Nitrous oxide from car exhausts is the most important source of acid rain. Although the car gives us tremendous personal freedom and mobility, such gains must be balanced by the damage to the environment that their ownership entails. it has been estimated that there are 350 million cars in use worldwide, and together they produce about 10,000 billion cubic metres of exhaust fumes annually. If it were not for the fact that most of the poisonous fumes rise up into the atmosphere, we would be suffocated by them and life would be annihilated.

Cars are ecologically unacceptable, but for most of us they have become essential. When politicians proclaim their green credentials they conveniently forget their own means of getting to Westminster or Whitehall. The *Sun* claims in shocked headlines that Greens would ban the car, yet even many members of the Green Party shy away from criticizing this deadly but necessary component of modern living. Greens would like to see fewer cars but realize that providing people with alternatives is better than forcing them off the road. Most of us commute to work; local schools have been replaced by inner-city colleges and village shops by out-of-town supermarkets. To work, study or eat we have to travel increasing distances. The isolation of those who have no access to four wheels, particularly the very young and the very old, is another forgotten but pernicious by-product of a society oriented around the car. Such trends need to be reversed. Decentralization must be used to restore clinics, schools, hospitals and shops to local communities, and Greens would discourage commuting (hardly a pleasurable pastime). We need to reduce travel by encouraging the development of communities in which employment, housing and other facilities are integrated. The *MFSS* states: 'Smaller, more self-sustaining communities would require much less transport. The emphasis would be on local provision of goods, services, leisure and commercial requirements. Planning procedures should be fully subject to democratic control' (TR 200). Ultimately, the most cost-effective, humane and environmentally sound solution to car chaos involves reducing the need to travel in the first place.

Positive steps would be taken to encourage the use of car-share schemes, such as pick-up points. A levy would be payable on certain roads when cars failed to meet such conditions as multiple occupancy, as is already the case in some cities abroad. Regular health checks for drivers, together with driving tests every fifteen years, would be requirements under the law. Driving while under the influence of alcohol or drugs would result in an immediate life-long ban.

Good cheap public transport, including buses, barges, trams and light railways within cities, would also reduce dependence on the car. Few people enjoy spending time in traffic jams, and in London travelling by car is rapidly becoming a nightmare, though at present public transport is worse. The Underground system is in crisis, with its increasing fares, lengthening delays and declining safety record. Three thousand staff have been cut from London buses, according to the *Economist*; the removal of conductors in such cost-cutting exercises has made buses 10–15 per cent slower. Even if they had to pay more for their petrol as a result of the levying of pollution taxes, many people would use their cars just as much as before. Many areas of Britain are served by poor, infrequent and expensive public transport or none at all.

The profit motive is an inappropriate basis for a green transport system. Community bus schemes, dial-a-ride and disabled transport will play a major part in any green transport policy. Greens would restore the Beeching cuts that decimated British Rail in the 1960s and would recognize the need for public investment in rail. Rail travel uses much less land and less energy and creates infinitely less pollution than the car. Freight too could be moved by train rather than by 40-ton juggernauts. Rail transport needs to be integrated with minibus services radiating out from rural railway stations, rather than ignoring timetables and stranding passengers. In short, Greens would make mobility without the car a real and far from inconvenient possibility.

Something like 70 per cent of journeys are less than 8 kilometres in length or, put another way, would take less than half an hour by bike. In inner London it is already faster to commute by bike than by car, bus or train. Sadly, casualties among cyclists are nine times higher per mile than among motorists – motor vehicles force cyclists off the road. In contrast to the billions of pounds spent on roads, as little as a few thousand pounds invested in cycle lanes would make cycling safer and would boost mobility. Bikes create no fumes or pollution, save on fossil fuels and are healthy to use. The carrying of bicycles on public transport could be free and the provision of cycle parks the duty of local authorities, which would also provide heavy-duty cycle locks free of charge.

Pedestrians need to be given a better deal as well. At present the rest of the community subsidizes the motorist in his or her destruction through tax relief on company cars and an open cheque from the Exchequer for the construction of new roads: poor pedestrians pay VAT to subsidize wealthier car drivers! Greens would end such allowances and use tax incentives to encourage non-polluting forms of travel.

Nobody denies the right to mobility. We should all have access to the transport facilities we need. Yet the truth is that today the system is stifling the society it is supposed to serve. Cars crawl at the rate of 8 miles an hour through London, Glasgow and other large cities. Our motorways are notorious for traffic jams, delays and repairs, and it is well known that new road schemes, far from easing traffic congestion, encourage drivers to use their cars for ever lengthier journeys. Already the Confederation of British Industry and the Road Haulage Association are calling for the construction of a new motorway to relieve congestion on the M25, which itself was built with the intention of relieving London of heavy traffic.

The Green Party would abolish the road-fund licence and increase fuel taxes in a move to persuade citizens to use public transport. We would include a third-party insurance levy in the price of fuel and ban the building of town-centre car parks. Where possible, the use of the private car in city centres would be banned. Citizens would benefit by having cleaner cities; there would be fewer accidents; and those who wished to use bicycles could do so without fear.

Modern agriculture is another sink of energy and source of pollution. Both nitrogen fertilizers and chemical pesticides are energy-intensive by-products of the petroleum industry, while farming becomes more like a form of heavy industry every day. Agribusiness clearly cannot sustain soil fertility on a long-term basis, let alone leave room for wildlife or allow rural communities to thrive. More energy goes into the ground in farming than comes out in food value. Soil erosion is becoming prevalent in Britain and across the world. Experts argue that, in energy terms, agriculture now is far less efficient than in pre-industrial days.

Pollution, from nitrates in water to pesticide-drenched farm workers, is yet another problem. It is hardly necessary to catalogue the destruction of hedgerows and the degrading of land over the last thirty years. Farming in Britain is a very visible reminder of ecological destruction on a far wider scale. Greens would scrap the present system of EEC subsidies that encourage farmers to rip down hedgerows and lay waste to wild heathland, phasing in a system of organic agriculture that would cut the food mountains as well as the tanks full of polluting chemicals. Money saved by cleaner rivers could be invested in research into organic land management, training for young farmers and conversion grants.

Greens believe that more people should have access to the land and would end the current stranglehold of large landowners by means of grants and a system of community ground rent designed to split up land holdings of many thousands of acres. At present, 52 per cent of all land is owned by a mere 1 per cent of the population. Greens do not believe that it is enough to 'set aside' small areas for wildlife while continuing to uphold a system of agriculture that is hostile to the natural world and to humanity. The Agricultural Development Advisory Service (ADAS) would be expanded, and the Soil Survey, sold off by Mrs Thatcher to Unilever, would be restored to public ownership. There would also be incentives to return substantial areas of Britain to deciduous mixed woodland, as a means both of countering the greenhouse effect and of producing wood on a sustainable basis into the future. Coppicing would be encouraged, as would tree planting in urban areas.

Greens would like to see a countryside with village schools and shops, convenient public transport, jobs and cultural opportunities arguing for the creation of 'self-reliant communities that retain the fruits of local investment and activity and preserve the conditions where people can live in ways that care for habitats and wildlife and allow them to fulfil spiritual, social and intellectual needs' (MFSS, C 110). While Greens would maintain the green belt and reject the expansion of uniformly ugly housing estates across the countryside, they would like to see more people living in rural areas and attempts to combat rural homelessness. Conversely, urban areas need to be greened and made pleasant to live in. The *Manifesto for a Sustainable Society* argues for a more natural balance between the two, noting: 'Rural and urban communities meet the many different needs of people in a healthy society. They are not separate from each other and one should not dominate the other. In a green society, towns will not grow beyond the ability of the countryside around them to provide fresh and healthy water and food, recreation, timber and wildlife habitats. There will be a constant flow of environmental, social and cultural information between them. Towns will return compostable materials to the countryside' (*MFSS*) C 102). With a sharp cut in vehicle emissions and the banishing of lead pollution, allotments would enjoy a renaissance, and urban food production, from city farms to mushroom growing in the basement, could be boosted.

But green politics is more than the political economy of landscape gardening, and any green government would have to find ways of drastically cutting our consumption of resources as a means of reforming agricultural practices and making cities into pastoral paradises complete with urban meadows. To survive ecologically and leave enough for the poor of this planet we must consume less. There is little need for the production of electric toothbrushes, Filofaxes or remote-control units for hi-fis, especially when the production of such goods directly depletes the Earth's store of scarce resources, adds to the greenhouse effect and causes us to cover more land in rubbish. Green politics goes hand in hand with green lifestyle changes, but living more simply does not mean going without. Items such as fridges and cookers could be made to last for longer, repaired with cheap, standardized spare parts and reused, finally recycled so as to reduce waste while maintaining what we have.

The average milk bottle is used forty times. If milk bottles, why not all other bottles? Recycling needs to be preceded by reuse instead of becoming a means of avoiding real conservation. Smashing up bottles in a bottle bank is like throwing away after just one year something that has a life of forty years. A Green government would swiftly introduce a Minimum Packaging Act with specifications for packaging that would ensure that waste was minimized and that the shape of bottles was standardized to allow for maximum reusability. A new Standards Commission, incorporating the British Standards Institution, the Design Council and the Patent Office, would make sure that consumer goods were produced in such a way as to maximize energy conservation, recyclability and long life while minimizing energy consumption and waste. Guarantee periods for goods would be extended, and innovators who came up with longer-lasting products would receive a royalty from central or regional government if their inventions were put to practical use. Trends towards the miniaturization of components would also be encouraged by government action.

The Green Party has long urged that local authorities be required to recycle municipal and domestic waste. Recycling is good for the environment and for our ailing balance of payments. The creation of rubbish leads directly to the destruction of natural habitats as a consequence of our search for somewhere to dump it. The transportation of waste by juggernauts disrupts the peace of city and countryside alike and is yet another form of greenhouse gas-creating energy consumption. Rubbish dumps produce methane gas that can lead to explosions, harbour chemicals such as PCBs that have been disposed of illegally and attract colonies of rats. Rubbish in a Green Britain would be a resource. In 1989 Avon County Council sent half a million tonnes of rubbish to a dump in Buckinghamshire at a cost of £14.35 per tonne. Members of Bristol Green Party have pointed out that the scrap value of glass at £15 per tonne, paper at £12, light iron and plastic at £20, and aluminium at an extraordinary £600 per tonne could make this rubbish into a major source of income for the community. Every tonne of lead, tin, aluminium or platinum recycled or reused reduces Britain's balance-of-payments deficit by hundreds of pounds and, in the case of many metals, thousands of pounds. The community-supported Anti-Waste Scheme in Cardiff estimates that on average each Briton throws away rubbish worth £1,000 every year and that 98 per cent of refuse could be reclaimed or recycled. Malcolm Williams, the scheme's director, believes that its collecting lorries could be run on methane produced from organic waste and garden clippings. Sheffield City Council, which has introduced the first large-scale recycling scheme in the country, estimates that 40 per cent of the city's population participates in some form of recycling and that if everybody reused 50 kilos of paper, this would save 250,000 trees every year. 10,000 homes in the city have been supplied with separate 'blue boxes' for organic, paper, glass and metal rubbish. CFCs from fridges must be recycled by local authorities instead of being allowed to escape and damage the ozone layer.

Greens are not Luddites (or, for that matter, Calvinists) who want to see people suffer poverty and want, but green politics is based on the fundamental realization that material growth, in the sense of producing and consuming ever more, cannot continue without wrecking the planet and causing massive social injustice. Greens believe in a different kind of growth – a growth in human well-being, achieved through technological and economic reforms – to put us back in balance with nature. We can conserve and recycle our way to the kind of society that sustains itself continually. Old-style politicians and economists have no idea what to do when the oil runs out. Greens have the ideas and the commitment to make the future possible. But what is feasible in scientific terms must be realized in terms of sound and sustainable economic policies. The Greens' greatest challenge will be to deliver prosperity without pollution, to create an economy that provides material security as well as fulfilling ecological aims.

We can solve the ecological crisis, but there is little point in conserving nature at the cost of economic chaos. We can make products last longer, conserve energy, share, repair and recycle our way to sustainable prosperity. We can halt growth by cutting waste and still live comfortably. Prosperity is possible without pollution, exploitation and the destruction of the rainforests. It will be more difficult, however, to maintain the economic cycle without economic growth.

A green economic policy sounds like common sense. It is 'good housekeeping' – though this point eludes Mrs Thatcher – not to fill the larder by taking from the poor and robbing the next generation. It is obviously superior to the Alice in Wonderland approach of conventional economics, which destroys nature, devours scarce resources, thrives on waste and leaves real human needs unfulfilled. But moving from one set of assumptions to the other, although inevitable, will not be easy. The present global economic system needs growth. Firms need to increase turnover to keep up with competitors, and bankers need to lend money on the assumption that businesses will grow so that the initial capital can be returned with interest. Most of us look forward to pay rises that are greater than inflation. We are all part of a system hooked on economic expansion. We can conserve energy and use less petrol, but what of the jobs of car manufacturers or electricity workers? The first Ecology Party manifesto bravely stated, 'The idea of a steady-state economic system based on limited consumption of resources is premature: thus, this manifesto is more than a statement of a new ideal and a list of steps by which it can be achieved. It is a challenge to the established view of the nature of our present social, political and economic system' (*MFSS*, PB 103).

While what seemed visionary in the 1970s looks likely to become common sense in the 1990s, the challenge remains. The most difficult task facing the green movement is how to move from one economic system to another. We have to break the cycle of increasing doses of addictive growth, providing a methadone programme to get through a period of fiscal cold turkey. The problems that bedevil current governments – inflation, falling exchange rates, unemployment and a trade deficit – will not disappear on the day that the Greens come to power. Greens must understand economic cycles as well as natural ones if they are to succeed.

New indicators of economic success or failure are needed. Rather than recording real increases in the standard of living, present indicators measure many factors that reduce our quality of life. Gross National Product (GNP) essentially measures how many goods are produced by the country, but Greens reject the simple notion that goods = growth = happier and healthier human beings. If goods could be made to last longer or could be repaired more easily, this would increase our standard of living in the most material sense, yet if goods were better made and didn't need to be replaced so often, GNP would fall. Goods produced with built-in obsolescence are part of economic 'progress'. As they are replaced, jobs are created, profits rise and the balance-of-payments position of the country producing them tends towards surplus. Real growth should take account of qualitative factors such as workmanship and durability rather than crude quantitive measures of how fast goods are consumed and destroyed. Where production takes place, the use of scarce resources, the contribution to the greenhouse effect and the creation of other ecological ills should be taken into account. At present, if factories pump toxins into a river, leading to increased spending by local water authorities, such spending is counted as 'growth'. If racism and poverty prompt inner-city riots, the resulting increase in police overtime is also regarded as 'growth'.

On the other hand, enterprise that creates real wealth is often ignored. Domestic work, such as cleaning, cooking, bringing up children and gardening, although it is the basis of just about all other economic activity, is undervalued because it is unpaid. Employ a cleaner, and you magically have 'growth'. Vacuum your own home and it disappears. DIY does not show up in the statistics, but the employment of a decorator does. Activity that is outside the monetary economy (usually involving women on what is effectively a domestic slave-labour basis) is invisible, yet the movement of shares or the flow of dollars in exchange for francs on the money market generates massive income and resulting rises and falls in GNP. City brokers burned out at the age of 25 but with £100,000 golden handshakes are hardly as productive, in real terms, as refuse workers or carers, whose activity is rarely recognized, let alone rewarded.

There are so many deficiencies in the present economic system that it is impossible to discuss them all in detail here. What if economic 'expansion' causes poverty (local people pushed out of villages by yuppie-induced house-price rises, peasants hungry because a Western tourist complex engulfs former fishing grounds)? What if growth measures the expansion of the military–industrial complex rather than consumer goods, as is so often the case in the less developed countries? What if growth today leads to poverty in the future by depleting scarce metals that cannot be replaced?

No set of economic indices can ever be perfect (and economists and politicians should stop treating them as such), but there is much that could be done to improve the ones we have. Other indications of human happiness, such as health statistics and housing standards, are just as important as monetary flows. Ecological indices should plot how well we are doing at reducing the greenhouse effect. Non-monetary forms of production should be estimated, however crudely. Qualitative factors, such as consumer satisfaction with goods, should be considered. Above all the negative effects of pollution and waste should be calculated and deducted from GNP.

Economics should be about more than consumption and production, dominated by the wishes of finance houses, advertisers and the money markets. It must be about human needs and happiness. A green economy, rather than concentrating on the current system of politics, which exploits electoral cycles by offering tax cuts and promises of increased expansion just before general elections, would set goals higher than the post-war consensus among the traditional parties of encouraging people to spend, spend, spend. We are all materialists; without food, housing, transport facilities and clothing none of us could survive. Most of us value telephones, videos, books, records, refrigerators and cameras, but life has to be about more than just devouring as many consumer goods as possible. A successful economic strategy needs to meet human needs on a basis wider than the merely material. Greens argue that one reason why people in the Western world consume so much is because they seek compensation for other needs that remain unfilled. If we find life boring and useless, lack channels for our creativity or feel that we have no control over the decisions that affect us, we seek solace in a second television or a compact disc. Real prosperity has to do with meeting real needs, providing good, useful work, interacting with nature, expanding intellectual, spiritual and practical horizons.

One of the most important of these is the need for good work. Creative work is one of the things that makes human beings human. We all need a niche in life. We all need to do something that we feel is worth while to give us a sense of self-worth. Work is a way of breaking down the barriers between people and building up a real sense of community. Finally, as one Zen proverb puts it, there is the concept of 'no work, no food'. We have to meet physical needs and create the goods that make human life possible.

Most people spend 20 per cent of their lives at work, yet most of us seem to hate it. Human life is a drab affair if it is dominated by useless toil and pointless, thankless labour. Huw Beynon, in his survey 'Working for Fords', found that most car workers he met would rather have done something else with their lives. They would like to have been PE teachers, craftsmen, journalists or sociologists like himself. Back in the 1920s, after introducing conveyor belts, mechanism and the science of time and motion that limited workers' tasks to the simplest, least creative actions imaginable in a system praised by apologists as diverse as Lenin, Harold Wilson and Mrs Thatcher, Henry Ford claimed, 'I have not been able to discover that repetitive labor injures a man in any way. I have been told by parlor experts that repetitive labor is soul- as well as body-destroying, but that has not been the result of our investigations.' He noted that one man who did the most monotonous task of all, shifting a single gear lever, time after time, to dip a steel hook into a vat of oil, refused to be moved even after eight years and had saved up some $40,000.

Greens would call such a process one of alienation and argue that unsatisfying, brain-numbing work is a source of frustration that leads to greed and dehumanization. But it isn't greed that motivates most car workers, simply necessity – no work, no food. A shop-floor worker at Halewood on Merseyside, considering why he had to work at a soul-destroying career, said to Beynon, 'You don't achieve anything here. A robot could do it. The line is made for morons. It doesn't need any thought. They tell you that. "We don't pay you for thinking," they say. Everyone comes to realize that they're not doing a

worthwhile job. They're just on the line for the money. Nobody likes
to think that they're a failure. It's bad when you know that you're just
a little cog. You just look at your pay packet – you look at what it
does for your wife and kids. That's the only answer.' High-tech has
made things worse rather than better: 'At Halewood, Dagenham and
Longbridge, men in the body plants work alongside the robots producing the shells of the Escort, Sierra and Metro . . . swearing, keeping
up with the robots, feeding the machines. For automation hasn't got
rid of machine-paced assembly-line work. If anything, it has intensified
it. And especially now, when "comparativeness" is the key word and
European workers are fed with warnings of the Japanese.' Yet Japanese
workers held up as paradigms of robotic obedience and, above all,
productive virtue are not necessarily happy with their lot. Satoshi
Kamata, author of *Factory of Despair: Diary of a Seasonal Worker*,
said of his time with Toyota (now moving into the UK to make
cars), 'How similar the labour in this auto plant is to slave labour!
How similar it is to Sisyphus! If it were punishment for some crime,
what kind of crime was it? Should it be a crime for a worker to try to
lead a normal life?'

It isn't just car workers or those in manufacturing industry who
have a hard time, however. Secretaries crouched all day over VDU
screens, otherwise unemployable teenagers, 40-year-olds in post-
Fordist burger bars, cleaners working long and unsocial hours, teachers taking on an increasing workload – all suffer from the fact that their
work is unrewarding. Executive stress and illnesses caused by work
are common enough to be clichés. Greening the work ethic and
creating good work for all is a target of economic policy ignored by
the conventional political parties. Economists forget that economic
systems are maintained by living, sweating, often bored and dis-
satisfied human beings. Real prosperity must put people first.

Pay is an issue closely allied to working conditions, and 'conditions'
is essentially another word for 'environment'. Greens would like to
see work assessed not just in terms of the market but on account of its
value to society. Today the advertising executive is often paid in
excess of £40,000 per annum while the hard-working care assistant in
an old people's establishment is lucky to receive £3 per hour.

Abolishing unemployment will be a major challenge for the green
movement. Present governments dishonestly use unemployment for
their own ends as a means of controlling inflation, of rupturing trade-

union organization and of social engineering. How many times have we experienced the constant cycle, under both Tory and Labour administrations, of spiralling inflation followed by mass unemployment and vice versa? Already at levels that would have astonished commentators in the 1950s and 1960s, unemployment would be likely to rise even more sharply if a Green government shut down polluting factories, halted the arms race and reduced the waste of today's society. Although there are many jobs that could be created – organic agriculture, community medicine, care for the elderly and disabled, recycling, conservation, public transport, insulation programmes, the provision of crèches and nursery care all spring to mind – the result, under the present system, would be a lengthening of the dole queues. Vital to the creation of a workable and fair economy is the concept of work sharing. If fewer people are needed to produce the same quantity of goods, it is better to redistribute work instead of creating a huge underclass of people who have no access to employment. Trainer, in his book *Abandon Affluence!*, argues ambitiously that we could make a green economy succeed on no more than a one-day working week.

At present part-time workers get a bad deal. Union organization is difficult, pay and conditions often poor. The 1980s have seen the substitution of full-time mass employment by part-time, low-paid work. A green 1990s could see the introduction of secure and properly paid part-time work for all. Much of what is known as the 'black' economy needs to be made legal. Unemployed people who do a little work but not enough to support themselves totally are criminalized by the Department of Social Security and forced into working covertly. Emergency tax makes part-time employment unrewarding. The taxation and benefits system needs to be overhauled to cope with the realities of work in the late twentieth and twenty-first centuries. Rather than penalizing part-time workers, Greens would pay everybody a basic income and housing benefit so as to pre-empt poverty, whether they worked full-time, part-time or not at all. The unemployed would have an incentive to seek work, as they would no longer lose out by working a few hours each week. Women would be financially independent. Worksharing would become a viable proposition, as people would be able to afford to work part-time only. Ecological and community ventures would thrive.

Basic income could be funded by cutting back Britain's huge

expenditure on nuclear weapons and power, by replacing current means-tested benefits and by reducing much of the bureaucracy associated with the present system. Coupled with higher taxes on luxury goods and progressive income tax that truly redistributed wealth, this scheme could be made to work.

The present tax and benefits system treats women as second-class citizens, yet they do most of the nurturing and caring that play a fundamental role in society. If we added the cost of caring for the future generation, the old or the physically disabled at home, it would be equivalent to 6 per cent of GNP. If we then added the cost of all other duties women do in the home, the present economy would collapse. Much of this in-built economic sexism could be changed by a basic income scheme that would encourage both sexes to work in the domestic but formally unrewarded economy. The scheme frees people to make choices.

A basic income scheme is no easy panacea, however. Set too low, it would merely reinforce poverty; set too high, it would discourage too many people from working to generate the taxable income necessary to maintain its existence. Yet a carefully judged system is the only way to cope with job losses, increasing numbers of pensioners and the needs of the self-employed who want flexible patterns of work.

Unecological and obsolete industries needed to be transformed. The jobs versus the environment dilemma can be overcome with investment and work-place participation. In the 1970s workers at Lucas Aerospace who seemed likely to be made redundant after a temporary downturn in demand for military aircraft found that there were over a hundred different products, from hob carts for children with spina bifida to road/rail buses that they could design and make without having to introduce new equipment or acquire new skills. Workers' plans for socially useful and ecologically necessary items could be used to preserve jobs and give workers a real stake in producing goods that are needed rather than those that generate short-term profit. A Green government would fund such research and work hard to make changes in the structure of employment as smooth as possible. Not all forms of work could be easily transformed, however: it is difficult, for example, to see how Sellafield could be made into a centre for manufacturing wind generators or a giant depot for tree planting, though it might just be possible to turn Dungeness power station, where Lord Marshall was keen to demonstrate the purity of radioactive water by drinking a tumblerful, into a purification plant. Many of the Ministry of Defence jobs concentrated in towns such as Plymouth, Bath and Barrow could be shifted swiftly and directly into alternative energy production. The conversion of the chemical industry would be a vital step in maintaining both employment and ecological balance.

All of us need to be given more say in the work we do, and Greens would be keen to boost collective ownership, worker cooperatives and self-managed employment. The Cooperative Development Agency would be funded more generously; investment grants would be made available to would-be cooperatives; business studies courses could give more practical advice on self-managed enterprises; while local authorities could help by buying from local cooperatives wherever possible.

Greens reject both nationalization and privatization. Neither, despite the propaganda of left and right, gives ordinary people any control over the means of production. Only a minority of Britons own shares, and where companies such as British Telecom have been floated few ordinary shareholders have any say in how they are run, despite Thatcherite rhetoric to the contrary. The big institutional investors and the super-rich continue to call the shots, while small investors have to pay their way to annual general meetings if they wish to question company policy. On the other hand, nationalization, while vital in the case of natural monopolies like water, gas and rail travel, cannot be seen as an unqualified success, let alone a means of promoting popular participation. British Rail cannot be said to have worked in the best interests of either the public or its work force, even though supposedly we all have a stake in it via state ownership. A self-managed BR would work very differently.

Industry needs to be gently cooperatized. Workers' control alone is not enough; the consumers who use trains and telephones also deserve to make their voices heard via elected local and national boards. But Greens must resist taking too rose-tinted a view of either coops or small businesses. In a society in which we are used to bosses and managers the shift to more adult ways of working, self-management or the election of others to do certain tasks, will not be achieved overnight or without pain. As anybody who has moved from a formal work pattern in an office or factory to self-employment knows, getting down to work on one's own, in a structured and serious way,

is far from easy. The failure of the cooperatives set up in the 1970s by
Tony Benn at ailing firms such as the Meridon motorcycle works was
caused by trying to move too quickly. Such ventures will thrive only
in a society that is more cooperative and more mature than the one we
have at present. Coops will need a lot of support, but the evidence is
that they have enormous potential to do well and create satisfying
work.

Small businesses are praised by all politicians (and by the Greens)
but also have failings. The fact that an enterprise is small doesn't
mean that it is necessarily beautiful. Small, local, 'ecologically' sound
sweatshops still exploit people, and small businesses struggling to
survive sometimes cut corners when it comes to pollution, health,
safety and employment law. Small concerns are likely to have better
labour relations, to enjoy the trust of the local community, but many
are far from perfect.

None the less, small businesses are generally preferable to big ones.
Greens feel that giant multinational companies are likely to cause
giant problems, many large corporations have more power than small
and medium-sized countries. The top 200 multinationals' turnover is
equivalent to a quarter of the planet's gross product. General Motors'
turnover is exceeded only by the GNP of fifteen individual
countries. (*The World Almanac*, New York, 1989)

Greens recognize that large multi- and transnational corporations
could not be dissolved overnight, but practical steps could be taken to
limit, discourage and minimize their operations in the United Kingdom
by means of 'a mandatory code of conduct with supervisory machinery
and sanctions, covering the worldwide operation of all transnational
corporations which might have constituents or associates in the UK.
At the same time the UK would press for such a code to be made
internationally binding through the United Nations' (*MFSS*, EC
429).

Small firms need to be given tax breaks and support while larger
ones are reduced to a manageable size. The American experience of
anti-trust law is depressing, and the British Monopolies and Mergers
Commission has remained largely toothless. Mergers that create stock-
market super-firms should simply be made illegal. Greens believe
firmly in the principle of economic democracy and support the argument that just as most adults have the right to vote, so we should also
have the right to wield commensurate economic influence. People

with multi-million-pound personal fortunes and controlling interests in major firms claim that some should have more say than others, but it is difficult to understand why anyone should have millions of times more economic and financial power than others. We all need a say in the economic decisions that directly shape our lives – often more drastically than parliamentary legislation or government action.

Businesses ultimately need to be controlled cooperatively by the community. Rather than allowing banks to lend money at high interest rates in pursuit of high profits, the extension of credit should be put into democratic hands via local community banks with elected officials. At present projects are invested in and loans given on the basis of profit alone. If a venture is likely to make money and is not obviously illegal, bank managers supply funds. Thus money placed in an account by any of us can be used to fund projects that directly harm us and the environment. All of the four large high-street banks have profited from Third World debt; all have had links with South Africa and some still do. Lloyds and the Midland have invested in projects that destroy the Amazon.

Local banks would have to be run on a prudent financial basis, but they could also assess loans in terms of what was best for the community – enterprises that were socially useful and tended towards conservation. First-time buyers might get lower rates of interest if banking boards elected by local people felt this to be a good thing. Community banking would give people a real say in how their money was used, halt much of the pressure generated by the financial system for ecological destruction and help to revitalize local communities. At present any money placed in accounts in banks in poor areas tends to flow elsewhere, but with community banking even the poorest communities would get some direct help.

Land reform would be another way of giving individuals more control over the means of production. Greens have pioneered the concept of a community ground rent that would encourage wider land ownership.

A green view of economic democracy coincides closely with that of William Morris, evident in a speech given in London on communism:

> The resources of Nature . . . and the wealth used for the production of further wealth, the plant and stock in short, should be communized. If that were done, it would at once check the

accumulation of riches. No man can become immensely rich by the storing up of wealth which is the result of the labour of his own brain and hands; to become very rich he must by cajolery or force deprive others of what their brains or hands have earned for them; the utmost that the most acquisitive man could do would be to induce his fellow citizens to pay him extra for his special talents, if they specially longed for his productions.

Greens see both monetarism and Keynesianism as failed economic experiments. Keynes was writing fifty years before knowledge of the greenhouse effect became common: Keynesian reflation demands exactly the kind of continuous, resource-hungry economic growth that Greens reject as a first principle. Growth as a tool of fiscal management is not sustainable. The economy cannot expand indefinitely without destroying natural systems, impoverishing the developing world or eating up scarce metals and minerals. Economic growth leading to a growth in the use of fossil fuels will be disastrous. Nuclear power is uneconomic, dangerous and unlikely to fill the gap. The economic logic of the post-war period no longer applies. Even if growth can be sustained in the long term, Keynesianism has few tools to deal with the economic challenge of today. What do Keynesians do about stagflation (the combination of high inflation and economic stagnation that is impossible according to Keynesian theory), international debt, European integration and exchange-rate instability caused by the money market?

Nor do monetarist approaches gain favour with the Greens Monetarism has failed to reduce inflation. Any fool can reduce the price of goods by creating 3 million unemployed and massively reducing consumer demand, but Mrs Thatcher's evil-tasting nostrums have done nothing to get inflation down in the long term. Inflation is most dangerous to those on low or fixed incomes, yet monetarists, in their abortive efforts to keep prices down, further impoverish the poorest in society by cutting benefits and services. A monetarism that reduced the public sector borrowing requirement by cutting the pay of top earners, abolishing tax relief on company cars and reducing genuine waste would find some support but would still be a long way from a real solution to inflation.

The policy of raising interest rates to lower inflation pioneered by Nigel Lawson and pursued by his successor, John Major, as an alternative to Milton Friedman's quack remedies, is likely to make inflation even worse. Trying to stop people spending by increasing interest rates is a crude and extremely cruel way of reducing inflation that hits first-time home buyers particularly harshly. As interest rates rise, so does industrial unrest: workers strike for higher wages so that they can meet rocketing mortgage payments. This in turn gives rise to wage-led inflation and government calls for higher interest rates to rein it in. High exchange rates make foreign goods, including raw-material imports, cheaper, reducing inflation but at the massive cost of bankrupting British firms and reducing the country's already shrinking industrial base. A 'strong' pound can be maintained only with the aid of climbing interest rates in the face of economies with real economic strength and appreciating currencies. It is remarkable that a supposedly free-market government should believe in massive intervention to defeat inflation. The fight, even if it is successful, will entail massive costs.

British exports have become comparatively expensive, and demand has dropped, causing a massive and growing balance-of-payments deficit. High interest rates and high exchange rates are a fatal hybrid for firms that have to borrow expensively and sell goods at prices far above those of foreign competitors. In 1989 Britain's imports exceeded its exports to other countries by a record £20 billion. Throughout the 1980s its manufacturing base shrank, shedding millions of jobs, to be replaced by services, the financial sector, insurance and other enterprises that can only live off the backs of industrial producers elsewhere. Paradoxically, we anti-growth, capitalist-hostile Greens believe that British industry is another endangered species in need of salvation. To maintain economic stability Britain needs to start making things again.

The principal cause of inflation is consumer demand. If more people spend more money, prices tend, other things being equal, to rise. Slater, putting it more bluntly, states, 'Inflation is an entirely logical outcome of an economy based on greed' (*Wealth Addiction*, Dutton, New York, 1980). We live in an era of consumer capitalism. Industrial production is mopped up through stimulating people to buy more and more by means of advertising, marketing techniques that play on their guilt about their role as parents or lovers, exploit peer-group pressure and convince us that happiness can be measured in terms of high-tech. The problem is that the goods are being imported and that they are being bought on credit. Credit is simply a way of spending money that does not exist, of expanding the effective supply of liquid cash and pushing demand higher and higher. Inflation will continue to rise unless credit is controlled.

To the extent that inflation is caused by increases in wages, such increases can also be seen as part of the ethos of economic expansion led by consumer-capitalist greed. If top rates of pay are obscenely high, the less well-paid will understandably ask for more as well. Housing – or, rather, the housing shortage – is the most direct cause of wage inflation because homes are so expensive and mortgages so high and because we all need to live somewhere. Any government that fails to get to grips with the housing crisis will fail both to reduce inflation and to meet a very basic economic need. Greens believe in discouraging second-home ownership, in expanding the rental market and in encouraging ecologically sensitive and economic self-build schemes. A society that meets needs and rejects greed will be a society with low inflation.

Britain is heavily dependent on raw materials and finished goods from abroad. If the value of the pound falls in relation to the dollar, mark or yen, prices increase, as such items become more expensive to import. In the long term we will have to pay more for commodities like coffee, cocoa and tea, foodstuffs, metals and minerals from the Third World. Inflation rates in the north are low because death rates in the south are high. We benefit from cheap goods, cheap raw materials and cheap labour, without which prices would rise very sharply. The south needs justice in the form of fair prices and sustainable local economic development. Eventually we must pay a just price within a structure of fair trade. But if we pay more, as inevitably we will, if we seek real social justice and a means of preventing poor people from ripping up the environment out of sheer desperate poverty, inflation will increase. Even without such a shift, minerals and metals are likely to become more expensive as they become more scarce. Resource depletion leads to inflation.

To overcome the balance-of-payments crisis, to keep inflation down and to maintain economic stability into the difficult next century, Britain must become more self-sufficient. We cannot produce everything we need, but if we don't revitalize our manufacturing base, we will be doomed when North Sea oil runs out. We certainly need to produce more of our own energy and food. Britain could give a lead in ecological manufacturing by producing goods that last longer and by developing alternative energy systems and non-polluting forms of production. If our government encouraged the production of conservation goods, such as fridges that run on 70 instead of 270 kilowatt hours of electricity, we could solve many of our economic problems and promote conservation. We need a programme of ecological investment in public transport, low-energy homes and industrial buildings, alternative energy and better community services. Weaning people off the car and making it simpler to get around by bus, rail and bike will ease our economic plight. Car imports make up £9 billion of our trade deficit, a figure that will mushroom if we are forced to import oil again. Manufacturing should not be abandoned but assessed on ecological and social grounds as well as economic ones.

As well as goods, money flows from country to country. Exchange rates are only partly determined by the import and export of goods: to an ever-increasing extent the value of a currency is determined by the activities of the money markets and the flow of 'hot' currency from one economy to another. Investors buy pounds with dollars or francs, in the hope that the pound will increase in value, and sell when they think it is likely to fall. International currency deals dwarf the amount of money that changes hands for goods and can have a major effect on any economy. This is why the question of the European Monetary System (EMS) not only brought down Nigel Lawson (and may bring down Mrs Thatcher) but is of vital importance to any green economic analysis. Mrs Thatcher opposes the EMS partly because it means that people other than herself and her advisers will be able to determine Britain's economic policy but mainly because she knows that the present system would bring any radical alternative to Thatcherism to its knees. Under the present crazy system, which gives financiers more power than voters, any really alternative government would be met by capital flight and the collapse of the pound. One of Mrs Thatcher's first acts on coming to power was to remove exchange controls, booby-trapping any future government that might be seen by the money market to be left of centre. The flow of capital out of Britain could destabilize a government intent on necessary but radical change. To maintain – restore – the power of the electorate, the UK should negotiate for international control of the money markets and promote a more self-sufficient (less easily destabilized) Britain. A Green or green-tinged alternative government would suffer the immediate wrath of the city but could be saved by a system of pegged European exchange rates. Politically motivated attempts to destroy an EMS-linked currency would fail because EMS commits its partners to supporting any such threatened currency. Greens reject plans for a European super-power, whether political or economic, and are rightly hostile to the concept of a single European bank and currency, but the changes that Greens would like to see will need European support.

The Green Party may not have all the answers, but conventional politicians and analysts are asking none of the fundamental questions. A Britain that is both ecologically and economically viable into the 1990s and beyond is the real issue at the heart of British politics, but only the Greens have begun to address it. Economic stability can be guaranteed in the long term only by grassroots regeneration and local control. Green alternatives will work not only now but into the future, which is more than can be said for the other policy choices on offer, but would they be fair? Concern for the environment has been seen by some as a middle-class luxury or a means of conserving greenery for an élite few. Those with wealth will gain from halting growth. Third World peoples are worried that they will pick up the bill for the First World's destruction. The pollution and resource taxes discussed in Chapter 4 would be regressive, hitting the poorest worst. If green politics is to work and gain popular appeal, it needs to end poverty here and abroad.

As the country that introduced the Industrial Revolution in the eighteenth century, Britain could promote the post-industrial revolution that is necessary to see the planet into the twenty-first.

6 SOCIAL JUSTICE

To millions of people talk about the politics of ecology that does not embrace social justice is meaningless. They are inseparable, just as feminism, anti-racism and anti-sexism are an integral part of green politics. The gap between the rich and poor is growing daily, not only in this country but all over the world. Homelessness, an inadequate diet and ill health are not just diseases of the less developed countries; they are spreading in this country and at an alarming rate. While the rich will continue to be able to buy services they can afford, the disadvantaged, people who are considered second class in the eyes of the state, will be left with sub-standard health services, polluted water and deteriorating educational, housing and welfare provision.

It is possible to co-opt the green argument in the cause of preserving the social and economic environment of Thatcher's Britain by protecting middle-class views from the intrusion of lower-class housing in green belt areas and the maintenance of green fields for the gentry to pursue sports such as fox hunting and game shooting. Zero or slower growth is often perceived as a means of maintaining wealth inequality, and a close relationship with nature is taken to mean country rambles and a gentle hack along a leafy lane. Campaigns on behalf of such issues as tree preservation, the desecration of our beaches, the pollution of our seas and rivers, although necessary and worth while, fail to take account of the social problems that are at the root of the ecological crisis.

Many argue that green politics is irrelevant to the vast majority of the world's population and that ecologists are, in the words of one former Labour minister, 'middle-class bastards'. It is important that the green message reaffirms at every opportunity its commitment to the poor and oppressed. Greens must not allow the media to promote a purely environmental image that maintains the hegemony of the present power structure.

The problems of life-threatening pollution and environmental destruction, such as the thinning of the ozone layer, are often dealt with in a way that hurts the poor. It is impossible to change the way in which people use resources without changing their relationship with one another and with their surroundings. In the UK each year over 1,200 people die from hypothermia because they live in old, poorly insulated and insufficiently heated houses, although we have the skill base and the resources to ensure that every house in this country is energy-efficient. However, Thatcherism prefers to leave energy conservation to market forces, allowing power to rise in price in order to ration its use and hitting the poor and disadvantaged most.

Advertising executives have been quick to take advantage of the food and water scare stories that abound, and the promotion of bottled mineral water and organic foods (which, incidentally, are often not organic at all but can be made to seem so by the inadequate labelling system in this country) has soared. For producers of bottled mineral water the trend is highly profitable. To Greens it is an expensive, energy-intensive way of supplying water. Nobody wants to do away with bottled water, but it should be considered a luxury, not a necessity. The danger of a free-market approach is that water filters and organic food become the prerogatives of the rich, while the poor make do with polluted tap water and listeria-infected food.

The recognition that poverty is linked inextricably with ecological destruction must guide green policies. A family living in a tenement block with a leaking roof and peeling wallpaper, and with £40 a week to feed four, can hardly be expected to make the environment a priority. Its basic material needs have to be met. The mother running away from yet another battering by a violent husband needs a safe refuge provided by the community before she can think of the dangers of the greenhouse effect. The child suffering from sexual abuse, the teenager without a home, the unemployed, the psychiatric patient discharged from an institution are all victims of a society that has forgotten a basic human right – the right to love, warmth, shelter, food and water.

It is estimated that there are over 2 million homeless people in the United Kingdom. Of this figure, Centrepoint estimates, approximately 50,000 are aged between 16 and 19 and living rough in central London. A return to the Conservatives' 'Victorian' values has brought in its wake the increasing use of the 1824 Vagrancy Act to detain contemporary beggars, whose untidy, guilt-provoking image sullies the façade of Thatcherite prosperity. Young homeless people fall outside the legal definition of homelessness, and their numbers need to be added to the 116,060 households officially recognized as homeless by the Department of the Environment. Comprehensive information about the number of homeless is impossible to obtain, as the legal definition of homelessness does not include those who, according to the law, have made themselves intentionally homeless, or are sleeping rough, or are sharing inadequate accommodation with relatives or friends. The most recent study of homelessness in London was completed by the Salvation Army, which concluded that there were over 75,000 'overtly' homeless people in London in 1988. The inadequacy of available information about homelessness and the need to rely on figures produced by charitable institutions demonstrate the low priority the issue is accorded by local authorities and government. Furthermore, discrimination emerges from the figures. Black and ethnic-minority people form a disproportionately small number of those recognized as homeless by local authorities and, when housed, suffer more overcrowding and tend to be placed in the worst housing. The London Gay Teenage Group found 11 per cent of young people had been made homeless because of their sexual orientation. In 1986, 35 per cent of households accepted as homeless in London were single-parent households, the majority of which were headed by women.

Everyone has a right to decent accommodation, yet the only area in which government investment has grown significantly has been home ownership. The cost of mortgage interest tax relief for 1988/89 was £5,500 million and estimates for 1989/90 run at £6,750 million (Hansard). The 'right to buy' sales of council houses amount to 861,729 over the period 1980–88, yet local authorities have been limited to spending only 20 per cent of receipts from these sales on new buildings and renovation. 'The ideal green solution would be for each town or village to contain all the facilities for work, social and cultural activities required by the community, and to be surrounded by an agricultural hinterland that feeds it. All such settlements should fit into the ecosystem with minimum disruption of it' (*MFSS*, B 202). To work towards this ideal will require radical changes to our present system.

We should commission, without delay, a survey of the real amount of homelessness in this country and emend the definition of homelessness under the Housing Act 1985. Homelessness is such a severe problem that we should consider requisitioning property that has been empty for a long time, with proper safeguards and adequate compensation, until we are in a position to release new housing on to the market. Local authorities should be free from restrictions governing the amount of money they can spend on housing. All income generated from housing sales should be released and spent on improving existing housing stock and providing appropriate new housing where necessary. However, it is imperative that housing provision should be linked with affordability: too often new housing is beyond the pockets of those on low incomes. Community-based housing associations and cooperatives should be a government and local authority priority, and security of tenure should be extended to cover rented properties in these sectors as well as alternative types of dwelling, such as barges, boats and caravans.

The phasing out of mortgage interest tax relief should be a priority for a Green government. The introduction of the basic income scheme, as outlined in detail on page 92, would make the need for tax relief on mortgages redundant. It would also remove the distinction between those who are able to afford private ownership and those who are obliged to rent.

There is an urgent need to improve and modernize existing homes, and funds should be made available for this. Long-term benefits would accrue in terms of energy efficiency and health. All new housing stock would be required to meet the highest possible energy-efficient standards, and make use of the latest appropriate energy technology.

We must also rescind the power of local authorities to sell housing estates in need of major repairs to private landlords. Instead they should be handed over to housing cooperatives and associations; with the removal of value added tax on repair work, and sufficient grants, good housing stock could be provided. When new housing stock is being built the needs of the community should be taken into account, and planning regulations should be adjusted so that work, services and leisure facilities are within easy reach. This in turn would lead to savings in energy and time. 'By allowing small part-time businesses, workshops, etc., to spring up in housing areas, incentives will be available for people to use their leisure time for useful part-time work at home, all of which will add to the national stock and add to the character of the community' (*MFSS*, B 504). A major priority of any government should be to ensure that everybody has adequate accommodation. Sadly, so far pressure to gain the electoral support of existing home owners has prevented politicians from taking the necessary long-term view of the country's housing requirements.

New social security legislation makes life even more difficult for young people and is yet another cause of poverty. The despair felt by many of today's young and long-term unemployed is crippling: crime and alcohol often become a solace. Job and youth-training schemes designed to help the unemployed have not had the impact that was intended; young people wander from scheme to scheme without any long-term benefit, and employers have used the schemes as a source of cheap labour. If the unemployed refuse to play the game on the government's terms, their social security benefit is cut, which contributes to the housing problems described above. The result of all this legislation has been to create sections of the community that feel more depressed, demoralized and divided than ever before.

In 1985 nearly 9.4 million people – that is, close to one sixth of the population in Britain – were living on or below the supplementary benefit poverty line. Poverty is, of course, subject to many definitions, and the present Tory administration would argue that the welfare state encourages dependence and apathy, while it wishes to promote self-reliance, initiative and achievement. A London Weekend Television Mori Poll, conducted in the mid-1980s to find out what constituted a minimum standard of living, found that two out of three people stated that the following were necessities:

self-contained, damp-free accommodation with an indoor toilet and bath
a weekly roast joint for the family and three daily meals for each child
two pairs of all-weather shoes and a warm, waterproof coat
sufficient money for public transport
adequate bedrooms and beds
heating and carpeting
a refrigerator and a washing machine
enough money for special occasions such as Christmas
toys for the children.

The latest published figures show that 15,420,000 people were living in poverty or on its margins, as defined by the government's own statistics. This total includes *29 per cent of all children*. It is the unemployed, the low-paid, the sick and disabled and pensioners who make up the main groups of people living in poverty or on its margins. In 1985 pensioners still accounted for the largest proportion (36 per cent) of those living in poverty. At the heart of the solution to this problem is the Green Party's basic income scheme, which releases people from the poverty trap, where a small pay rise can often lead to the withdrawal of benefit, thus negating any potential rise in the standard of living.

The Green Party would introduce a basic income scheme payable as of right to all, regardless of status. It would ensure that everyone, whether in paid employment or not, would have a guaranteed income high enough to support a full and independent life, regardless of circumstances. Three basic rate are envisaged: a standard rate for adults and people on occupational retraining courses; a lower rate for children; and a higher rate for those currently receiving pensions, the disabled and those with special needs. Payment for children would go to their legal guardian. The basic income scheme would replace all existing welfare benefits and tax allowances and would not be withdrawn if a recipient had income from other sources, though remodelled tax structures would ensure that only those on low incomes would receive any net benefit.

Alongside a basic income scheme there must be policies that protect women and minorities.

The contribution that women make to the family, the community and the economy is enormous. They do most of the work in the home, most of the child rearing, most of the caring for the sick and the dying and most of the voluntary work that underpins our social services and economic system. Little of this work is acknowledged, let alone rewarded. Icelandic women went on a twenty-four-hour strike in protest at the unequal position that they hold in society. On average women earn 40 per cent less than men. Even the President, Vigdis Finnbogadottir, stayed away from her office to show solidarity with the women. Men whose partners refused to prepare their breakfast rushed to restaurants only to find the whole system in chaos. When businessmen tried to place calls telephonists responded, 'We can! We dare! we will!' Iceland demonstrated that a country cannot function without women.

Sadly, the social, economic and political oppression of women is still an undeniable feature of our culture. Women are exposed daily to injustice, exploitation, violence and discrimination. On top of this they are promoted by the media and the advertising profession as sex objects that are freely available to men upon demand. This is the result of the persistence, for hundreds of years, of male-dominated values that have structured society around the subordination of women, which young girls experience from their very first days at nursery school.

However hard they pretend to deplore the system, men still remain in positions of power and dominance. (Any woman who has had to work in Westminster, the seat of power in Britain, can testify to the lack of facilities and consideration given to women there.) Because their experiences are so different from those of men, women can bring a new dimension to politics. For women it is possible to reject the hierarchical structures and aggressive nature of traditional politics. Since women have entered the modern world of industry and commerce they have learned to juggle jobs, child-care, housework and a wealth of other activities. They are able to rationalize the importance of work versus the home in a way that men cannot.

Die Grünen once issued a fact sheet explaining why anti-discrimination laws are needed for women and presented it to the West German public at large for discussion. They pointed out that although Article 3 of the Basic Law, the constitution of the Federal Republic of Germany, states, 'Men and women shall have equal rights,' that has not prevented women from being exploited. The story repeats itself across the globe, from the United States to the USSR. In the United Kingdom we do not have a written constitution; the need for a feminist perspective is therefore crucial. Women do not want 'equal opportunities' or token participation; these are man-made concessions that keep women dependent within a patriarchal society. Margaret Thatcher has done nothing for women's rights. Her 'traditional family values' led her to take on a patriarchal role, and all evidence points to her having mastered it better than former male incumbents.

We want empowerment for everyone. We want to liberate both men and women from sexual stereotyping. We need to remind society that women constitute over half the world's population and are rewarded for performing two thirds of society's work by being paid for a third. Women earn, on average, 30 per cent less than men. Most women are excluded from economic and political influence.

A Green government would create a Ministry for Women's Affairs that would ensure that women were represented at all levels of decision-making. Although legislation to end patriarchy and sexism is impracticable, a Ministry for Women's Affairs would actively challenge such attitudes throughout society, ensuring particularly that the education system was free from the influence of male-dominated ideas. It would advise women about their rights and require all local authorities to provide safe places of refuge for women and their children in times of need. It would support women by providing more community policing, adequate health care and proper screening facilities, free of charge.

New policies for women must ensure equality under the law. One in six women is likely to be raped in the United Kingdom, and only one in twelve rapes will be reported to the police. Over 1 million children under the age of 15 will be sexually assaulted or raped, many of them by members of their family or so-called friends. The present legal system is weighted heavily in favour of men. Recent rape cases in this country have shown that judges do not accept women as free, independent people. 'Women who say no do not always mean no. It is not just a question of saying no; it is a question of how she says it, how she shows and makes clear. If she doesn't want it she only has to keep her legs shut' (Justice Wild, 1982). Unfortunately, this is not an isolated statement by one of Her Majesty's judges. Consider this, from another judge: 'It is the height of imprudence for any girl to hitch-hike at night, that is plain. It isn't really worth stating. She is, in the true sense, asking for it.' Another custodian of the nation's morals, Justice Leonard, stated in 1987, 'The trauma suffered by the girl was not so great.' This girl was raped by two burglars, tied up and had a knife handle inserted in her vagina, all within earshot of her father and boyfriend. The two rapists received shorter prison sentences than a third, who had committed only burglary. Recently another judge 'quite understood' how a father could sexually abuse his daughter while his wife could not perform her 'conjugal' duties because she was pregnant.

Sentencing policies concerning sexual assault on women are scandalous and further show the contempt in which women are held by the legal profession. The old idea of women as men's property, to do with what they will, is reinforced by the attitude of many senior old men in the law courts. The maximum sentence for indecent assault on a woman, including forced oral sex, is two years, five if the victim is under 13. Yet if a man commits indecent assault on another man, the maximum sentence is ten years. There is no minimum sentence. The truth is that sexual harassment and sexual violence are experienced almost exclusively by women. In the eyes of the law-makers the violation of women is not a serious crime. Rape within marriage is not yet an offence in England, although one in eight women states that she has been raped by her husband.

We still have a long way to go. Clare Short, the Labour MP, tried to get a Bill passed that would prevent daily papers from treating women's bodies as objects of sexual desire. She, along with millions of women, feels that the practice is degrading and obscene and contributes to violence against women, especially of a sexual nature. The display of women's bodies on posters, on television and in magazines to advertise products gives the impression that women are available and accessible. It encourages sexual harassment. Typical of the response to her Bill was that of Norman Tebbitt, who claimed that he could not differentiate between a page 3 nude and a Rubens.

Lesbian women are discriminated against by the courts when applying for custody for children. One woman was limited to seeing her daughter three times a year, and then only under supervision, because she had been brave enough to declare her homosexuality. The fact that her ex-husband was violent and sexually abusive to her daughter weighed less heavily on the judge's mind than the woman's chosen sexual orientation.

Abortion is another area where men think they know best. David Alton, MP, introduced a Bill to restrict the time span during which women could have abortions. In March 1988 the Green Party supported an emergency motion brought to the spring conference supporting the existing 1967 Abortion Act and opposing the Alton Bill. The Green Party stated that it was 'opposed to any amendments to the Act which would further restrict the reproductive freedom of women'. It instructed the Green Party Council to issue a statement of support for the Fight the Alton Bill Campaign. No woman thinks that abortion is an easy option. Greens believe that it is a woman's right to choose. Sex education, together with readily available contraceptives for both sexes, should be obtainable free of charge. There should be free condom machines in clubs, pubs, fifth-and six-form schools, colleges and work places. Every baby should be a wanted baby.

It is time that the institution of marriage was re-examined. Matrimony remains a patriarchal institution and no longer reflects the aspirations of many women. Women are not men's property, yet the matrimonial laws still expect a woman to take her husband's name and assume that she is no longer an individual. Although the tax laws changed in 1990 to allow married women to be taxed in their own right, the married man's tax allowance did not change. A man is still assumed to be the head of a household, and the law still contains provisions relating to sexual access and financial control.

Racism is also an undeniable feature of British society. Intolerance and prejudice are commonplace, both in individuals and in institutions, despite recent anti-racist laws. If our society is to be truly free of racism, we must examine and radically alter our social attitudes. It has been said that racism cannot truly be understood unless one has experienced being black in Britain today. We have sympathy for that view, but it must not stop the Green Party looking at itself and asking why there are not more black faces among its members or in other political parties.

The Green Party believes in a multi-cultural society and is not afraid to face the challenge, 'making its anti-racist policy clear through the images and statements it deploys, and . . . its social and political programmes are addressed to all ethnic and cultural groups in society' (*MFSS*, RS 109). Members representing the Green Party pledge to ensure that all their statements are free of racism and take positive steps to open channels of communication with ethnic and cultural groups within communities. Local green parties are doing much to involve themselves in community-based initiatives that combat racism. All Green Party working groups have an obligation to address ethnic and cultural issues when formulating new policy for Conference to approve.

Greens recognize that racism is not an isolated issue with a single solution. Decentralization would do much to return power to the local communities, and an emphasis on grass-roots democracy would benefit the oppressed in society. The basic income scheme would offer real choice and action to communities where racial hostility thrives on deprivation. Professional training in the needs of a multi-cultural society in all walks of life, especially the police, the judiciary, education and the social services, would promote much needed respect and awareness of different cultural values.

Greens believe that cultural diversity enriches our society. Until we believe that attempts to enforce heterosexuality as the only 'normal' behaviour of men and women are as much a violation of human rights as racism, we will never truly believe in the right for people to choose their own sexuality. Lesbians and gays suffer discrimination in their communities, the courts, the local authorities, education establishments and work places. For years we have been told that homosexuality is a pre-determined medical condition and that we should feel sorry for gays because they 'can't help the way they are'. This blatant nonsense, propagated by religious communities and educational establishments, belies all historical evidence: when people previously defined as heterosexual are confined to single-sex institutions they often take up homosexuality temporarily or even permanently. Peter Tatchell, a gay activist, argues very strongly for the abolition of the homosexual as a distinct catègory of person:

> Instead of exclusive heterosexuality and exclusive homosexuality, and in place of self-identified and separate heterosexual and homosexual people, lesbian and gay liberation affirmed the universal potential for everyone to experience both the homosexual and heterosexual dimensions of their personality.
>
> Given the plasticity and social determination of human sexuality, if the institutional restrictions and ideological pressures against gayness were removed and if homosexuality were positively promoted as an equally valid form of sexual and emotional expression, then homosexual experiences could become part of the typical range of erotic desires for the whole population, on a par with heterosexuality. (*Seven Days*, 24 June 1989)

The Green Party programme puts forward the following policies:

1. The age of consent for homosexuality should be lowered to that of heterosexuals, which is sixteen years of age.
2. Sexual orientation shall in no way determine or reflect upon ability and worthiness to care for children.
3. Discrimination on the grounds of a person's sexuality shall be illegal and all local authorities, work places and building societies should adopt a general statement prohibiting any distinction between heterosexuals, lesbians and gays in publicity, housing advice, allocation, transfers and mortgage provision.

4. Young people have the right to be brought up to understand that they may experience homosexual or heterosexual feelings or both, and that either or both are to be welcomed as having potential to enrich their lives and those of the people around them.

In the 1989 European elections the German Die Grünen decided to put a gipsy at the top of its list. Recognizing that travellers are disadvantaged and discriminated against, Die Grünen sought to highlight their plight; consequently one of the sitting members in the European Parliament is a gipsy. British Greens have always acknowledged the right of people to decide their own way of life, and members of the Green Party have been leading campaigners in the struggle for alternative communities that the state has tried to thwart.

Brig Oubridge, a former co-chair of the Party Council and now a dweller in Tepee Valley, Wales, has being fighting both national and local authorities for the right to allow the present inhabitants to retain their lifestyle. As a result the Greens now have a comprehensive travellers' policy, which insists that those who choose alternative ways of living should be accorded the same rights as any other citizen. In 1989 British Greens highlighted the inconsistencies in international policy by opposing the forced repatriation of over 700 Eastern Bloc gipsies from West Germany while the same country was accepting other refugees from behind the Iron Curtain with open arms. Such double standards form no part of green solutions to the break-up of the former communist empire. Greens also oppose Britain's racist and repressive immigration laws.

Local authorities should have a statutory duty not just to provide services but also to guarantee proper protection for those who choose a nomadic way of life. Travellers should also have rights regarding the education of their children. Local education authorities often turn a blind eye to the needs of children of travellers; travellers who wish to secure education for their children should be able to do so without fear of discrimination. Special on-site educational facilities should be available.

Community-care programmes are underfunded and hopelessly inadequate. We institutionalize children and adults and then expect them to form part of the community without a care in the world. Youngsters, even at the tender age of 7, when life should be a joyful experience, are placed in old people's homes because resources are stretched. Once our young have reached eighteen years of age, no matter what their personal problems are, they are no longer the responsibility of local authorities. However caring our professional social workers, probation officers, health visitors and community nurses are, without adequate resources their hands are tied. We are quick to blame social workers and other professionals when things go wrong, yet slow to praise them when they have achieved miracles. Putting financial resources into community schemes often pays dividends and, in the long term, provides benefits for both the community and the recipients.

Children are individuals, not possessions of their parents, yet we still fail to recognize that fact. The advertisers' portrayal of the nuclear family – two parents, two children, one dog and a large detached house in the country – is a myth. In 1985 there were over 3.5 million children living on the margins of poverty and 1.5 million in single-parent families. A Department of Health and Social Security survey found that 56 per cent of couples with children living on income support ran out of money most weeks. In 1986 an analysis of the average expenditure of a family with two children living on benefits showed that the average diet was 6,500 calories short of nutritional adequacy per week.

In such conditions, is it any wonder that abuse is directed at the most vulnerable in society? Most violence against children takes place in the confines of the home, and sexual abuse of the young is on the increase. The Cleveland child-abuse episode demonstrated how many children are at risk. Child Watch, set up in November 1986, invited children to phone, in confidence, about experiences of sexual assault. It received over 60,000 calls in the first few days.

The Green Party would ensure that children were informed from an early age of their rights under the United Nations Declaration of the Rights of the Child. The United Kingdom, as a signatory to the Declaration, should act to uphold them. Children should be taught these rights in schools, and every classroom should have them pinned up on a wall, together with the telephone numbers of advisory bodies. All schools should have staff especially trained to recognize and deal with the social needs of children. It is worth stating in full the rights enshrined in the United Nations Declaration:

the right to affection, love and understanding

the right to adequate nutrition and medical care
the right to free education
the right to full opportunity for play and recreation
the right to a name and nationality
the right to special care, if handicapped
the right to be among the first to receive relief in times of disaster
the right to learn to be a useful member of society and to develop
    individual abilities
the right to be brought up in a spirit of peace and universal fellowship
the right to enjoy these rights regardless of race, colour, sex,
    religion, national or ethnic origin.

The Green Party would introduce family courts, where divorce, separation, custody, domestic violence, access, wardship, care, guardianship and the rights of unmarried cohabitees could be dealt with. Judges and court workers would be expected to undertake further training in these areas. A children's ombudsperson will be established to defend these rights and act on children's complaints.

For too long we have relied on the good will of relatives (mostly daughters, who give up their careers) to look after sick and ailing parents. Most relatives gladly provide the time and care needed, but often the carers themselves become ill because of the twenty-four-hour nature of the job. Hospitalization for the elderly, or a permanent place in a residential home, then becomes the order of the day. This crazy way of doing things benefits nobody.

Greens believe that disabled and elderly people wish to live as independently as possible but need the support and advice of the care services to do so. We would extend community-care programmes, ensuring that the provision of financial resources was enough to meet the needs of the scheme. There should be choice of housing for disabled and elderly people within their community, as it is often traumatic for them to move away from friends and relatives. Proper support must be given to carers who look after the disabled and elderly; that means ensuring that they have regular breaks and holidays, including daily or weekly visits from professional services when requested. The basic income scheme, together with special payments, would ease the financial burden often carried by carers. Grants should be made available for those who wish to adapt their homes for the comfort and convenience of elderly or disabled people. Telephones and alarms should be supplied free of charge, and a direct connection with the local surgery or emergency services should be available for those who need help. Self-help and support schemes should be set up in all local communities.

However good the home-support system, there will always be those who require constant attention in residential units, which should be small and very much part of the community. The units should be run cooperatively and with the involvement of residents, staff and the local community. Schools and colleges should be encouraged to open their doors to all those who wish to further their education, remembering that elderly or disabled people often have valuable knowledge to impart.

There are over 10 million people of pensionable age in Britain today. By the end of the century there will be 4.1 million people aged over 75. Some will be lucky enough to have good occupational pensions, and their retirement will be joyful; many will feel that they are a burden to the younger generation. British pensioners are among the worst-treated in Europe – the standard pension is a disgrace, and it is likely to get worse for millions of our elderly. Private pensions mirror the inequalities in the labour market, leaving in poverty those who worked intermittently or had low-paid jobs. More than 2 million elderly people live on income support, unable to afford proper heating or food. Nearly half of our most deficient housing is inhabited by old people. Over 30 per cent of all pensioners live alone, receiving no regular visitors, in the certain knowledge that they will end their days in the geriatric ward of a large hospital.

Being old and poor in Britain today means being thrown on the scrapheap: nobody wants to know. Charities such as Help the Aged struggle to compete with more glamorous causes and are increasingly having to provide basic facilities. Thatcherism seeks to expand the work of charities, thereby letting government off the hook when it comes to providing for the disadvantaged. The Green Party believes that no elderly person should suffer because of a lack of amenities, that the elderly have a valuable role to play and need real support. Attitudes also have to change. The old will always suffer in a society with ageist attitudes constantly portrayed in advertisements and in the media. It would become illegal to discriminate on grounds of age. Greens also believe that their vision of small, decentralized, self-reliant communities would do much to integrate the elderly into society. The Green Party believes that the elderly should have a choice of housing, ranging from single accommodation to group living. It should be made simple for a disabled or elderly person living in housing with inside and/or outside stairs to move to a flat to maintain his/her independence. If needed, practical cash help should be available from the state for such a move. If a person would prefer to remain in his/her existing accommodation, this should be facilitated by providing adaptations. Local authorities should not discriminate against owner-occupiers who wish to move into council sheltered housing. Grants and loans available to the elderly and disabled owner-occupiers should be fully publicized to enable the adaptation, maintenance and renovation of their homes.   (*MESS*, S 501/2/3)

Elderly people in Britain are organizing themselves to press for a better future and are talking of putting up candidates at the next general election. With millions of votes at stake, it makes political sense to listen to them and act upon their requirements.

Greens believe that people should be allowed to choose the age at which they retire, and again the basic income scheme would enable this to happen. The knowledge and expertise of our senior citizens is undervalued, and we would encourage those who choose early retirement to participate in schemes that benefited their local community. We also acknowledge that retirement shock is a genuine condition and would introduce legislation to enable people to reduce their working hours gradually up to retirement if they wished. Seventy years of age can be a new beginning: Michelangelo was 71 when he began work on the completion of the new St Peter's in Rome in 1546.

We would ensure that all citizens had access to information about themselves held by welfare authorities, schools and colleges, doctors. In appropriate cases counselling should be provided before the disclosure of distressing information.

A green society is one that is just. The long-term aim of the Green Party is to ensure healthy, thriving communities and material security for all, regardless of status. We believe that government has responsibility for those who are disadvantaged in this society, in whatever way, and must make provision for them through a welfare system that is accessible, flexible and non-paternalistic, and that safeguards the rights of the consumer.

7 GLOBAL JUSTICE

Every day of our lives we are bombarded by literature telling us of the plight of those on the other side of the world. We are subjected to harrowing pictures of starving children and informed of oppressive regimes, yet somehow we remove ourselves, sanitize the information, retire to our living rooms with another cup of coffee and resume the business of daily living.

Robert McNamara, a former president of the World Bank, described absolute poverty as 'a condition of life so characterized by malnutrition, illiteracy, disease, high infant mortality and low life expectancy as to be beneath any reasonable definition of human decency'. Nearly 1 billion people on this planet live in the conditions described above. In Bangladesh alone 75 per cent of the population lives in 'absolute poverty'.

The notion that, by increasing their own wealth, the industrial countries actually help the world's poorest is a myth. The trickle-down theory, so beloved of Western leaders, just does not work. Brazil is perhaps the best example of this failed theory. Its economy is the largest in the Third World; it is the top exporter of coffee, soybeans and sugar; and it has a thriving export market in cattle and cocoa. Yet two thirds of its 150 million people go hungry. Wealth remains in the hands of the few: 20 per cent of the people control 70 per cent of the wealth. Successive governments have opened up lands to the poor to try to resolve the inequalities but at the expense of the environment and indigenous peoples.

Zambia, on the other hand, handles its economy on a resource-dependency basis. Reliance on copper exports and manufacturing led to a decline in agriculture. In 1955 Zambia imported 20 per cent of its food; today the proportion is nearer 50 per cent. Predictably, copper markets slumped, and Zambia was forced to take on huge loans. Debt service went up from 6 per cent of exports in 1970 to 59 per cent in 1987 (*Third World Quarterly*, January 1988).

South Korea's 'economic miracle', by which cheap manufactured goods have found markets in the developed world, has not been without cost to the people. Multinationals control 30 per cent of South Korea's exports, and there is still strong dependence on foreign capital. Twelve-hour, six-day-a-week jobs with low wages are common, and it is difficult to see how conditions will improve, as the government is reluctant to give in to demands that may affect export prices and allow competition from other Third World countries.

The gap between the world's rich and poor is growing daily. Ted Trainer points out in his book *Developed to Death* that the decade of the 1980s has seen a marked decline in the standard of living of the world's poor. Over one tenth of the world's population has not experienced any increase in income. Many writers and workers in non-governmental organizations have pointed out that, far from leading to real prosperity, economic 'development' in the southern hemisphere has more often been about creating profits for foreign multinationals or financing local élites than about ending poverty.

New roads and transport infrastructure make it easier to get cash crops out of starving countries, while continually falling commodity prices allow the rich of one half of the globe to make even more wealth out of the poor of the other. In the Filipino province of Batan the connections between poverty, power, natural resource depletion and hunger is obvious. Production of black tiger prawns for the Japanese market reaps a rich harvest; for every $5,000 invested $30,000 returns as profit within three years. Such production might be thought of as an excellent and environmentally friendly means of boosting economic growth and local development. It has drawbacks, however. The prawns require a delicate mix of salt and fresh water, which can be maintained only by pumping huge amounts of water inland so as to lower the water table and cause salt water to be sucked in from Manila Bay. Seventy per cent of the local population who are below the poverty line are becoming even poorer, despite such 'growth', as their main source of protein, fish, is being displaced by prawn ponds. They cannot afford the prawns, therefore the Japanese gain while Filipinos become even more malnourished. Only the richest fifty families on the islands can afford the investment and profit from their outlay. President Aquino's promises about land reform have not been fulfilled. The people power that ousted Marcos, who exploited the Philippines to boost his Swiss bank accounts and Imelda's vast collection of shoes, has done nothing to change the structure of Filipino society or to end the destruction both of people and of nature.

The destruction of Filipino forests is equally fuelled by profit and hurts the poorest most. A heavily pregnant woman who is active in the campaign to promote citizens' arrests of trucks illegally logging the forests of the Philippines explained that she was acting for her children: 'Without trees there is no food, and without food, no life.' Logging is a source of secular power. As the authors of this report from the Philippines note in *Capitalism, Nature and Socialism* (No. 2, Summer, 1989), legislation, diplomacy and gentle lobbying have little effect where large sums of money are concerned.

Control of natural resources, be they forest, minerals, fishing grounds or land, renders enormous economic power, which translates into political power. Forest covers 68 per cent of Palawan. But one wealthy logger has forest concessions controlling 61 per cent of those forests, and he is tearing down 19,000 hectares of forest each year. His annual income of $24 million stands against a provincial budget of $1 million and an average annual income of $400 per Palawan family.

The logger is also the principal backer of the most powerful politician on the island, House Speaker Ramon Mitra, whose ambition is to be the next president of the Philippines. Mitra, in turn, has bought the governor, most of the mayors and the top military. Potential opposition to the rape of the forests by the Church has been sidetracked by the logger; he donates wood for parish chapels. Mitra's people control Palawan's one newspaper and the one radio station. They censor opposing views. One day during our visit all copies of a Manila newspaper carrying an article critical of Palawan's power structure mysteriously disappeared. A person quoted in that article was physically assaulted.

Developmental experts acknowledge that poverty, the debt crisis and the patterns of world power have to be addressed if we have any hope of solving the global environmental crisis. A new imperialism has developed, one that may not rule directly but insidiously controls less developed countries' economies and people's lives. And who can blame the countries, when multinationals offer the hope of desperately needed jobs or funds for health and education schemes? But there is a price to pay. Wanjiku Kariuki from Kenya describes it thus, 'This country's in the hands of the nationals now, so it's not colonized. But the foreigners still have a lot of influence on the government. This influence works through aid: we have to toe the line. Also this country is not as democratic as it should be; it's more like a dictatorship. You can't just say what you think or you'll be inside. The foreigners aren't always there to be seen: but they are there in the background' (*New Internationalist*, No. 167, January 1987).

The USA likes to think of itself as the international protector of justice and to that end has intervened in the internal affairs of other countries on average once every eighteen months since 1945. Its most recent intervention has been in the internal politics of Panama; its aim was to capture General Noriega and take him to the USA for trial on drug charges. Yet Noriega, a former CIA operative, enjoyed American support for years because he was useful as an opponent to the Sandinistas.

Soviet military intervention has been little better, ranging from Hungary in 1956 to Afghanistan in 1979.

The developing countries are beset with problems, not least the one of population and the First World's attitude to it. One of the great myths of the twentieth century is that the childbirth patterns of less developed countries are to blame for the world's population crisis. The issue of population must be acknowledged without hysteria because if the figures that are projected by demographers are accurate, we shall be facing a world population of 10 billion by the end of the next century. We have to face facts: even with the most successful family-planning programme imaginable, there will be population increases in the twenty-first century. We must ensure that we have the means to provide the social programmes necessary to eliminate world hunger and, at the same time, to promote self-sustainable communities in both the northern and the southern hemisphere.

In his 'Essay on Population' (1803), Malthus examined what would happen if the world's population were to continue to grow without check. He likened human beings to plants that jostle for a bare minimum of soil and light, and he warned that humans would eventually fill all available space. This position was taken up by various environmental groups following the influential report 'Limits to Growth', issued by the Club of Rome in 1972. The US Agency for International Development argued that people in the Third World were poor simply because they had too many children, and it advocated vigorous birth-control campaigns.

In order to examine population growth critically we must also look at the allocation of resources and consumption. At present 25 per cent of the world's people consume 80 per cent of the world's resources. In the United Kingdom the average person eats three times as much, consumes forty times the amount of fossil fuels and industrial products and uses 100 times as many cars, items of household equipment and paper as a person born in the less developed world. In the September/October 1974 issue of *Development Forum*, a United Nations publication, René Dumont likens the rich white man to a cannibal: 'By consuming meat, which wastes the grain that could have saved them, last year we ate the children of the Sahel, Ethiopia and Bangladesh. And we continue to eat them this year with undiminished appetite' – a harsh statement designed to point out global inequalities. To blame the Third World for its poverty and over-population is merely an excuse for the richer countries to do nothing about the way in which resources are distributed globally or, indeed, their own population problems. The fact is that the Netherlands is twice as densely populated as India, and Britain is two and a half times more densely populated than China. Western Europe has a population density of 94 people per square kilometre in contrast with the average less developed country of 34 people. The 16 million or so babies born in the developed world will have an impact on the world's resources that is four times greater than that of the 109 million born in the poor world.

Yet the myth persists. Why, we ask, do the poor keep having more children? By Western standards the more babies we have, the more expensive it is to support them. It has been calculated that the cost to a Westerner of supporting a child to the age of 18 is over £50,000, and that is a conservative figure. Young married couples often state that they cannot afford to have a baby. Mortgage payments and second incomes come first. In other words, children are a financial liability in Western states. Contrast this with the experience of a family in Bangladesh, where by the age of 10 children are already producing more than they consume, and they have repaid their parents' investment in their upbringing by the age of 15. There is no welfare state, no one to provide for people in their old age except their children. If children were an economic necessity for us, would we be so keen to have small families? If infant mortality were high, and the chances of our children living beyond 5 years were less than 50 per cent wouldn't we plan large families? It is a statistical fact that no country has managed to achieve a low birth rate while infant mortality has remained high. UNICEF estimates that if it were possible to prevent the death of 7 million babies in less developed countries each year, this could lead to the prevention of between 12 million and 20 million births by the end of the century. 'My children are my wealth' is a cry commonly heard in countries that fail to provide any social services. The East–West Population Institute has looked at the reasons given for having children in three countries with high, medium and low birth rates:

	Birth Rate	Economic Support	Love, etc.	Other
Mexico	High	72%	16%	12%
Singapore	Medium	19%	65%	16%
USA	Low	4%	73%	23%

Just as Western riches have brought about a more stable population, so health care, the redistribution of wealth, education and land reform could reduce the population of the less developed countries. Kerala, a state in India, has cut its birth rate by 50 per cent in ten years. Money has been directed towards local health-care centres, available to all; consequently Kerala has the lowest infant-mortality rate in the whole of India. Girls are educated, and literacy among women is accorded high priority. Land reform and a minimum wage has ensured the redistribution of wealth. And Taiwan has reduced its national birth rate from 41 to 26 per thousand, not by handing out condoms and IUDs but by means of land reform and higher incomes.

We are beginning to see a crisis in West Germany, and no doubt the trend will follow in other industrialized countries. West Germany has the lowest population growth in the world (− 0.3 per cent); if population levels continue to decline from a peak of 63 million in 1973, by the year 2030 there will be one retired person for every one person in work. The implications for the social services are beginning to worry governments, and West German politicians have been urging couples to have more children. A target of 200,000 babies a year is the current figure. Ironic, isn't it, that at the same time Western governments are pouring money into family planning in the less developed countries? Rather than preaching to the less developed countries about population levels, an examination of the global distribution of wealth would do more to aid the population crisis than all the money spent by the First World on family-planning programmes. The selfishness of the developed countries, which analyse issues in their own terms and disregard global perspectives, is legendary. They should be considering alternative social systems designed to sustain life for all.

No country scores 100 per cent when assessing its human rights record. The *World Human Rights Guide*, which rates countries according to their observation of the International Covenant on Civil and Political Rights, varies from a high of 98 per cent in such countries as the Netherlands (the UK scores 94 per cent) to 13 per cent (Ethiopia). Article 1 of the United Nations Declaration of Human Rights states, 'All human beings are born free and equal in dignity and rights.' Article 25 states, 'Everyone has the right to a standard of living adequate for the health and wellbeing of himself and his family, including food, clothing, housing and medical care and necessary social services, and the right to security in the event of unemployment, sickness, disability, widowhood, old age or other lack of livelihood in circumstances beyond his control.'

When we think of human rights abuses South Africa and countries in the Middle East are the first regimes to come to mind, and they seize the headlines. Native peoples of the less developed countries suffer terrible abuses but are ignored by the world's press. The exploitation of resources has caused Guatemala's Indians (who, incidentally, have a life expectancy eleven years shorter than that of the European Ladino majority), Bangladesh's Buddhist tribespeople and Chile's Mapuche to lose land and life in the name of 'progress'. An estimated 100,000 Guatemalan Indians have been killed and 400 Indian villages destroyed by a ruthless military in search of rich lands now occupied by cattle ranchers and timber and mineral companies. The Karnafuli reservoir in Bangladesh displaced over 100,000 tribespeople, robbing them of rich agricultural land. In every corner of the globe native peoples have been abused and exploited by colonialists and imperialists, national governments and multinational corporations, which uphold the traditions of the past. Native peoples have the worst health, housing, income and social services; they are imprisoned more, and consequently suicide and alcoholism feature more prominently in their lives. The Green Party would ensure that 'development schemes where the British Government has influence take place only with the permission and control of indigenous people, when influencing their lands' (*MFSS*, FP 322).

The Universal Declaration of Human Rights was adopted by the United Nations General Assembly in 1948 without a dissenting vote. What has gone wrong?

International codes seem non-enforceable: human rights depend upon national laws and public will. However, around the world atrocities and abuse continue, and all the evidence points to greater abuse as resource depletion continues. It would appear that once a nation state has internal problems, its willingness to listen to international opinion and observe international codes is suspended. We have seen this happen not only in places where we traditionally expect to see the violation of human rights but also in countries that continually barrack other states about their human rights records, namely the United States and the United Kingdom. The Thatcher and Bush regimes constantly take other countries to task while at the same time operating double standards.

The ever-growing debt crisis in the less developed countries is one of the world's most pressing problems. For every £1 given in aid, £2 is owed in debt repayment. The developing countries transfer over $35 billion a year to the rich nations. To put this into context, USA net capital imports in 1987 amounted to $154 billion, equal to $2,400 per American household and more than the total income per head of 3,500 million people in the less developed countries. The poor of this world help to finance the deficits of the rich. Conditions in the poor countries are rapidly deteriorating. Western governments are well aware of this; financiers and transnationals are collaborators; World Bank presidents make worthy statements; yet urgently needed remedies are absent. This situation is manifestly unjust, and every reasonable and humane person should be outraged. Resource flows from north to south must be a priority.

The causes of the debt crisis are complex, and any reader who wants further information would do well to read Susan George on the subject. Her book *A Fate Worse than Debt* exposes the injustices of the international system and puts forward positive proposals for debt relief. Suffice it to say here that much of the Third World's mounting indebtedness is due to First World protectionism, crippling world interest rates and money lent for totally unsuitable projects, all of which are wholly beyond the control of developing countries. Add to them the worsening ecological conditions in many debtor countries and you have the potential for global ecocide.

The debt crisis came about because in the 1970s there was a glut of money in the First World, caused by rising oil prices, and therefore banks lent indiscriminately. Prestige projects and the arms trade have both benefited from the debt crisis; in fact, two thirds of arms exports are destined for the less developed countries. Third World debt amounts to approximately 1 trillion dollars; present annual world-wide expenditure on arms is roughly the same. With a little imagination and huge political will the debt crisis could be wiped out.

At the request of the American Association of Jurists, the Permanent People's Tribunal was called to consider violations by the International Monetary Fund and the World Bank of international law concerning the self-determination of peoples and to make proposals for change. The Tribunal was convened in West Berlin in September 1988 and concluded:

1. The World Bank and International Monetary Fund are in breach of the Charter of the United Nations in that they have not promoted higher standards of living, full employment and conditions of economic and social progress and development, nor have they promoted a universal respect for the observance of human rights and fundamental freedoms for all, without distinction as to race, sex, language or religion, as required by Article 55 of the Charter. Furthermore, they have violated the right of sovereignty of individual states and rights of peoples to self-determination.

2. The World Bank/IMF are in breach of their own constitutions in that they have not contributed to the promotion and maintenance of high levels of employment and real income and to the development of the productive resources of all members as primary objectives of economic policy as required by Article 1, Articles of Agreement of the World Bank. Furthermore, the credit granted to dictatorial governments has often been diverted to armaments used against the people, invested in foreign banks without being applied to development, health, education or food programmes.

3. The World Bank has been negligent in that it has made loans without properly examining the needs of the debtor nations, nor has it considered fully the ability of the debtor nations to repay such loans. The structural adjustment policy of the World

Bank/IMF caused a growing net transfer of resources from indebted countries into the creditor countries. Consequently, lives and living standards in indebted countries have deteriorated. The environment has been irreversibly damaged and living areas of indigenous peoples have been destroyed. The payment of reparations should therefore be considered. Through such practices the IMF/World Bank give illusory legitimacy to the accumulation strategies of the industrial countries, multinational corporations and international finance capital, which led to the present debt disaster, a disaster imperilling not only the present but the future of most nations.

4. Considering the political and economic conditions that generated it, the repudiation of debt can be justified by the 'defence of necessity' which is accepted by the international courts as a valid defence when payment of financial obligations would gravely impair the living standards of a nation's population – as is the case with Third World countries.

And what is the World Bank/IMF's reply to these findings? They claim that the developing countries ought to have adjusted to new world market conditions and that their failure to do so caused the crisis. They allege that the debt crisis in the Third World is primarily a consequence of the policies of governments. A World Bank report released in December 1989 revealed that debt relief arranged for Third World countries amounted to only $14 billion in 1989 compared with $22 billion in 1988, and the banks projected a rise of 0.5 per cent in total debt, bringing it to $1,189 trillion at the end of 1989. 'It's time for realism,' commented Stanley Fischer, World Bank Vice-President for Development Economics. When asked how the Third World could cope with the limits on debt relief, Mr Fischer said that the debtor countries would have to meet part of their needs by generating trade surpluses (*Herald Tribune*, 18 December 1989).

And who suffers most? More often than not, it is the women in the poorer countries, as 'structural adjustment' means cutting health and education programmes. The biggest killer of women under 39 in Latin America is illegal abortion. In Brazil infant mortality rose by 12 per cent between 1982 and 1984, and in Zambia hunger-related deaths among children doubled. Nearly ten years of investment in education, health and social services has been lost, and the prognosis for the future is critical. The thorn in the side of the Third World is vested interests.

Would Western capitalist economies want to promote self-reliance in the Third World? The present picture would indicate that they do not.

During the European elections the Green Party called for an international forum, comprising all countries involved in the Third World debt crisis, to agree a mechanism for the withdrawal of debt-repayment agreements in favour of local-currency investment in democratic, ecologically sound community projects, supported by grants, expertise and training where needed. Non-governmental organizations and local communities must have an input into any such discussions. Greens further called for the cancellation of any bilateral aid/trade agreements that would bring money from the lending organizations back into the pockets of Western industrialists. They demanded support mechanisms so that cash-crop exporting countries could revert to self-reliant food programmes. Together with cancellation of all bank loans that contribute to the exploitation of natural resources and cooperation at an international level to monitor the activities of the transnational corporations, the Green Party's policies are well on the way to a comprehensive plan to beat the inequalities of the debt crisis.

And so back to global social justice. We have shown that social justice at home leads to less environmental pollution. On a world scale that is even more true. Putting people first, empowering them to make the decisions that affect their lives and the redistribution of land and wealth would be the first steps in creating a world geared to peace and harmony with our environment. Nearly three quarters of all the land in the world that can be owned is controlled by 2.5 per cent of the people. Around half the people living in less developed countries have no secure home. In Bombay it is estimated that half a million people live on the pavements. Huge tracts of land in Brazil are owned by multinational companies that exploit and abuse indigenous people. Yet land reform can and does work, provided it is supported with credit, fair prices and appropriate technical help. Gandhi said, 'There is enough land for everybody's need. But not for everybody's greed.' And there is plenty of land: about 21 per cent of the world's surface is arable, yet only 8 per cent is actually farmed.

Of all countries China has succeeded best in eliminating malnutrition. Before the revolution millions of people starved each year, and flood and droughts were common. China supports one fifth of the world's population on half as much arable land per person as there is in India. While Greens abhor the political oppression of the Chinese people, the fact is that with a system that takes ecology into account China has excelled in mastering techniques to feed its massive population. The Chinese leave little to waste and have evolved a decentralist system in harmony with their environment. Bio-gas stoves and digesters, fed mainly with waste, human, vegetable and animal, ease the energy crisis. In some communes they supply two thirds of the energy needed. Because of the huge human labour resources, organic farming takes on real meaning. Biological controls keep down pests, and instead of the intensive chemical monoculture of other nations, integrated crops are grown with symbiotic advantages. A high degree of communal self reliance is achieved through a mixture of light industry and agriculture. Many Chinese cities feature farm plots, which reduces the conflict between countryside and city.

There is no doubt that the Chinese have used political oppression and expended much blood and sweat to achieve this remarkable feat. What we need to do is to find ways to emulate Chinese agriculture while at the same time preserving that most precious commodity – personal freedom. But is anyone free who does not have the means to feed him- or herself? The Chinese model could serve as a model for agriculture of both less developed countries and the First World and could help us all to take the first steps towards emancipating the world from hunger.

We need to understand, however, the reliance on the present system by multinationals and what they would lose if the system were changed. The desire for more and more profit and ever-increasing expansion seems to go beyond basic common sense and certainly shows no concern for the welfare of the planet or its peoples. The following statistics summarize the position of multinationals.

In 1986 the top 500 multinationals were operating from these areas: USA 216; EEC 140; Japan 87; and others 57. Multinationals control 90 per cent of all pineapple and forestry-product exports; 85–90 per cent of all wheat, coffee, corn, cotton and tobacco; 85 per cent of all cocoa; 80 per cent of all tea; 70–75 per cent of all bananas and natural rubber; 70 per cent of all rice; and 60 per cent of all sugar. ICI, a British-based multinational, stated in its annual report of 1988, 'The resource-rich countries of South East Asia offer a growing market for the Group . . . Strong agricultural commodity prices led to higher demand for ICI products such as fertilizers, agrochemicals and paints.' In Mexico ICI won government permission to build an agrochemicals plant. In Brazil national corporations such as Volkswagen, Mitsubishi, King Ranch and others own lands the size of king-doms, where they provide pasture for beef cattle for export. As a result of taking over Brooke Bond, Unilever owns land in Kenya, Tanzania, Malawi, South Africa and India, making money out of democracies and dictatorships alike. When enterprises are not profit-able, it simply closes them down, making thousands of people redund-ant. It controls plantations in the less developed countries, which in turn make those countries dependent upon it. Corporations such as Unilever create a tangled web, and when a country is enmeshed it is virtually impossible for it to cut the strings.

The issue is not as simple as giving land back to the people: what they do with it is important too. For instance, Nestlé gets 50 per cent of its turnover from the use of land without owning any. It contracts local growers to produce coffee, milk and cocoa at a fixed price on a given date. The company controls the production and income of the Third World farmer (ensuring that we get our nightly fix of cocoa at the cheapest possible price) without having to take the risks that ownership of land entails. This means that the community cannot use the land to grow the food that it so desperately needs. Multinationals are growing fast and fat on the backs of agribusiness in the Third World.

The power of the multinational transcends that of governments. Multinationals move into less developed countries where wages are lower and pollution controls less stringent. They plunder the less populated areas such as Antarctica for resources and control a turn-over equivalent of one quarter of the planet's gross product. They continue to manufacture pesticides declared illegal in Western countries and sell them to less developed countries, causing over 10,000 deaths each year from *application* alone. (We do not know the total number of deaths caused by the *consumption* of food polluted by these chemicals.) And so the pattern goes on. More and more consump-tion, and more and more pollution. These large corporate industries are not called to account for their plundering of the Earth's resources, the mountains of waste, the degradation of more than 75 per cent of the world's populace. For it is the poor of the world who suffer the brunt of the pollution. The rich can move, buy purifiers, invest in unpolluted lands and leave the poor knee-deep in mess created by wanton greed. The time is nearing when there won't be anywhere to run to. The whole planet will be in a state of explosive turmoil. And as if the foregoing were not indictment enough, consider who owns and controls most of the world's transport systems, telecommunications, science and technology information and the ugliest trade of the lot, the huge arms-manufacturing industry. Yet we have been led to believe that what is good for big business is good for us. What hope for change, you might ask, when faced with such overwhelming odds?

The problem is that the capitalist economies are quite happy to concern themselves with environmental reform, providing it does not harm their profits. Governments in the industrialized countries will bring in environment-protection laws that will force both public and private enterprises to clean up their acts. They will endorse new technologies that are able to limit ecological damage. But the underlying wealth inequalities will remain the same. The instability of the planet will not change, and private profit will remain the goal, though constrained by stricter environmental controls. The emphasis will not be on prevention but on limited cure. The needless consumption of dwindling raw resources will continue. And the gap between rich and poor will grow.

Until now human beings have had new places to exploit, new markets to explore, and the extent of the ecological crisis had not been realized. Although from the late nineteenth century onwards warnings about global warming have been publicly sounded, they have not been taken seriously by the forces that control production. Globally we need to move towards economies that are based on shared concerns, not private or national greed. We need what Murray Bookchin calls a 'moral' economy. Bookchin argues in *Remaking Society* that the present economic system is grossly immoral: 'Price formation, to take only one example, is not merely an impersonal "amoral" computation of supply versus demand. It is an insidious manipulation of both supply and demand – an immoral manipulation of human needs as part of an immoral pursuit of gain.' Bookchin goes on to say that the whole world of market transactions has become so impersonal that we no longer feel any responsibility towards our fellow citizens and the only words that enter the market economy are 'interest', 'cost' and 'profitability'. A moral economy, on the other hand, would be one in which we cared for each other's wellbeing, a participatory system of distribution based on ethical concerns. Unless we are prepared to get to grips with the wealth inequalities across the globe and penalize severely those who trade in human misery, the greed of the few will bring about the slaughter of the majority, and our tenancy of the planet will be at an end.

Animal liberation is a huge issue. The amount of pain and death meted out every day in Britain by human beings to other species is unimaginable. Factory farming, vivisection, 'humane' slaughter, hunting, shooting and the destruction of wildlife habitats are merely the most visible signs of a holocaust of cruelty at the heart of our society. Animals cannot vote or lobby; they cannot be offered the rights that human beings should enjoy; but they *do feel pain*. Yet human beings unthinkingly inflict pain upon them in thousands of ways and often for quite trivial reasons – new cosmetics and floor cleaners, sport and entertainment. It is impossible to talk about justice without talking about justice for animals.

Animal liberation, more than any other issue, is the one that makes green politics different. The other political parties show relatively little interest in other species. Labour's Gwynneth Dunwoody, a former shadow minister, continues to receive each year a £4,000 fee as a Westminster 'consultant' to the British Fur Trade Association. David Clark, a Labour environment spokesperson at the time of the 1988–9 outcry over salmonella, was concerned to defend factory farming as a source of rural employment and cheap eggs. The Conservative Party has been the traditional friend of the huntsman and has its campaign coffers filled by vivisecting chemical and pharmaceutical companies. In contrast, Greens promote not just human progress but animal rights as well. Other parties measure animal rights against the yardsticks of human benefit and economic expediency. Greens don't. Even if better drugs could be discovered through animal experiments (a view that we believe to be plainly wrong), this would still be no justification. Greens argue that we have to share planet Earth with its other creatures. We should cease to behave as if the natural world had been put in place purely for our benefit, stop warring with other species and learn to live in harmony. Humanity is one species among many, and we are just one part of the web of life. We will not survive if we arrogantly place ourselves above everything else.

Between 1600 and 1980, 350 varieties of bird and mammal have been made extinct. The European lion that used to roam through the Balkan forests disappeared with the Romans in AD 80. Steller's sea cow (*Hydrodamals stelleri*), described by its discoverer as showing 'signs of a wonderful intelligence, indeed, an uncommon love for one another, which extended so far that when one of them was hooked, all the others were intent upon saving it', was totally exterminated in 1741, within twenty-seven years of first being sighted, its 10-metre length and 4 tonnes of meat used to feed hungry English sailors. Since the *Mayflower* arrived in North America with its crew of Puritans escaping persecution 500 American plants and animals have disappeared. A population of some 60 million buffalo, with a territory that extended from California to New York State, was reduced to just *twenty-two* by over-zealous hunters, who left decaying corpses strewn across vast tracts of prairie. The sea mink (*Mustula vison macrodon*) was last sighted in 1880 before being hunted out of existence for its fur. The passenger pigeon that once blackened the skies has gone the same way as the dodo, the moa, the Great Auk, the Caribbean monk seal, the Tasmanian Wolf and many other species. The African mountain gorilla, a cousin of its destroyers, is reduced to 200 individuals. (The British have an unenviable record as destroyers of nature and abusers of animals. King Alfred the 'Great' organized the first commercial whaling expedition in AD 890.) Native human populations have also been made extinct, victims of plague and gun. The Caribs of the West Indies and the Tasmanian Aborigines are two examples. Cruelty to other species also breeds cruelty between members of the human species.

As animals and plants disappear, ecological stability is upset and human beings suffer as well. There is much public sympathy for baby seals, tiger cubs, African elephants and Great Blue whales, but even the most unappealing species play a part in the growing ecological imbalance. The removal of ugly, human-eating crocodiles from African rivers has led to a fall in fish catches, and hence human hunger, because crocodiles prey on the predatory fish that eat the kind of fish that we like to eat. Ecological systems work like intricate pieces of machinery, bolted together by both animals and plants. Take away certain species and the systems collapse, causing famine, soil erosion, climatic change, poverty and a plague of other ills. Yet despite a more enlightened attitude to nature than our forebears had, we continue to destroy with little thought for the future.

Greens argue that even when human beings gain from abusing animals, such abuse cannot be justified. Many, if not all, forms of animal abuse are linked with the abuse of human beings. The exploitation of women by men, men by men and animals by humanity all stem from a common root – a rationale that regards others as belonging to economic categories that may be exploited for our own benefit, women doing the domestic labour, Third World peoples sweating in factories, the mahogany of the Amazon chain-sawed for our furniture. As Tom Regan puts it in *The Case for Animal Rights*, 'The fundamental wrong is the system that allows us to view animals as *our resources* here for *us*, to be eaten, or surgically manipulated, or exploited for sport or money.' Human beings are part of nature. Human beings are also animals. Our genetic material is very close to that of a gorilla or a chimpanzee. More separates mammals from other taxa than human beings from other mammals. Vivisection could perhaps be justified morally if animals were different from humans, if they felt less pain and were less worthy of concern. But the practice is justified by some on medical grounds precisely because they are identical to us. Such philosophical niceties can have been of little interest to the animal experimenters who carried out 3.5 million pieces of research on living, struggling creatures in 1988. According to the HMSO statistical survey *Scientific Procedures on Living Animals, 1988*, the roll-call included 1,850,463 mice, 860,384 rats, 269,496 birds, 131,796 rabbits, 12,129 dogs, 4,111 cats, 1,090 horses and an unrecorded number of ferrets. Britain has only nineteen inspectors to regulate millions of experiments and tens of thousands of premises licensed for vivisection. Their 7,000 visits each year allow them to see only the tiniest fraction of experiments. We do know that two thirds of the experiments they witnessed were performed without anaesthetics, and some 2,313,100 procedures were performed without any kind of painkiller. Two million of the 3.5 million experiments were performed by drug companies replicating earlier trials or by industrial firms seeking to create new food additives, pesticides or household cleaners; 86,000 animals were subjected to ionizing radiation, while 1,000 were submitted to 'physical trauma to simulate human injury'. That the number of experiments declined throughout the 1980s is, according to Richard Ryder, 'probably a function of the general economic recession rather than the result of the introduction of non-animal techniques' (in Peter Singer, ed., *In Defence of Animals*, Blackwell, 1985)

All British drugs have, by law, to be tested on animals. The pro-vivisection Research Defence Society argues: 'Faced with a severe illness or a critically ill relative, most people would not hesitate to have their doctor prescribe an animal-tested medicine. Likewise even an ardent anti-vivisectionist would not want to see his [sic] pet dog die if an animal-tested antibiotic could save its life.' But animal testing is not the medical panacea its supporters claim it to be. Penicillin kills bacteria: it also kills guinea pigs. It would have never been developed if it had been tested on these animals. Morphine sends laboratory rats mad but is a human painkiller. Chloroform is vital as an anaesthetic for humans, but it is toxic to dogs. Aspirin causes birth defects in a large number of animals, including rats, mice, guinea pigs, cats and dogs, but is a useful and safe painkiller for humans. Other drugs that have produced horrifying side effects, including Thalidomide (10,000 birth defects), Opren (70 deaths, 3,500 cases of damage to skin, eyes, circulation, liver and kidneys) and Clioquinol (30,000 cases of blind-ness), were said to be safe after extensive animal testing. Indeed, when Professor Aygun of Turkey tested Thalidomide prior to its release, using cell culture, he found it to be teratogenic (causing birth defects), but the medical and scientific world chose to ignore his advice in favour of the evidence provided by animal experiments. The World Health Organization argues that only 200 drugs are necessary, yet there are nearly 20,000 licensed drugs (i.e. tested on animals) on the UK market. Far from being pioneering forms of medication, most are merely slightly altered versions of commercially successful phar-maceuticals produced by rival firms. The advances in health that are claimed to be the result of vivisection by the Research Defence Society – such as longer life expectancy, reduced infant mortality and a decline in diseases such as polio, tuberculosis, diphtheria and pneumonia – have been achieved largely through changes in lifestyle, including the introduction of better sanitation, housing and nutrition. Lifestyle change, according to all medical authorities, will be central in curing the killer diseases of the 1990s – cancer, heart disease and stress.

Bizarre experiments are gratuitously barbaric and totally un-necessary. (One of the most often repeated psychological experiments is the separation of mother and baby in order to study the effects of maternal deprivation.) Some are particularly cruel. The LD50 test works by administering a dose of a chemical under test until 50 per cent of animals are dead. In 1988 100,000 LD50 experiments took place, and a similar number involved what the HMSO report describes as 'chronic whole-body toxicity tests'. Today scientists are beginning to question the validity of the LD50 test; many of them consider it irrelevant and unscientific. As part of a supposed investigation into the effect of oil spillages by some far from conservation-minded scientists, three polar bears were forced to swim through a tank containing a mixture of crude oil and water. After the polar bears had licked their fur in an attempt to get clean and had died of resulting kidney failure, the scientists reached the astonishing conclusion that oil pollution has a negative effect on white-furred animals – and all at a cost of £120,000 to the Canadian taxpayer. Between 1971 and 1990 the French government gave researchers $5 million to kill baboons and pigs in carefully rehearsed car crashes. Part of the study involved using hammers to break the skulls of live macaques in order to replicate auto injuries.

The constant invention of new chemical compounds for shampoo, lipstick and hair gel is a way of boosting company growth but is hardly vital to human progress. New products can be introduced without animal testing, as has been shown by the success of the Body Shop. The creation of thousands of new chemicals demands the extermination of hundreds of thousands of animals but tells us little of long-term value. Whether humans differ in their reactions from mice, or whether substances may react dangerously with other exotic, human-created chemicals are questions that cannot be answered by vivisection. Greens believe that it is unhealthy to release a stream of new chemicals into the natural environment and fear that vivisection is being used to justify the production of many potentially dangerous chemicals. Legal 'safeguards' mean that tests are duplicated in different countries by different firms.

Even for supposedly vital experiments there are alternatives to animal cruelty. Human-scale articulated dummies, rather than farm animals, are used by car manufacturers to cut accident rates. Rabies vaccine can now be cultured from human cells, whereas the first vaccine, developed by Pasteur in 1885, involved killing hundreds of rabbits. Since 1970 the Hadwin Trust for Humane Research has invested nearly £400,000 in developing alternatives to animal experiments in work on cancer research, rheumatism, liver failure, drug side effects, cataracts and diabetes. Cancer research can be carried out on human cells cultured outside the body, though cell culture on its own is not always effective because a substance that isn't initially poisonous may become so after being broken down in the liver or affected by other organs. But the arguments against the use of cell culture and for animal experimentation take no account of the fact that biochemical processes are likely to vary from species to species and are far from reliable. Cells from different human organs, including diseased ones, enable the direct study of cancer, leukaemia and other conditions, while cancer researchers cannot replicate human tumours in animals. A Green government would outlaw animal experiments, reform the drugs industry and fund alternative forms of research.

Vivisection is only the visible and much protested against tip of a particularly bloody iceberg. Factory farming affects billions of animals. Most eggs are produced in battery units, where chickens have little more space in which to move than the area occupied by two pages of this book. Forty per cent of birds are debeaked at between five and eight weeks to prevent cannibalism. According to a Ministry of Agriculture, Fisheries and Food advice leaflet, 'An upper blade has a sharp edge, is electrically heated and closed on to an unheated lower blade. A portion of the beak is thus removed . . . Great care is needed with very young birds not to damage the tongue or nostrils' (ADAS advisory leaflet No. 480, available from Tolcarne Drive, Pinner, Middlesex, HA5 2DT).

Factory farming is bad for the environment. It is highly energy-intensive. It produces tonnes of concentrated manure, which causes pollution and is one reason why UK nitrate levels are higher than those permitted by the EEC. It is bad for us as well as for our environment. It reduces rural employment and creates the hazards of dust and disease for workers in giant sheds. It remains cheap for reasons of false economy – cheap energy and expensive land. The most rudimentary understanding of disease ecology testifies to the fact that factory farming kills. If you pack together any population, human or animal, in close proximity to excrement, disease will spread rapidly. Many factory farms contain a staggering 50,000 birds, a single building housing tens of thousands. The means of disease control, whereby at least 40 per cent of birds are dosed with antibiotics, is bound to increase the resistance of bacterial strains including salmonella. It is common knowledge that most poultry is contaminated, and cases of poisoning from *Salmonella enteritidis* have increased from 392 in 1981 to 12,522 in 1988. According to the *New Scientist* (17 December 1988), 40 per cent of egg samples in 1988 contained the bacteria. The prime source of infection is feed. The British Egg Information Service says, 'According to our guidelines, our producers do not feed their chickens any chicken waste,' yet the codes of practice are purely voluntary, and feed mills are checked only once a year. We know that 5 per cent of feed includes meat and bone meal. Said one vet in the industry, 'Contaminated fishmeal isn't turned away: if it were, we'd have nothing to feed the animals.' As the Ministry puts it, 'It is not our policy to prosecute.' This isn't good enough.

Pigs are increasingly housed in closely packed indoor units as well. In the USA many cattle are put into feed lots, where they never see the sun or eat grass. 'Humane' slaughter simply does not exist. A pathologist writing in *Meat Magazine* (November 1986) reveals that the bolt method used to stun cattle rarely works as it should: 'It is a horrifying fact that approximately one third of the cattle shot in this way are not stunned, but stand grievously wounded and fully conscious while the pistol is reloaded.' While Britain remains a meat-eating country the conditions of animal husbandry and slaughter are in need of reform. The case of Hilda the Hippo, a zoo animal involved in a road accident during the first weeks of this new decade, is an illustration of why the transport of live animals over long distances should be ended.

If meat presents moral dilemmas, then milk production too creates suffering. Cows grazing in green fields or gently chewing the cud do not look as if they are in need of liberating. But the commercialization of the dairy industry has put enormous pressure on cattle herds to yield greater quantities of milk as swiftly and as cheaply as possible.

While it is possible to argue for food production via animals, the use of animals to produce luxury clothes is something that Greens find unacceptable. Thankfully, public pressure over the wearing of fur is causing a decline in the sale of fur coats and has prompted the closure of Harrods' department. For this we must thank the campaigns of Lynx and Greenpeace. However, the fur trade is retaliating by saying that fur is 'environmentally friendly' and that fake fur involves the use of harmful chemicals in fabric production. Greens have no truck with either type of fur – if fake fur involves harmful manufacturing processes then its production should cease. Greens state firmly that nothing can justify the slaughter of animals just to put a luxury item on a human back. The breeding of animals for their fur alone or the catching of wild animals would be a crime in any green society.

Greens would end all bloodsports. We all abhor the bull fighting in Spain, yet we condone shooting, calling it a 'gentlemanly sport'. What is gentle about killing millions of pheasants, specifically bred, by blasting them out of the sky with a shotgun? What is gentle about deer stalking, angling or any other so-called sport that involves the murder of animals? The shooting gentry claim to be conservationists, but study shows this claim to be false. Grouse shooting – incidentally, a favourite pastime of Prince Charles and other royals – means that heather moorland is burned every year to create the right conditions for grouse to breed. The burning exposes soil to erosion and causes the pollution of our water systems. To add to this, far from ending their days on the dining table, millions of game birds are burned or buried because there is little demand for lead-infested birds. In the past, banning cruel sports has not necessarily proved successful: those who are caught indulging in badger baiting and dog and cock fighting often receive paltry fines, indicating that the abuse of animals needs to be taken seriously by lawmakers and magistrates. Where others pay lip service to the issue, the Green Party has an excellent animal rights working group, whose aim is to stimulate public awareness of the rights of animals. A motion put to the Green Party Conference in April 1990 states, 'The Green Party believes that only a robust campaign of non-violent direct action can liberate the animals tortured, imprisoned and abused in our society.' A Green government would ban fox hunting, hare coursing and similar abominations.

Pythagoras noted, 'For as long as men massacre animals, they will kill each other,' but forgot to note that human war also leads to the massacre of animals. This century has seen the development of a form of biological warfare that uses animals as weapons. The US Navy has been developing the concept of killer dolphins and whales to destroy enemy vessels. The USSR has long trained explosive-laden anti-tank dogs, which in the event of conflict would have a short life expectancy. The US 82nd Airborne Division at Fort Bragg, North Carolina, has experimented with parachuting dogs into the front line. During the Vietnam war elephants and water buffalo 'suspected' of helping the Vietcong rebels were machine-gunned into submission. David Day, in his book *Eco Wars*, reveals that 'Entire forests came under "suspicion" as wilful collaborators, and were consequently fire-bombed and pulverized into swamplands.' The 125 wars that have beset the world since 1945 have all destroyed habitats and decimated wildlife populations. Peace is a prerequisite for the protection of animal rights, while respect for human life is enhanced by respect for the life of other species.

It is difficult to see how zoos can be associated with such respect. The Green Party believes that it is wrong to keep social animals in solitary confinement and argue that the conservation of rare species should rest principally on preserving habitats from industrial pressure. Zoos, introduced by powerful pre-Roman monarchs as a way of flaunting their wealth and power, have an unhappy history. Entire collections of animals were exterminated to demonstrate a ruler's power over not just human subjects but other forms of life as well, a practice that persisted until as late as 1719, when Elector Augustus II of Dresden personally slaughtered his menagerie of tigers, lions, birds, bears and boars. While zoos today are concerned in theory with conservation and in practice with gate money, things remain far from perfect. Ten chimps die for every one delivered to Europe. Malnutrition, cannibalism, infanticide and fighting are all documented in Lynn Grinder's fourteen-year study *The Pathology of Zoo Animals*.

Commercial pressures threaten many of the species we commonly see in zoos with extinction in the wild. In thirty years' time the only elephants left may be those in zoos and safari parks, separated from their own social and environmental setting, consigned by human villainy to the equivalent of our long-stay mental hospitals and prisons. Every year 100,000 elephants are killed for their ivory. Botswana, South Africa and Zimbabwe all oppose a ban on this trade and profit from the hunters. Rowan Martin, deputy director of the Zimbabwe Wildlife Department, claims that, thanks to his 'excellent management', the African elephant population is on the increase and 'closing the illegal trade gaps . . . [would be] a waste of time'. According to the Environmental Investigation Agency, the Zimbabwean census has been boosted by the migration of thousands of elephants from Botswana to escape the drought that has dried up their watering holes. The EIA argued in September 1989, 'Both countries now want to "cull" what appears to be virtually the same herds of elephants.' Other countries have a greener approach to the plight of the elephant. Tanzania, for instance, has banned the ivory trade, the only sure way of protecting elephants from criminals who launder ivory as a legal product in centres like Hong Kong or move it from one African country to another so as to evade detection. In the first half of 1989 the country arrested 1,000 poachers, dealers and middlemen; but, as Constantius Mloy, the director of the country's Wildlife Department, points out, the legal ivory industry is exerting international pressure to continue the killing. Mloy comments, 'As long as someone in Europe, the USA or Japan is going to buy ivory, someone in Africa will kill elephants. We cannot stop the poaching of our elephants for illegal ivory unless big men in Hong Kong, Singapore, Taiwan and Japan are put out of business.'

The plight of the elephant neatly illustrates the philosophy behind a green policy of animal liberation. However much pleasure people take in owning ivory objects, this can never outweigh the suffering caused to even a single elephant killed for its tusks. At present human needs, however minor, are always placed above the most essential need of animals – to be allowed to live without the threat of suffering or extermination. To justify animal abuse in exchange for human gain, Professor Bernard Williams has argued that animal suffering is 'qualitatively' different from that of humans. Greens believe the opposite, arguing that, morally and ecologically, 'The present assumption that animals can be used for any purpose that benefits human beings is not acceptable ... Suffering and disruption to other species has to be justified in the strongest terms' (*MFSS*, AN 100).

Dilemmas will always remain, even for those most convinced of the case against animal cruelty. Where the choice is between supporting native hunting people and conserving local fauna, Greens would argue that to stop such people eating meat would lead to the extinction of endangered human beings. But such situations, where potential human suffering is great enough to justify harm to other forms of advanced life, are rare. Bernard Williams, when pressed, argues that there are some extreme uses of animals that might be unacceptable, claiming that it would be wrong to use them as 'fire lighters'. Yet this is almost exactly what we do by vivisecting them in the cause of creating new cosmetics or replicating old drugs.

Western culture is particularly at fault. The *halal* meat condemned as 'religious slaughter' by Europeans was specifically introduced by

Muslims and Jews to fulfil God's prescription that slaughter should be as swift as possible. Our approach is to turn a blind eye and pretend that Cellophane-wrapped meat is just another grocery item, like a tin of beans or a sack of potatoes. McDonald's, the burger chain now invading Eastern Europe and the USSR, once produced TV commercials explaining to North American children that hamburgers 'grow in little hamburger patches'. We have all seen the advertisements that show happy cartoon sheep and pigs happily looking forward to their arrival on our plate. An animal rights activist in Quebec recounted to a local magazine that a school friend believed that steaks were surgically removed from cows, which returned to peaceful meadows (presumably to be left in peace until the steaks grew back).

Humans can live without meat, and many members of the UK Green Party see meat eating as akin to cannibalism. But while the Greens believe that the promotion of a vegetarian diet is vital, meat eating neither can nor should be legislated away. What should be recognized is that meat eating starves the Third World. As only 42 per cent of the body weight of animals can be consumed, meat production is also an inefficient use of the Earth's scarce resources. The English meat-and-two-veg diet, with its resultant waste, cruelty and nutritional deficiencies, has to go. The trend towards eating smaller amounts of meat and towards veganism and vegetarianism – in short, towards a varied, healthy diet – should be encouraged and applauded. Suffering can be kept away from the dining plate.

The emotion that fuels cruelty is more often greed than anger or ignorance. It is not the philosophers but the accountants who decide the fate of vivisected rats and caged pigs. The Protection of Birds Act 1954 makes it an offence to keep any bird in a cage that is too small to allow it to spread its wings (any bird, that is, except one reared commercially for table or omelette). As Dr Desmond Morris put it in the *Sunday Telegraph Magazine*, (23 May 1982) 'The moral of the story, if you happen to be a bird or a mammal, is not to provide mankind with any valuable form of food. If you merely provide companionship as a pet or beauty as a wild creature, you will be well treated; but if you give more – if you provide your eggs, or your meat, for human sustenance – your reward will be a life sentence in an animal concentration camp.' The extension of such logic, which puts gain before anything else, can be found in biotechnology. The splicing and splitting of DNA has already led to entirely new species of animals and plants, which can be patented so that they belong to specific organizations. Nature may be on the brink of being redesigned on a grand scale for human benefit – or at least for the benefit of some humans.

The concept of human dominance that falsely places us above nature will, if it is allowed to persist, drag us to our collective doom. Human liberation equals animal liberation, and the sum of both is green politics. Animal liberation won't be easy, and the Green Party accepts that those who care about other species are up against ingrained habits and powerful commercial interests. But the struggle must go on. As Frederick Douglass, a black leader of the movement for the abolition of slavery stated, 'If there is no struggle, there is no progress . . . Those who profess to favour freedom, and yet deprecate agitation, are people who want rain without thunder and lightning. They want the ocean without the roar of its many waters. Power concedes nothing without a demand. It never did and it never will.'

Animals in our society are either in prison or under sentence of death. They need liberating.

Greens have an unambiguous approach to defence: you cannot love the planet and love the bomb.

Nuclear and other weapons of mass destruction must go. Real defence can be based only on a policy of peace, and that means much more than being in a continual state of preparedness for war. 'Armed truce should not be mistaken for peace . . . A defence policy based on the willingness to commit genocide, and to wreak incalculable destruction on the planet, is unacceptable' (*MFSS*, DF 101).

According to the tabloid papers and the Murdoch press, a Green Party in control at Westminster would leave us defenceless in a dangerous world. In spite (or perhaps because) of this, the Greens gained 15 per cent of the vote as a totally anti-nuclear party. Just when Labour rejected unilateralism because the stance was thought to be too unpopular, voters deserted the Conservatives in droves for the Greens. The real enemies of security are those who have ignored the destruction of the environment.

There can be no room for compromise in a world facing ecological death; defence of the Earth must come before territorial squabbles. We cannot afford to spend billions of pounds on weapons of mass destruction while ignoring the threats of poverty and environmental damage, which are far more dangerous than foreign 'enemies'. It is impossible to campaign against environmental destruction and ignore the fact that the Earth would be destroyed many times over by nuclear war. Environmental campaigners point to the risk of industrial accidents such as those at Bhopal or Seveso, but any nuclear mishap would be far more dangerous. The Green Party would 'unilaterally' destroy all of Britain's nuclear weapons, getting rid, in the process, of the bases that make us at present the USA's 'unsinkable aircraft carrier'. We would pull out of NATO and call for the dissolution of super-power military blocs. The revolution that started in 1989 in Eastern Europe and the introduction of democratic processes behind what used to be an iron curtain vindicate our long-standing policy: 'to encourage all European states, East and West, to establish a doctrine of collective neutrality as an essential step towards defusing the Cold War'.

Greens believe in ridding the world of all weapons of mass destruction, chemical, biological and conventional. The nastiest of the non-nuclear weapons can be very nasty indeed. The so-called 'fuel–air explosive' (FAE) releases over a wide area chemical vapours that can then be ignited to grotesque effect. The American CBU-55, comprising three bomblets, each containing 33 kilograms of ethylene oxide that will burn without oxygen, can be dropped from a helicopter at a height of 500 metres. At a certain distance above the ground the vapour is released and detonated by a delayed-action device within the bombs, creating a huge fireball that kills all life within its wide range. Smaller FAEs were used during the Vietnam war to incinerate areas of ground covering 600 square metres. What such a device would do to an Asian village or a shopping centre in North London or the West Midlands truly does not bear thinking about. Attempts to ban the FAE, along with its military cousin napalm, have floundered during disarmament talks. A Green Britain would scrap all such infernal weapons and shift to a position of defensive weaponry. It would resolve to attempt to settle disputes by non-violent means but would understand that at present we need to maintain defensive weapons, scrapping tanks in favour of anti-tank weapons, scrapping submarines but maintaining anti-submarine helicopter squads. Defence does not have to mean killing millions of civilians with whom one has no direct quarrel, whether they live in Kiev, Krakow or Kentucky.

Yet such pragmatism is swept aside by a torrent of hostile cold-war rhetoric by Cabinet ministers masquerading as high-tech warlords. Mrs Thatcher proclaims that unilateralism is one-sided disarmament. The Green Party points out that her multilateralism is a form of no-sided disarmament. The truth is that every state must disarm unilaterally, as no nation state has the means or the power to remove forcibly the weapons of others. The Iron Lady, alone in Europe on so many issues, is also alone in her advocacy of high defence spending despite the thawing of the cold war. Mrs Thatcher continues to praise Britain's 'independent nuclear weapons capability', no doubt arguing that even if détente had reigned for a century to the West of the Urals, we would still need a few 'nukes' just in case.

It is strange that anyone could discern virtue in a state of armed nuclear terror, but British politicians will, in the words of Gaitskell, 'fight, fight and fight again' to maintain military supremacy. Even at the height of 1950s tension the idea of an independent nuclear deterrent was deeply irrational. Amazing as it is that former unilateralists and CND supporters Neil Kinnock and Paddy Ashdown have gone nuclear, the nuclear disease is one that many formerly peaceful individuals have fallen victim to. Kinnock stated after Labour's adoption of multilateralism, 'I will never be put in the position again where I argue for a unilateralist policy.' Trident, Polaris, Cruise and all the rest are a source of prestige and power. They give Britain (that is, British politicians) a place at the negotiating table and an excuse for pretending that Britain is still part of an empire, albeit a radioactive one. In the popular and the political imagination nuclear weapons are compensations for the loss of India and all the other colonies – perhaps even the American one that went in 1776. None the less, nuclear weapons have to go. Electoral expediency is no justification in the face of Armageddon.

Because the nuclear nightmare is so frightening we rarely think about it. The killing power of Britain's 'defences' is almost unimaginable. The Hiroshima bomb dropped in 1945 killed at least 160,000 people outright, yet was minuscule by comparison with today's missiles. A single Trident submarine, the replacement for Polaris backed by former disarmers Kinnock and Ashdown as well as Owen and Thatcher, contains 408 warheads with a total explosive capacity 1,200 times greater than that of the bomb dropped on Hiroshima. Yet such an apocalyptic weapon is defended as a bargaining chip by Britain's nuclear politicians. A single 40-megaton bomb would be equal to twenty times the explosives used in the Second World War. The damage that just one weapon would do to its target – a city in Europe, North America or the USSR – is difficult to comprehend. A single Poseidon submarine could effectively destroy Russia at the touch of a button. In 1981 Frank Barnaby of the Stockholm Peace Research Institute claimed that every major city within the territory of the NATO and Warsaw pact countries was targeted by the equivalent of 2,000 Hiroshima bombs. Even with the advent of INF and the destruction of Cruise missiles, we have the capacity to wipe out every member of the human race many times over.

Nuclear weapons kill in a dozen ways, not just with their explosive capacity. A 20-megaton bomb dropped on Westminster would ignite clothing 34 kilometres away, cause serious skin burns at 50 kilometres and first-degree burns at 72 kilometres. The Hiroshima bomb burned everything within an area of 11 square kilometres. A much larger Westminster attack might do similar damage over 40 square kilometres. Millions of smaller fires would break out spontaneously, and the idea of fire fighting would be a joke. The blast would be strong enough to hurl cars into the air 20 kilometres away. The explosion would create a chasm 80 metres deep, into which would fall Westminster Abbey, Buckingham Palace, the Houses of Parliament and the former GLC building on the other side of the Thames. It goes without saying that few fish would be left in the Thames after it had been boiled away by nuclear fire and thrown halfway across Europe by the blast. Numbers 10 and 11 Downing Street would vanish, along with their bunkers. London would burn away, and commuters lucky enough to survive in the deepest Tube station, Hampstead, would emerge to find themselves in a fire storm strong enough to starve them of oxygen.

Survivors would die of radiation sickness right across the home counties, although they would gain temporary hope from the classic sequence of recovery followed by swift relapse and fatality. Millions of people in southern England, the Midlands and (depending on the wind patterns) either the North, Scotland and Ireland or France and the Low Countries would be bathed in radioactive dust and would eventually succumb to leukaemia and other pernicious cancers. Dr Richard Lawson, a Green councillor, became notorious in the national press when he declared that he would prescribe suicide pills to his patients in Congresbury, near Weston-super-Mare, in the event of a nuclear war. Despite such an assertion, Dr Lawson has been returned with a greater majority each time he has sought re-election.

The Chernobyl accident, which released only a fraction of the fission product that would be created by a nuclear explosion, will cause tens of thousands of untimely deaths throughout the Soviet Union and even in Britain. To date, three years and 5000 miles away from the Ukrainian nuclear accident, Welsh sheep are still too contaminated to be taken to market, and there are regular radiation scares. A nuclear war would spew forth the contents of 1 million Chernobyls. Plutonium and other deadly isotopes would take hundreds of thousands of years to decay, and generation after generation would suffer horrifying mutations. Sternglass, a critic of the atmospheric nuclear tests of the 1950s and 1960s, argued that these had killed up to 1 million people through cancer.

Some species thrive on a little radiation. After the event the rat population of London's outer suburbs would grow dramatically. Rats can triple their numbers in just a few months and would proliferate among the bodies, rubble and smashed sewerage systems. Radioactive rodents would busily spread typhoid and a host of other plagues throughout the remnants of Reading, Winchester and Luton, ready to pick out the already radiation-weakened population. Most victims of nuclear war die not from the initial explosion but from its vicious and varied after-effects.

Road and rail links would be smashed. Emergency services would find it impossible to negotiate pitted and rubble-strewn streets. An electro-magnetic pulse would cripple radios and wipe computer disks clean of vital information. Communications would fall apart. Food would soon run short, and those with revolvers would fight gun battles for the last mouldy loaves of Mother's Pride.

The detonation of a single bomb would be bad enough, but what if Britain were caught up in a full-scale nuclear exchange that blasted not just London but also Bristol, Birmingham, Manchester, Glasgow and other major cities? What if the dozens of American bases and domestic military installations in Britain were targeted – as would be inevitable in a full-scale nuclear war? It is easy to see how the surface of a small island like ours, bristling with bases, could be destroyed by a nuclear assault that would leave few, if any, people alive.

Nature, as well as humanity, would be fatally wounded. After a period of initial prosperity even the rats would find the going tough. Paul Ehrlich, who coined the term 'nuclear winter', argues that dust thrown up by the blast, smoke from massive fire storms and water vaporized into the atmosphere would black out the light of the sun. For months after an attack the temperature would fall sharply, perhaps to as low as 30 degrees below freezing, thereby inducing an artificial Arctic-style winter. Life would become extremely difficult. Crop failures and icy conditions would prevent attempts to restore life to some kind of post-holocaust normality. The ecological components of the Earth would fall apart. Photosynthesis would be impossible, and plant life would die, in turn starving our herbivores and killing their predators.

Nobody knows how long a nuclear winter might last or whether it would lead to major damage or just fatal inconvenience. Nuclear winter might be followed by a radioactive summer, as a massive release of carbon dioxide from billions of tonnes of burned debris boosted the greenhouse effect.

Whatever the climatic consequences of nuclear war, we can be sure that survivors sheltering in their underground bunkers for the HMSO-recommended period of fourteen days would find themselves in an unrecognizable landscape of charred vegetation, decaying corpses and rubble. Kent County Council produced documents, written by Colonel 'Blick' Waring and Flight Commander 'Bunny' Warren, on how to survive the effects of nuclear war and construct garden shelters from recycled household waste. Such advice, although possibly comforting, would not on its own guarantee long-term survival. Without food, clean water or accommodation, existence (even for Messrs Waring and Warren) would undoubtedly be nasty, brutish and short. Such would be the consequences of a marriage between foreign policy and advanced physics.

Even a 'minor' nuclear conflict could destabilize global ecosystems enough to wipe out higher forms of life. J. Schell argues in *The Abolition* (Knopf, New York, 1984) that the ozone layer could be reduced by 70 per cent in the event of nuclear war, blinding all animals and insects and making it impossible for humans to stay out of doors for more than ten minutes. A 20 per cent reduction in the ozone layer would blister skin exposed to direct sunlight for just two hours. Insects that locate flowers visually would be blinded by ultra-violet light and would find themselves unable to pollinate plants.

There are many other frightening effects of nuclear fission that could dislocate the ecosystems of the Earth: massive floodings if missile bases adjacent to the ice sheets of Iceland and Siberia were hit; the migration of hungry survivors to the forests and semi-desert areas of the 'developing world'; the wiping out of oxygen-producing sea plankton; the destruction of grain belts; the extinction of thousands of species of plants and animals; the gross distortion of vital geo-chemical cycles. A nuclear war could turn the biological clock back millions of years or overwind it to the point of final destruction. The disputes between super-powers, however important they may have once seemed to us, are impossibly trivial by comparison with the release of the payload of one Trident submarine.

The overriding moral arguments against nuclear war and the manufacture of nuclear weapons have been made time and time again by commentators as diverse as the novelist Martin Amis and the late Lord Louis Mountbatten. They hardly need labouring. Yet defenders of the balance of terror argue that nuclear deterrence is the best guarantee against nuclear attack and the devastation we all fear so much. Apologists for nuclear terror claim that we need weapons to prevent war, that an armed West is the best guarantee against Soviet aggression. Our present government argues that the rise of Gorbachev and the destruction of short-range missiles has been possible only because of its robust defence strategies and that we need deterrence in case the present amenable Soviet leader is toppled by a new Stalin. They allege that, whatever the circumstances, any attack will be met by instant and devastating retaliation in the aptly named game of MAD (Mutually Assured Destruction) and that to fail to be serious about making ready for mass destruction, or even to be seen to fall behind in the race to develop new and deadly weapons, is to risk having one's bluff called. Deterrence means that to defend a country one must be prepared to destroy the whole world. To prevent war, the argument goes, one must prepare for it. Yet preparation for war has its own risks. It is not difficult to see how the theory of deterrence might lead to the reality of war during a period of high tension. Faced with a major international crisis – perhaps triggered by the struggle for Middle Eastern oil or conflict in Central America – in which both sides are playing for high stakes, it is easy to see how the threat of nuclear attack might be used to gain an advantage. According to Ellsberg in the *Monthly Review* (vol. 33, no. 4, 1981), the Americans have used their nuclear weaponry to threaten developing countries into submission on several occasions. If the Falklands war had gone a different way, Mrs Thatcher might have been tempted to use Polaris to persuade the Argentines to go back home. The step from nuclear defence to nuclear war is no doubt a very short one.

Cruise and its Soviet equivalents can fly just metres above the ground and, with the aid of complex guidance systems to avoid detection, could be used to launch a first-strike attack, wiping out the enemy's silos to prevent retaliation. The concept behind the Strategic Defense Initiative, popularly known as Star Wars, sounds innocent but has equally sinister potential. An 'umbrella' set up to prevent enemy weapons from striking US territory could be used aggressively to cover North America in the immediate aftermath of an assault on the Soviet Union. The danger is that an arms race based on the risky concept of deterrence might be replaced by one based on the fatal concept of first strike. Each super-power would strive to develop the perfect protection of the undetectable missiles to prevent the other from getting hold of either first. Expenditure would soar, and the temptation on either side to mount a first strike to prevent the other from doing so could become terrifyingly irresistible. And the possibility of accidental apocalypse should not be ignored. In 1983 there were two false alarms of impending nuclear attack every three days, according to the *Guardian*, 2 August 1984. Computers are as fallible as the human guardians of weapon-delivery systems.

Star wars or the older idea of anti-missile missiles would provide no real protection, even if the American rhetoric were to be believed, because nuclear weapons destroyed in the upper atmosphere or repelled into the Atlantic would still blanket the Earth in radiation, fragment ecosystems and erode the already fragile ozone layer. Nuclear war cannot be won, only prevented. Luckily, with the exit of Reagan and the arrival of *glasnost*, the arms race has slowed and may even be reversed. However a little disarmament can be a dangerous thing, reducing public pressure for peace, while retaining the essentials of the radioactive status quo. A non-Green government might lower the political heat by giving in to some of CND's demands and scrapping obsolete missiles merely to make way for new weapons technology.

The joy of SDI is it allows the USA to go on spending ruinously large quantities of money on defence while getting rid of some nuclear weapons. In *Protest and Survive* (Penguin, 1980) E. P. Thompson shows that, until the recent bout of *perestroika*, the Soviet system worked in a way very similar to capitalism as far as arms spending was concerned. Right across the world there exist scientists who gain prestige and pleasure from developing new systems. According to Dr Theodore Taylor, a brilliant young physicist in the 1950s who devoted his waking hours to making nuclear bombs 'smaller and more efficient', 'There are people in the labs who are hooked on testing, and do not want any inhibitions.' Hugh de Witt, another nuclear-weapons physicist who has spoken out against the arms race, warned, 'The weapons-labs people enjoy very great influence with members of Congress and the higher level of the US government, and they always have. They are the experts.' Such experts in East and West make up a powerful military–industrial complex with a certain commitment to an accelerating arms race. Few politicians stand up to them. They have done their best to make disarmament unacceptable to the voting public.

War is used as a way to divert internal political pressures. There are economic pressures for the production of weapons and their use. The arms industry is a powerful lobby, and weapons making is a sure-fire route to profits. At 1986 prices the cost of the manufacture of US warheads and delivery systems came to a cool \$218 billion. Gore Vidal, the American novelist, has described in cynical but accurate terms how the military–political–industrial cycle maintains its rhythm, claiming that arms manufacturers donate generously to the campaign coffers of both Republican and Democratic presidential candidates, who in turn feel obliged, in the name of security and freedom, to increase arms spending and to give the Pentagon a larger budget, which is spent on new aircraft, missiles and naval equipment. The resulting funds are again recycled into political donations that maintain the equilibrium of arms spending. Even if the Soviet Union didn't exist (and, given the changes going on at this very moment in Eastern Europe, it certainly won't exist much longer as a 'Red threat' intent on world domination and the destruction of McDonald's and apple pie), it would have to be invented to keep companies in profit and to create jobs. Forty per cent of workers in California are employed by the defence industry. Thirty per cent of US engineering contracts are paid for by the Pentagon. In Britain a similar story could be told of whole communities (Barrow, Faslane, even Bath) that are almost totally dependent on the military. 'For corporations which are "defence-dependent", the drive for new contracts becomes compelling. By the time a firm has developed the personnel, complex equipment and expensive facilities to handle programmes budgeted for hundreds of millions or billions of dollars, the management must keep the firms operating at or near full capacity or risk serious losses' (*New Statesman*, 10 April 1987).

The arms trade is a source both of profit and prestige. Britain is at its centre. We are the second largest arms-selling country in the world after the USA with 20 per cent of the market. Mrs Thatcher is an enthusiastic saleswoman who does her best to boost the government's Defence Sales Organization (DSO) on foreign visits. On coming to office the Conservatives vowed to boost arms sales from £36 million to £1,800 million per annum and more than succeeded. Britain now exports £3,500 million worth of weapons a year. Approximately 15 per cent of Britain's aid to developing countries consists of weapons of destruction, such as tanks, missiles and machine guns. The roots of Britain's record of aiding Third World conflict lie in the soil of earlier governments. Dennis Healey, as Labour Defence Minister, was instructed by Harold Wilson to set up the DSO so as to 'ensure that this country does not fail to secure its rightful share of this valuable commercial market'. During the 1970s the Shah of Iran, it is said, went to bed every night with defence magazines to prepare the next day's shopping lists. The items noted included his Chieftain tanks, and the torture equipment used by SAVAK, the secret police, helped Britain's exporters. The argument that if we didn't sell weapons to the poorest countries of the world, then somebody else would is the logic of the heroin dealer. It is a logic that rebounds on Britain. Between the election of the Conservative government in May 1979 and the start of the Falklands war, Britain sold £180 million worth of arms to Argentina, including an aircraft carrier, destroyers, ship-to-air missiles, surface-to-air missiles, Lynx helicopters, bomber aircraft, armoured cars and sub-machine guns. Many of the 255 British servicemen killed in the conflict died at the hands of British arms manufacturers. (To take one example, HMS *Ardent* was sunk by a jet aircraft propelled by Rolls-Royce engines.)

Greens believe that it is evil to export to the developing world arms that are used to fight futile wars, silence critics of undemocratic regimes and keep the poor quiet. The *Manifesto for a Sustainable Society* states unambiguously, 'The UK shall cease immediately to participate in the commercial arms trade, or to export other military technology and expertise, as an important step to demilitarizing' (DF 307). The Green Party is also committed to converting the economic, technical and scientific resources used to feed the international arms race to socially and environment-friendly uses. The process initiated by the super-powers to remove short-range nuclear weapons should be extended to end the international arms trade.

Nuclear weapons kill through poverty as well as cancer. To put arms spending into terrible perspective as we in the so-called developed world spend billions and billions of dollars on armaments – $1 million a minute world-wide – each year over 15 million people die of starvation and 5 million children die of contagious diseases that would be preventable by a programme of immunization. Ken Livingstone notes in *Livingstone's Labour* (Unwin Hyman, 1989) that if we lowered our defence spending to that of West Germany, we would release £9 billion to be spent on other priorities: the health service, aid, senior citizens – the list is endless. We as a nation should be ashamed that we dare spend money on killing machines rather than on healing machines when so many ills abound. We spend more on defence than on any other area of government expenditure bar the nation's welfare system: £19 billion in 1988, 43 per cent of which went on equipment, from Tornado jets to new missiles. Trident will cost £9 billion alone. Less than 1 per cent of spending is used to protect the environment or to give aid to the developing world. Twelve pence out of every £1 of tax paid in Britain goes on defence. If only a fraction of the amount of money spent on nuclear weapons world-wide were invested in health care, food production and housing, the number of poor on this planet would fall dramatically. One of the reasons why economies have to grow, eating up irreplaceable resources and disrupting nature, is because we *want* to spend money on such weapons. The arms race is an economic as well as a technical contest between super-powers trying to prove their superiority by pushing each other into ever greater spending on armaments. The winner is the side that becomes bankrupt second rather than first.

Even if the race finished today, its consequences would be felt for centuries. Missiles containing highly radioactive weapon elements are not easily disposed of. A nuclear submarine like Poseidon or Polaris produces a lot of low- to medium-level radioactive waste that has to be put somewhere. Disarmament cannot disinvent plutonium. The radioactive spin-offs of political squabbles will curse us far into the future. A number of nuclear submarines, both American and Russian, have been lost at sea and will gradually release their radioactive poison as hulls decay and break apart. (Some incidents may have been caused by illegal drug taking. Indeed, a local journalist visiting the US submarine base at Holy Loch in Scotland was offered 'a stunning cocktail mixture of cocaine, LSD, mescalin, marijuana, "uppers" and "downers" by US Navy men in 1972'. Despite denials from the US Navy, a former civilian employee found court-martial papers of drug cases on a local rubbish dump. Perhaps President Bush would be better engaged fighting his drug war among US servicemen than in Bolivia or Peru, where at least local drug abusers are not in a position to blow the world up many times over.) Nuclear submarines are lethal. According to Duncan Campbell, water discharged from Polaris cooling systems has seriously polluted Holy Loch on the Clyde as well as nearby mud flats. Answering allegations of danger, the commander of USS *Proteus*, Richard Lanning, proclaimed, 'Danger of radiation is practically non-existent. In fact, we could drink the water from one of the primary systems.' Sympathetic newspaper headlines pronounced, 'Polaris ship radiates only good will.' The authors are sceptical of this view. Seaborne nuclear weapons are a horrifying idea. Yet US sea-launched Cruise missiles are now operational. Britain has twenty-two nuclear-powered submarines equipped with sixty-four nuclear missiles, all waiting for an accident that will make the Irish Sea boil with radiation.

Yet another risk of retaining nuclear weapons is proliferation. We are a bad example – a small nation that insists it can survive and preserve the security of its citizens only by threatening the rest of the planet with annihilation, a small nation that cannot be taken seriously when it asks other small nations (Israel, South Africa, Libya, Argentina and Chile) not to take up the nuclear arms that it claims it could not do without. Nuclear weapons have to go. There are no plausible arguments for their retention by Britain. The risks of bearing nuclear weapons are far greater than those that might come from disarming.

Scrapping nuclear weapons is not enough on its own, however. Real defence rests on the creation of real security and the establishment of a peaceful world order. While millions of people are without access to food, clean water, shelter or basic educational facilities there is bound to be conflict. World peace must go hand in hand with world development. There are rational reasons for the most irrational of wars. Poverty is perhaps the most important. If half the globe starves, there is bound to be vast unrest. If the money spent on arms were transferred to development spending to end such poverty and injustice, there would be far less pressure to propel conflict. We should be spending on peace instead of on war. Making it possible for everybody in the world to have access to food, shelter and basic goods would be the best security for all of us.

Wars will be fought over scarce reserves of oil and strategic metals if we continue to use them up at ever-increasing rates. The disputes between Israel and the Arab states, war-torn Lebanon and the bloody Iran-Iraq conflict continually threaten to draw in super-powers concerned to maintain supplies of oil. Some have suggested that the real issue in the Falklands war was not sovereignty over the islands but sovereignty over huge mineral deposits that might be harvested from the surrounding seas and the Antarctic. One report to the European Parliament from the European Democratic Group (which contains mostly MEPs from our own Conservative Party), calling for a European Army, notes, 'The economic growth of the industrially advanced nations depends more and more on added value in the expansion of high technologies for new products and services ... [that depend on] exotic and rare metals and their alloys, sourced mostly in countries distant from the European Community,' going on to remark that European security should be viewed not purely in terms of the Soviet Union 'but also in terms of ... economic dependence on trade and ... continued free access to raw materials and broad international respect for codes of conduct such as international law and multilateral and bilateral treaties and conventions'.

Territorialism, patriotism and nationalism are all evils that can be used to whip up conflict. Across the planet countries and would-be nations of Sikhs, Croats and Basques fight over borders. The most arid deserts have become prizes for tribal groups to win. Mrs Thatcher versus Gualtieri in the south Atlantic. Somalia and Ethiopia in the Ogaden. Egypt and Israel in the bleak Sinai. Many of the conflicts in the developing world emerge from the gerrymandering of traditionally defined and long-agreed borders between tribes. In Sri Lanka the British deliberately gave positions of power to the Tamil minority as a way of inflaming and oppressing the Buddhist Sinhalese majority and directly caused the conflict that has torn the island apart. In countries such as Nigeria dominant tribal groups have been given hegemony over other groups, which naturally causes resentment. (The British, with their love of pomp, princes and royal babies, should beware of labelling other manifestations of tribalism as irrational.)

Nationalism of all kinds needs to be understood and, if possible, discouraged. Green politics certainly demands international cooperation, and the green movement encompasses supporters from all races, all major religions and all classes. But declaring ritually that one opposes nationalism does nothing to reduce the problem. A partial solution will come through regionalization, granting rights to as many self-defined groups as possible and reducing dangerous concentrations of power.

One cause of future war may be environmental. Having had green consumerism, we may next have green wars. The greenhouse effect will create millions of refugees from low-lying countries such as the Netherlands and the Maldive Islands, creating in turn international tensions. Soil erosion will also displace peoples. Disputes over pollution, fishing rights and natural-resource control could well lead from diplomacy to conflict. Green politics is the answer.

Greens argue that we must remove all nuclear weapons from British soil because, even without the threat of war, they are just too dangerous to keep. Nuclear weapons are part of a nuclear cycle that involves uranium mining and reprocessing and the transport of radioactive substances from one side of the globe to another, a cycle that causes pollution and cancer deaths at every stage of the way.

The British civil nuclear-power programme, which Greens strongly oppose because of the danger of accident and the problems caused by the disposal of waste (to name just two of many dilemmas), is intimately linked with the production of plutonium for nuclear weapons. However uneconomic, nuclear power is supported by governments as a convenient and relatively uncontroversial way of providing raw materials for the bomb. Far from protecting lives and keeping the peace, nuclear power demands that we process and transport large quantities of radioactive material, creating cancer blackspots and increasing 'natural' background rates.

Stronger international peace-keeping institutions are needed to promote and maintain peace. To be effective and to gain real trust such institutions need to be both non-aligned and recognized as such. The post-war international establishment, which includes the International Monetary Fund, the World Bank, the Bretton Woods agreement on currency as well as the United Nations, are dominated by the USA. This should change: there should be a far greater role for developing countries and a far smaller one for the USA, the USSR, the UK and China. As the Green Party Manifesto puts it, the UN is 'more often an arena of international conflict than co-operation ... The United Nations system needs a complete overhaul, which should include: the decentralization of its functions to regions; reduction in its numerous agencies; abolition of permanent Security Council membership.' The United Nations should be able to act as an arbiter between countries and regions, so as to defuse the risk of war, in just the same way as industrial arbitrators prevent strikes and lock-outs by negotiating between workers and bosses. At present the UN is still seen by many small nations as a means of supporting American foreign policy by other means. Such perceived bias must end, and the UN must stand above sectional interests, whether economic or territorial. The UN needs to be able to police peace settlements if conflict is to cease. The presence of British troops on the streets of Ulster will always look like a colonial invasion to a large section of the local population, yet some Catholics fear even worse bloodshed if they go. The indigenous Ulster Defence Regiment and Royal Ulster Constabulary have been linked with sectarian murders and contingents of police or soldiers from Eire would upset Loyalists. The obvious answer would be a well-trained UN security force drawn from Europe or North America. The UN should also have a role in preventing environmental damage and in working for a new economic order that ends poverty in the developing world.

While a more peaceful world is the priority, Britain will still, at least in the short term, need to maintain the armed forces to guarantee security.

The Green Party would give priority to the development of a realistic strategy of non-violent resistance to potential aggressors. A peace broadsheet produced by the party states, 'This envisages the detailed advance planning and carrying out of non-violent resistance of all sorts, from non-lethal sabotage to the disruption of communications and the invader's administrative services, from the organization of strikes and boycotts to propaganda, from non-cooperation to the subversion of enemy troops. Such advance preparation, combined with the armed defensive forces, would indeed constitute a formidable deterrent against invasion.' Combined with policies on decentralization and self-sufficient communities, it would be possible to make the country effectively impossible to invade.

While recognizing the need for armed forces at present, it is vital to ensure that our military is democratic. Our armed forces are supposed to uphold British democracy, yet they are still driven by outdated class divisions and remain among the least democratic institutions in Britain. In 1988 a grand total of fifteen non-white officers entered the armed services. The role of any military should be about conflict resolution and effective security rather than 'blowing away' the opposition.

Any student of history can see the results of a world where militarism has gone mad, from the early Egyptians with their iron weapons to the sophisticated nuclear arsenal we have today. The world system has been structured around the principle of violence, be it state or individual. Domination by oppressive, exploitative, hierarchical and militaristic forces is a way of life experienced by the majority of people alive today. Whether it be the Pentagon, the Soviet and Chinese military leaderships or the French or British Defence Ministries, each has the capacity to influence all manner of decisions, including energy choices. Top military personnel head productive and trade sectors, maintain international links and orientate scientific research. It has been estimated that 80 per cent of science graduates enter defence-related industries, which consume enormous quantities of raw materials, energy, space and money. They divert human capacities. Armies fear that decentralization will threaten defence as they see it. At present, at the top of each nuclear state a few people have the power to decide about the life and death of the human and other species. Peace cannot be just the absence of war. We must rethink our attitudes and values. Peace requires genuine trust, cooperation, mutual support and the free exchange of information. It means material security for all the world's people, regardless of sex, colour or age. It means realizing that we are all one – only now some have more advantages than others. Any defence that does not promote trust and security is increasing, rather than reducing, the risk of war. Disarmament must be an intrinsic part of a world-wide movement towards a sustainable economic, social and political order.

Peace will not be an easy option, but it is possible. For a long time the world has been dominated by militarism in its efforts to procure peace. Any policy designed to create a peaceful world needs to break down the power structures so beloved by politicians and generals and give back to the people the incentive to find the inner core of peace that is within us all. Millions of people the world over are part of a grass-roots peace movement, and it is this uniting force that can change the destructive forces that are in evidence today.

To this end the Green Party would give priority to implementing plans for the conversion of military industries to socially useful production and would base its foreign policy on principles that are co-operative, non-aggressive and non-exploitative. Its defence policy is designed to create peace – a peaceful Britain and a peaceful world in which disputes are settled by international machinery for negotiation and mediation.

Disarmament is about political will. The concept of the nation state depends upon the assumption of an enemy from whom we need protection, which in turn is a justification for state secrecy. Psychologically we have been taught to accept a potential enemy. As relations are warming between the Eastern European states, Conservative politicians in Western Europe and the USA are looking for new excuses to love the bomb. Now that it is impossible to see the Soviet Union, under Gorbachev, as any kind of 'Red menace' or 'Russian bear' intent on domination, Mrs Thatcher argues that instability in the East and events like the Romanian revolution mean that we must retain our vast armouries. While the collapse of the Soviet empire has already led to bloody conflict between Armenia and Azerbaijan, such disputes will not be helped by UK rearmament: on the contrary, a strengthened UN and support for Soviet attempts at reconciliation on our part would be far more constructive. With peace breaking out with the USSR, top American military personnel are looking for external or internal enemies to justify political élitism and state secrecy – crack dealers, Japanese financiers or Panamanian generals all fit the bill. There will be no peace without social justice, participatory government, freedom of information and life in balance with the environment. We should all be talking peace because if we don't, we will be stuck, as now, in the old expansionary and patriarchal society that we so desperately wish to change.

In conclusion it is worth quoting Green Party policy in detail:

Violence underpins our social fabric, and international relations depend on the use or threat of force. Our whole world can be described as already at war. Nuclear weapons are the tip of the iceberg in a world built and sustained on the principles of violence, exploitation and domination. To rid ourselves of all weapons of mass destruction, we have to transform the material and cultural foundations of society. Lasting peace is impossible in the context of a patriarchal social and political system based on domination, a denial of feelings, and an unquestioning obedience to authority. An economic system that exploits people and the entire planet, that fosters excessive competition, aggression and consumerism, cannot be the basis of a peaceful world. (*MFSS* DF 102.)

The National Health Service (NHS) is in crisis. There are ever-growing hospital waiting lists, the closure of local clinics, an all-time low in staff morale, climbing drug bills and patient dissatisfaction. In some areas of Britain hospitals are finding it difficult to treat even the direst of emergencies. Every sector of the service has been in revolt. Even the far from militant British Medical Association has launched an imaginative and vitriolic advertising campaign against government plans. Health policy in Britain is a suitable case for treatment.

While insisting that the NHS is safe in her hands, Mrs Thatcher trumpets the virtues of privatized, US-style health care. Essential to her plan is the idea of getting hospitals and doctors' surgeries to compete for patients within an internal market. The more patients an institution gets, the more funding it receives from the public purse. Those who don't satisfy the customer go under. In theory this sounds like a way of increasing choice, but it has obvious draw-backs. There is no incentive for GPs to take on patients with chronic and expensive illnesses. Without very strict regulation the elderly, the disabled and those needing long-term treatment will lose out in such a market. AIDS victims and those who suffer from related syndromes may find it impossible to get care other than in expensive private clinics, or they may be moved from practice to practice, hospital to hospital. Doctors will become accountants first and carers second if they are to survive the harsh climate of competition.

The internal market has led to an enormous growth in paperwork, administration and non-medical costs in the American system. There is nothing to suggest that the situation would be any better here in Britain. Indeed most health professionals, from doctors to hospital administrators, believe that it would be a great deal worse. The USA has the 'most litigated against, second-guessed and paperwork-laden physicians in Western industrialized democracies' –

until NHS reforms bring the US system to Britain, that is. Dr Robert Elkeles, a London consultant, has claimed, 'The motive in business is to make a profit. The Health Service cannot make a profit. The Health Service in this country has been very successful. I'm not sure the same can be said of British business.'

The present government rejects such criticism as the plea of a special-interest group afraid of losing power and argues that it has poured money into the NHS. The facts tell a different story. While there has been a 24 per cent increase in real spending on the NHS between 1978 and 1987, most of the money has gone on increasing still pitiful wages and meeting the demands of a rapidly growing number of old people. There has been little or no growth in hospital services. Health Secretary Norman Fowler was cheered loudly at the 1986 Conservative Conference after producing a computer printout several metres long that contained a list of 380 new 'large hospital schemes'. The list was unrolled impressively over the rostrum and newspapers critical of the government's record on health spending were instructed to photograph it by the triumphant minister. The list was long only because projects over £1 million were included for the first time (the former definition of a large hospital project had been £5 million), and it contained such items of essential patient care as a car park at Medway Hospital, Kent, and new reception offices around the country.

But it is not enough to reject the internal market and claim that all of the NHS's problems are of Mrs Thatcher's making. Even without free-market medicine, the NHS would be in genuine crisis. To save the NHS we have to go the roots of why people get ill and treat the causes (often social or economic in origin) instead of suppressing the symptoms.

One major cause of ill health is the environment. Cutting lead out of petrol, controlling pollution and improving the inner-city environment are all vital forms of preventive medicine. From 'sick buildings', in which office design causes a host of maladies from headaches to legionnaire's disease, through to the links between petro-chemical production and leukaemia, our surroundings make us unwell in dozens of ways. While the killer smogs of the 1950s have gone, new invisible 'cleaner' forms of pollution persist. Acid rain emitted by the super-tall chimneys designed to remove such smog causes ill health. Radioactivity, which cannot be seen or smelt, is far more dangerous than other more visible forms of effluent. Cars churn out a whole host of pollutants, which, even when lead is finally banned, will still make the lives of those living near trunk roads and motorways unpleasant. Medical maps that chart the geographical spread of cancers show blackspots around nuclear power plants and factory complexes. Upwards of 1 million cancer deaths have been caused by atmospheric testing of nuclear weapons in the 1950s, and even the official Soviet report on the Chernobyl accident suggested that it would cause 49,000 extra cancer fatalities (some estimates put the figure at 100,000). Pesticides, although less of a problem in Britain, kill thousands in the developing world, where 2 million people are poisoned by pesticides every year and 40,000 die as a result . Five per cent of all cancers are said to be caused by workplace hazards, especially carcinogenic chemicals. Ozone depletion may make sunglasses necessary in order to prevent cataracts. With nitrates in our drinking water, pesticide residues in our fruit and vegetables and caesium in our lamb chops, Britain deserves its unsavoury reputation as the dirty man of Europe. We need a greener, cleaner Britain, without nuclear power and dioxins and with far stricter controls on pollutants.

It is probably not an exaggeration to state that the British diet is the most unhealthy in the world. The best way of cutting hospital waiting lists would be to change it drastically. A supermarket chief, addressing a meat industry conference, once summed up the attitude of the food industry when he said, 'The bad news is that a pork pie is a ball of meat with a fairly high fat content, wrapped in an envelope of fatty pastry. The good news is that people enjoy pork pies and will continue to do so. Logic might anticipate the demise of the pork pie, but we must not. What we eat is a matter not just of personal preference but also of political choice. Salt, fat, sugar and additives are all bad for us but good for company profits. They help to preserve goods and extend their shelf life; they provide cheap bulk; and they make food easier to mass-produce consistently. They are highly addictive as well.

The food industry has enormous power. It condemns critics as 'food Leninists', makes generous donations to political parties and spends millions of pounds on advertising. The provision of cheap, wholesome, unadulterated food and the promotion of a less calorie-intensive diet that is not based on meat is clearly not in its interest. Its influence over home economics curricula in schools and catering colleges and even over advisory bodies concerned with health policy is all-pervasive. A European Community ban on growth hormones for cattle was another 'Luddite move in the face of scientific advance', according to one government minister and Professor Lanning of Nottingham University claimed that the move was 'dangerous and politically motivated'.

West Germany's refusal to allow imports of British beef because of the fear of transmitting bovine spongiform encephalopathy (more popularly known as 'mad cow disease'), after 7,000 obviously affected cattle had been slaughtered, was condemned by government speakers as a manoeuvre to improve the country's balance-of-payments. John Selwyn Gummer stated, 'Beef is entirely safe. The Germans should realize I wouldn't let it out if it did harm.' The disease, which originally affected sheep, infects cattle via contaminated feed, and some scientists believe that it could spread to humans through offal. Health Secretary Kenneth Clarke admitted that the disease had got into the human food supply between 1985 and July 1988. Tim Lang of the London Food Commission claimed, 'It's virulent, it's dangerous and it's threatening', and he warned that to destroy BSE, infected food should be pressure-cooked for sixteen minutes at a temperature of 160°C.

Colin Spencer, the chair of the Guild of Food Writers, rages at the way factory farming abuses our health and that of chickens. 'Nothing is so barbaric as the way we treat our poultry. The muck and chemicals given to boost them is unimaginable. The birds are killed at forty days but they need at least three months to reach adult size. I think it is vile, and you end up with a very inferior product. Eight out of ten chickens have *Salmonella enteritidis*. It is carried in the cavity and in the edible offal, and the onus is on the consumer to kill it – by making sure the chicken is fully cooked' (*Independent on Sunday*, 28 January 1990).

Far from wanting to ban fish and chips or repress the pork pie (on second thoughts, perhaps not such a bad idea), the Green Party would seek to ensure that healthy food is available to all. At present, locally produced and fresh food is difficult and expensive to come by for many, particularly the poorest communities in Britain. Inner-city greenhouses, allotments and city farms could provide low-income families with cheap in-season vegetables and local jobs and would help to green urban areas. Lead needs to be banned so as to make such a plan viable. Start-up grants for urban growers could be provided and links between hospitals, schools and other community facilities set up.

While such plans may be something for the longer term, a Green administration, or even backbenchers via a cross-party-supported Private Member's Bill could do much to make the great British diet less deadly. Labels on foods are ambiguous and unhelpful. A packet of sugar (the subject of John Yudkin's classic book *Pure, White and Deadly*) is marked additive-and preservative-free. White bread is hyped as part of a healthy diet. McDonald's claims that its burgers form part of a well-balanced diet – presumably on the basis that if the rest of the day's intake is cholesterol-free on balance things may not be too bad. All food products, however unhealthy, can be sanitized in some way. Lard, for instance, becomes 'a traditional product taken from the British countryside and free of all sugar, salt or chemical additives'. Even a sausage made of mechanically retrieved 'meat', comprising crushed testicles, gristle and the run-off of semi-melted bones, can surely be sold as 'wholesome' by a marketing person somewhere. We need clearer labelling for the right indication of nutritional value, and food advertising should be subjected to far closer scrutiny.

Medical research confirms that allergies and hyperactivity in children are linked with the chemical content of food (though food manufacturers deny this). Yet food additives are consumed in large quantities: over 200,000 tonnes of additives are eaten every year in the UK at a rate of 4.5 kilograms per adult. Nine tenths of these are used purely for cosmetic effect – to make steaks look redder, batter more golden or otherwise grey instant-soup mixes more appealing. While some additives are valuable, enhancing the quality of food or preserving it, the majority are at best unnecessary and at worst dangerous. Britain has a poor record of endorsing additives banned by other countries. Potassium bromide was used for three decades in white sliced bread but banned in November 1989 after it was found to be carcinogenic. Food-processing workers are also at risk and are likely to come into contact with all manner of chemicals. Calcium proprionate (a mould inhibitor added to bread) causes irritation to the eyes and nose. Sodium bisulfite, which prevents fruit and vegetables from becoming discoloured, causes painful blisters. Additives need to be cut back drastically and research into their harmful effects stepped up (though not at the expense of vivisecting animals). At the moment

Britain lags behind nearly every other industrialized country in its outdated attitude to food safety.

Far from being a 'scientific breakthrough' or 'new advance in food technology ', irradiation should be seen for what it is: a way of killing bacteria in food that has been stored for too long or shipped too far. Like additives, irradiation helps industry but does little for the consumer, who deserves food that is good to eat without the dubious benefit of high-energy ray treatment. On the domestic front, November 1989 brought warnings of the danger of some microwave ovens, which were inadequately insulated, and we have all become aware of another danger, PVC clingfilm, from which di-2-ethyhexbadinate migrates into food if the film is inadvertently heated.

Listeria and salmonella are both forms of micro-life that have received regular coverage on television. Before the advent of Edwina Currie, the odd stomach ache or abdominal pain might be dismissed; we now know the full extent of food poisoning epidemics. Mrs Currie, although far from being a Green where the health of pensioners is concerned (her advice to them was to take up knitting and wear woolly hats), deserves all of our praise for tackling agribusiness head-on. Her outspokenness, at the cost of her ministerial career, pointed to the need for proper sampling and regulation of the food industry. At present there are far too few food-safety inspectors, and the rules can often be broken with impunity. Green Party policy would ensure that the work of all government advisers on food and health was subject to a Freedom of Information Act. A register of advisers' interests would be published annually.

If food is one environmental reason for ill health, poverty is another. Poverty, it has been said, is the worst form of pollution: bad housing conditions and an inadequate income inevitably make people ill. It is estimated that a healthy diet costs at least 35 per cent more than many pensioners and those receiving benefit have available to spend. Nearly 7 per cent of senior citizens suffer from malnutrition: to keep themselves solvent they spend less and less on food. Cheap housing has always tended to cluster around the areas of worst pollution. Pollution and resource taxes, unless accompanied by a national campaign to insulate homes, could become hypothermia taxes. Decaying housing, especially when damp, is known to cause or exacerbate many ailments. Meningitis, which is a growing menace – there have been significant outbreaks around Manchester, in the Cotswolds and in the south-east

– has been clearly associated with poor living conditions. People on low incomes may not have access to fresh produce (no local shops plus expensive bus travel), and tinned food, often the cheapest and least nutritious, may be the nearest they ever get to fruit. Increasingly, food retailing is geared to the needs not of the poor and old but the owners of credit cards and cars. Many local shops are being forced out of business by the huge hypermarkets that dominate the outskirts of large towns.

Recent surveys have shown clearly that poorer people die earlier than the well-off. We need to stop taking from the poor and giving to the rich. In the struggle to pay the iniquitous poll tax, many people will be forced to turn down their heating, spend less on meals and suffer illness as a consequence. A real redistribution of wealth is essential if we are to promote health and cut hospital waiting lists.

We need to redistribute work as well. Both unemployment and high-pressure over-employment can cause mental illness, physical problems and alcoholism. Work sharing would help. In the long term a Green government would promote satisfying work for all and encourage everybody to take part in tasks that exercised both mental and physical capacities. In the short term the Health and Safety at Work inspectorate needs to be restored to its pre-1979 strength. Too many of us have to put up with dangerous working conditions, and in areas such as the construction industry the fatal-accident record climbed sharply through the 1980s.

Stress is a cause of ill health, from headaches to cancer. One such cause is racism. Protasia Torkington, a black nurse who escaped from South Africa so that she could marry her white husband, completed a thesis entitled 'Racism in the National Health Service' after finding that black nurses are given the hardest work and are rarely promoted. Black women in the medical profession have been forgotten even when they have had the opportunity to do useful work. During the Crimean War, of the 20,000 fatalities 17,000 died of cholera and typhoid. Mary Seacole treated soldiers with drugs made from herbs that she learned about from her mother, a doctor in Jamaica. Torkington argues that explanations of why such figures are forgotten are 'always culturally and genetically presented, without looking at the racism of the system'. She also described how racism causes ill health: 'Racism cripples people's reaction to diseases. Stress will contribute to high blood pressure, and the immune system can be weakened if you are under stress. Black people are continually under stress from racism.'

Other sectors of the community are also under continual and health-endangering stress. Twenty per cent of women in industrial societies take tranquillizers, indicating that feminism has a very long way to go before it can be seen as successful. Women get a very raw deal, yet women's issues are ignored in the NHS debate. Billions of pounds are spent on drugs to keep women quiet and capable of coping with domestic drudgery and boredom. The cure will come not from spending more on putting women to sleep but from waking men up. The average mother works over sixteen hours a day, looking after children, cleaning, preparing meals, shopping and acting as unpaid slave. Most women suffer from stress. Despite the advent of the new man, male partners rarely do the washing-up or change nappies. Advertisements for anti-depressants feature women predominantly and play heavily on the social origins of mental illness. An ad for the 1970s drug Serenid-d, showing a woman pushing a pram outside a tower block, proclaimed, 'She can't change her environment . . . but you can change her mood with Serenid-d. Whilst neurotic illness has been shown to occur with greater frequency in women flat dwellers, it should not be forgotten that it is an increasing problem in the community at large. Serenid-d helps to control neurotic symptoms, anxiety, tension, irritability, etc., rapidly and with minimal risk of drowsiness or other untoward effects, thereby helping to restore serenity and calm to your patients' lives.'

'Serenity and calm' should be replaced with social change. There are ways of improving women's health and acting for a fairer deal for over 50 per cent of the population. Paternity payments and leave should be automatic, so that the bringing up of children can be a shared experience. The basic income scheme would provide women with a weekly payment, giving them some freedom of choice. For those women who choose to continue their work outside the home massive investment must be made in infant care and proper nursery education. At present child care is not even tax-deductible. Anti-sexist education should stress that 'real' men are fully rounded human beings who are able to cook and look after children. Both sexes would gain from the change.

Medical technology should be used with caution. General practitioners are seen by many patients as tribal witch doctors with almost supernatural curative powers, from whom they expect miracle cures. Many people are not satisfied unless they walk out of the surgery with some kind of pill or potion, but they should be taught instead how to involve their natural processes of healing. The medical profession has for too long provided a 'sickness service' rather than promising a genuine health service. Medicine is too often used to 'cure' socially created ills – screaming babies, jammed lifts in tower blocks, domestic violence, lack of self-worth, insomnia caused by mortgage arrears or late-night traffic – as this is both 'easier' and more profitable than attending to real causes. Pills keep us quiet and stop us complaining. Valium is the adult equivalent of gripe water and the legal version of cannabis. We live in a deeply drugged society, and as consumers we have come to expect high-medication health care, forgetting that pills cannot cure ills created by bureaucrats and politicians rather than by bacteria.

The problem is that drugs companies make their money by selling as many drugs as possible, giving doctors an incentive to over-medicate and create patients dependent on drugs or damaged by their side-effects. Firms like Glaxo, Beecham's and Wellcome spend millions of pounds on promoting their products to general practitioners. In January 1983 the television programme *Panorama* revealed that doctors were being offered a free trip to Venice via the Orient Express by the makers of a new drug for treating arthritis. Doctors are frequently invited to receptions designed to promote new pharmaceuticals. According to one London pharmacist, Jerry Shulman, 'The present volume of drug promotion has reached the point of over-kill. A doctor needs to be blind, deaf and dumb, and to lock his office, if he wishes to avoid being swamped by direct-mail advertising, visits by reps and heavy promotion in throw-away journals which serve as advertising vehicles.' Every year the drug companies spend over £5,000 per general practitioner promoting their products.

Such an excess of promotion can be paid for only by an excess of profit. Brand-name drugs often sell for five, ten or even fifteen times the price of generic drugs that have exactly the same function but lack the famous (well-advertised) name. In 1983 the government's head of pharmaceutical services listed eleven drugs that, if substituted for brand-name products, would save the NHS £29 million a year. Aldomet, which keeps blood pressure down, costs £27.23 for 500 pills; its generic identical twin, which is chemically no different, could be bought for £9.75 per 500. Lasix, a diuretic normally costing £53.81 per 1,000 pills, could be replaced by an identical generic drug costing just £4.00. The present government, to its credit, has tried to introduce generic drugs but has met with limited success. Given that one third of NHS spending is taken up by the drugs bill, it is essential that the drug manufacturers' profits should be reduced drastically and the savings used to supplement pay, boost hospital building and promote preventive medicine.

Over-medication creates illness as well as increasing the bills. About 5 per cent of hospital admissions are patients made unwell by prescribed drugs. The Royal College of Physicians claims that the side-effects of drugs are a major source of ill health. It can be argued that tranquillizers, laxatives and cough medicines are all useless. £30 million a year is spent on 'peripheral vasodilator drugs', despite the fact that there is no evidence that they work, and tranquillizers have created a far bigger addiction problem than heroin.

Prevention is better than cure. Hypertension causes raised blood pressure in many middle-aged men, increasing the possibility of heart attacks or strokes. The total bill for a man who is treated for hypertension with Navidrex K between the ages of 40 and 80 will be £164 at 1989 prices, but he runs the risk of developing diabetes or gout, and there may also be psychological side-effects. If the newer Capozide were used instead, the bill would rocket to £8.356 over forty years; while side-effects are *likely* to be less damaging, no one can be certain because the drug has not been prescribed long enough for a proper statistical analysis of patient reaction. On the other hand, hypertension can be treated at zero cost by reducing salt intake, cutting alcohol consumption, losing weight or taking up relaxation techniques such as meditation. This example could be matched by many similar cases of cheap, effective, non-pharmaceutical treatment. Sadly, medical training tends to forget such alternative approaches.

But even without the distortions created by the profit motive, the NHS would be far from green. Brigid Brophy has described hospitals as 'the most rigidly hierarchical society to be found in Britain since the Middle Ages'. Even if we were to ignore the epidemics caused by freeze/thaw catering – very much a feature of Thatcher's cut-price Britain – there are many other reasons why hospitals are far from healthy. Vast and uninviting, they hardly make us feel at home or encourage the natural rhythms of healing. Hospitals need to be rehumanized. Caring should be emphasized rather than high technology. The Green Party would reverse the trend towards even bigger hospitals and fund hospitals on a local level. Community health care is one area where Greens would like to see some economic growth and an increase in funding. The number of district and community nurses would be increased, particularly to cater for the needs of the very elderly and others who, though infirm, rightly reject institutionalization. At the other end of the age spectrum, home births should be encouraged and women given more choice. Sally Inch, in her powerful book *Approaching Birth*, challenges the hospital orthodoxy to reassert the wisdom of the community midwife, arguing that home or the general practitioner's unit is the best place for all but a minority of births.

We need to put alternatives into the NHS: acupuncture, herbal medicine and traditional techniques all have a role to play, but they need proper regulation and proper funding. Herbal remedies are the basis of many high-technology drug formulations but have fewer side-effects and have been tested by centuries of use. Acupuncture has been shown to increase levels of enkephalins, the body's natural morphine-like substances, aiding healing and killing pain. Osteopathy works by manipulating muscles and is similar to many of the techniques found in sports medicine. Many people gain relief from techniques that fall outside medical orthodoxy, yet at present alternative therapies are just as much a middle-class luxury as BUPA. Greens insist that they should be available for all and that proper research funds are provided for their development. Obviously a broken leg will never be cured by herbs (although they may soothe the pain and accelerate the process), but depression has never been cured by drugs or cancer totally eradicated by conventional drug therapy. But alternative forms of care are not, on their own, enough to solve the problems of the NHS; far-reaching political alternatives are needed as well.

All of these changes will demand an upheaval in training. GPs need an exhaustive knowledge not only of anatomy and pharmochemistry but also of nutrition, environmental health, sociology and psychology. Medical training needs to become holistic, with an emphasis on root causes rather than chemicals. GPs should be educated not as élite controllers of somewhat esoteric knowledge but as people who serve others and accelerate naturally occurring processes of well-being.

The NHS needs more resources. Nurses need better conditions and ambulance workers more pay. The public is prepared to forgo tax cuts so that money can be invested in well-funded public-health care. Money, though, is only part of the problem and increased public spending only part of the solution. Green health policy is about putting people before profits and rejecting the simplistic approach of the old-fashioned parties. Above all it is about tackling vested interests, letting people stand on their own feet without the malicious nannying of the drugs companies or of the multinationals that adulterate our food. It won't be easy, but if we don't green the NHS, it will wither and die.

11 GREENING EDUCATION

If we really want to make the world a better place, the way we nurture, educate and respond to our children's needs is vital. Education is central to the changes we need to make to our society. Greens believe in education for life.

The education system in the United Kingdom is under great stress. Teachers are demoralized; schools are closing because of the lack of educators; and, consequently, pupils are suffering. The GCSE examination, in theory a great advance on the old O-level, is suffering because too little money is available and there is insufficient preparation.

The national curriculum introduces a rigid structure, limiting many subjects that were previously part of the syllabus with a resulting loss of comprehensive understanding. Extra administrative work puts a strain on teachers and prevents them from playing a complete role in the all-round education process. Pay and conditions, not only of teachers but also of ancillary school workers such as cleaners and caretakers, are inadequate.

While all children are entitled to a free education, the quality of such education differs vastly according to where they live, their parents' financial status, their sex and their ethnic origin. Local education authorities' expenditure per pupil varies enormously. (The Conservative-controlled Kent County Council proudly announces its competitiveness when it comes to administering education finances. Indeed, in 1988 it was the third lowest spender in the league and was prepared to allow sixth formers to be employed as school cleaners, as the pay failed to attract other staff.) The United Kingdom lacks the facilities or the will to introduce a comprehensive nursery-school programme, falling a long way behind European counterparts. The proportion of children under 5 who received education in the maintained sector in 1988 was 45 per cent, a paltry 5 per cent up on 1983. Yet the role of women in the work force will become increasingly important and unsupervised, 'backstreet' nursery care will flourish to the detriment of our children.

At present only 3 per cent of university entrants are drawn from the families of 'blue-collar' workers; just 7 per cent are accepted by polytechnics and colleges of further education (the same percentage as in 1939). With the introduction of student loans the figure looks set to decrease. Student grants have fallen in real terms by more than 20 per cent over the last decade. Answering a parliamentary question, the Secretary of State for Education revealed that he expected mandatory awards to rise by a mere 5 per cent in the 1989–90 academic year despite inflation at over 7 per cent. The net institutional expenditure per student at university decreased from £5,508 in 1982–3 to £5,276 in 1986–7 in spite of rising costs. Most students are already operating on an overdraft, some even before the end of their first term of study. In 1989 undergraduates at the University of Kent were obliged to camp in the grounds because there was not enough suitable accommodation at a reasonable price, yet the university is building luxury housing to attract wealthy overseas students from Japan and Hong Kong. Some students at Manchester University are living in hotels for the same reason.

Of the 57,000 overseas students entering Britain annually approximately 22,700 receive government grants. Far from helping the poorest countries with their higher educational requirements, the Foreign Office has stated that its objective is to 'win influential friends overseas by enabling future leaders, decision makers and opinion formers from all walks of life to study in the United Kingdom'. When Mr Michael Jopling, MP, asked about the grants made available to students from developing countries, he was told that approximately 18,000 students come from such countries. Upon further investigation it transpired that Hong Kong, with a relatively high proportion of affluent people (and hence better categorized as a 'newly industrialized country'), supplied the greatest percentage of this figure. The conclusion to be drawn is that grants made to overseas students are of a political, not developmental, nature. Poor students, whether they come from home or abroad, are gradually being squeezed out. Higher education, far from being freely available to all, is fast becoming a prerogative of the rich.

Green solutions to these problems are informed by a very different conception of education. Greens believe that 'education should result in the development of each individual personality and of the potential, which all possess, to serve the community in a variety of ways' (*MFSS*, ED 100).

An American educator, Mario Fantini, when trying to define the requirements of a modern education system and the role of the teacher stated, 'The psychology of becoming has to be smuggled into schools.' That is to say, the examination system works against any teacher who wishes to try out new ideas, and the philosophy of hierarchy typical of most of our schools and our society means that pupils are the lowest priority.

As long ago as 1928 Ernest Barker, Professor of Political Science at the University of Cambridge, had this to say of schooling:

> Any system of education must be a training not only for work, but also in appreciation of poetry and music and literature and art, the things which belong to leisure and the secret life which is the true life of every man that cometh into the world. And so in every school, whether it be Modern School or Grammar School or whatever it may be, I should desire to see these things set in the foreground, and laid in the foundations, and digged into the soil, and made substantial and essential ingredients of every soul. And for this reason I would also include adult education in any dream and in any scheme of the training of the nation, believing that the spirit, at all stages, must be kept alive, and fed with pure nutrient which belongs to nature, and led day by day to enjoy more and more the things which belong to its peace. ('Social Ideas and Education')

Today, as we approach a new millennium, we are still far from achieving Professor Barker's dream.

We have been fed the false notion that the purpose of education is to ensure that the needs of the industrialized and capitalist society in which we live are met. In other words, the primary function of the modern education system is to ensure a continuing supply of workers and managers, with appropriate skills in appropriate numbers, for corporate capital needs. Children are taught that the purpose of education is to prepare them for a lifetime of paid employment. We compartmentalize our children at an early age, expecting them to make decisions that direct their future work patterns at the age of 16 –

in some cases as young as 11. Recognizing the dangers of early specialization Greens state, 'We wish to see developed a broad, holistic type of education and, although later specialization may be necessary, we should strongly advise against the dangers of students becoming blinded, by that specialization, to the wider implications of the subjects being studied' (*MFSS*, ED 105).

Education today is about making us fit the economic system instead of self-enlightenment. Unless parents are wealthy enough to buy the kind of education that is provided at Summerhill (see below), they have very little choice but to send their children to a conventional school or to educate them at home.

For thousands of children the daily business of going to school is a nightmare. Bullying at school has led young children to commit suicide. Children who do not feel that they fit quickly become demoralized, often substituting truancy for tuition.

All parents have the right to opt out of formal schooling for their children, but it is a difficult choice unless they have the means, motivation and know-how. Parents living in an inner city on income support, no matter how much they wished to educate their own children, would be under tremendous pressure from the authorities to send the children to school. Today's society regards those on low incomes as somehow incompetent, and education authorities are required to be especially vigilant about the school attendance of their children. Teaching children at home is normally an option only for middle-class parents. (Education Otherwise, a self-help group for parents who wish to teach their children at home, has over 2,000 members throughout the country.)

Schools such as Summerhill in Suffolk, founded in 1921 by the late A. S. Neill, have tried to break the mould of traditional education but are, alas, available only to those who have incomes running into tens of thousands of pounds. Describing how Summerhill started Neill said:

We had one main idea: to make the school fit the child instead of making the child fit the school. We set out to make a school in which we should allow children freedom to be themselves . . . My view is that a child is innately wise and realistic . . . I seldom hear a child cry because children, when free, have much less hate to express than children who are downtrodden. Hate breeds hate, and love breeds love. Love means approving of children, and that is essential in any school. You can't be on the side of children if you punish them and storm at them. Summerhill is a school in which the child knows that he is approved of. (*Summerhill*, Gollancz, 1962)

Greens would wish to see the present system, under which parents' wealth can buy their children's education, replaced, but they would not wish to interfere with the right of parents to organize home education or the setting up of non-profit-making alternative educational establishments, providing they were ecologically conscious and non-exclusive.

Education should be part of a continuing process for all of us. In the past, education had to provide skills for life rather than for narrow economic necessity. In rural areas this meant detailed knowledge about husbandry, land management, meteorology and horticulture, linked with purposeful activity that was essential to community survival and grounded in sensitivity to the physical and natural world. It was essential that knowledge was shared not only between generations but also between peers, that skills survived and that the best use was made of local resources. For example, buildings were constructed with local materials – and many of the results survive today (modern houses have a pathetic sixty-year life span). Such skills came under increasing pressure as capitalism and industrialism intensified, removing populations from their relationship with nature and the community. The past two centuries bear witness to the rise of schooling for capitalism as opposed to education for life. This is not to say, of course, that life was idyllic for the vast majority of the population or that we should return to oppressive feudalism. The point is that in our rush to industrialize we have forgotten to teach our children about the importance of a relationship with nature.

Thomas Huxley, talking at the South London Working Men's College in the 1860s, stated, 'We allow education, which ought to be directed to the making of men, to be diverted into a process of manufacturing human tools, wonderfully adroit in the exercise of some technical industry, but good for nothing else.' A century on from Huxley all mainstream political parties believe in schooling as a means of directing children and shaping them into flexible work units for future employers. Education at present enforces dependence; we learn to become subservient so that we will fit comfortably into our future social niche. By contrast, cooperation and self-management are the qualities that are necessary for an ecological future: schooling has to be changed to meet the needs of a new society based on empowering the individual. It has to invite pupils to question, challenge and contradict. Teachers need to understand why they are asking pupils to undertake certain tasks and to be prepared to justify their own actions and demands. Good teaching requires the mutual respect of pupil and teacher. (How many teachers have been told while training 'not to smile until Easter'? Start the year strictly, they are instructed, and you can always relax later.)

School uniform is relevant in this context. The idea behind a uniform is to deprive children of individuality by forcing them all to look the same. Many teachers argue that without school uniform discipline would be unmanageable, pupils would forget their 'place' and there would be competition in the fashion stakes. The argument that uniform abolishes class distinction is false, as it ignores the difference between patched and pristine clothes. Even today, in some schools it is considered a privilege for young adults of 18 not to have to wear uniform. Although many Greens reject the commercialism of the fashion industry and argue that it is repressive, school uniform is equally bad.

Teachers who value their career prospects quickly learn that it is very important to know their place and to respect the structure. Large schools are run by a headteacher with maybe one or two deputies. Then there is often a head of senior school and a head of junior school, along with their deputies. Next come heads of departments and possibly year heads as well. Then there are head boys and girls, prefects, form leaders and deputies. This centralized, hierarchical structure provides an efficient framework for the ambitious teacher. (The top rungs of the ladder are occupied predominantly by men.) Outstanding teachers become administrators because career structures determine that route for advancement. Every time a good teacher is plucked from the system to become an administrator, education is the loser. Within such a bureaucratic nightmare the needs of pupils are secondary.

In order to create internal democracy we must look at new ways of governing schools. Joyce Millington, convenor of the Green Party Education Working Group and herself a teacher until her retirement, tells the following story about the power of the headteacher of a large comprehensive whose absolute control resulted in misery for a teacher of long standing.

On Thursday afternoons the maths staff taught the sixth first period and then had a double with the fifths. Towards the end of the summer term there were two Thursday afternoons when they had no classes, the sixths being out at work experience and the fifths having already left after their O-levels and CSEs.

Mrs R., who had taught maths at the school, conscientiously, for fifteen years and had been employed by the local education authority for well over twenty-five years was retiring at the end of term, three months before her sixty-fifth birthday. Because she had taught under the authority for more than a quarter of a century she was invited to join other retiring teachers with long service at a reception at the Council House, to be held on one of these above-mentioned Thursdays, starting at four o'clock in the afternoon. Mrs R. asked the headmistress some weeks beforehand whether, in view of the fact that she would have no classes on that afternoon, she might leave at the end of the morning school so that she could go home and change before the event. The headmistress said she would see nearer the time. The day before the reception Mrs R. again asked for permission to go home at 12.30 p.m. The headmistress repeated that she would have to see. The other three members of the maths staff offered to cover for Mrs R. should she be required for any stand-in job, but still permission was not granted. Mrs R. became annoyed. At 12.30 p.m. on the day of the reception, nothing more having been said by the headmistress, she told the other members of staff that she was going and left. (In point of fact, the other three maths teachers were not called upon for any duties that afternoon.) The next morning, upon arrival at school, Mrs R. was summoned by the Headmistress and rudely reprimanded. She was also informed that a complaint had been sent to the local education authority and that she would be docked £6 pay for absenting herself without leave. This was an unpleasant end to a school career.

After her retirement, a week or so later, Mrs R. wrote to the

LEA inspectors complaining of her treatment. The reply stated that the inspectors upheld the headmistress's action.

An isolated case, you may think, of an extreme headmistress. Sadly not. Joyce could cite many other case in which headteachers have abused their power, and she quite rightly asks, 'Can you be a head without its going to your head? A few can but many can't.'

We have a very long way to go to change the hierarchical structures that are evident in our schools. Headteachers should be replaced by annually elected school representatives, who should include parents, students, teachers, representatives of ethnic and cultural minorities and ancillary workers. Greens believe that it is vitally important that all those who are affected by decisions at school should play an active role in educational administration. Even today, when parents can play a more active role, very few feel that they participate in decision making. Governing bodies in schools are still remote to the vast majority of parents, and little effort is made to inform parents and workers regularly about the decisions made at schools. An annual public governors' meeting, at which the results of recent examinations are the main topic under discussion, is inadequate. Members of the local community should be encouraged to participate in the administration of schools. This would require much more than the simple Thatcherite populism of parental involvement. It would mean creating centres where members of the community could acquire the necessary knowledge to become involved in the learning process. Real involvement can be achieved only by informed, democratic participation.

It is important that student–teacher relationships should be structured around meaningful activity with useful ends. This does not mean community service schemes, which so often fall short of real, long-term involvement in the community. Social science students, for example, could lead campaigns for land reform, exposing local landowners who threaten to vandalize hedgerows, meadows and marshes. Learning linked with the needs of environment and community must begin at primary and nursery level.

Discrimination must be abolished in all learning establishments. The right to celebrate one's own religion and culture must be protected, and all pupils should study different cultures and religions. Ways to overcome racist and sexist attitudes should be explained and practised. Clearly, this is a very difficult area, as some religious teaching can and does involve personal oppression. The dilemma must be acknowledged and sympathetically dealt with. (An example that comes to mind is female circumcision: the freedom of the parent is in conflict with the freedom of the child. An estimated 74 million girls in all parts of the globe are subjected to this operation; while it is illegal in this country, it is practised with impunity in others.) Students should be taught to understand the needs of all members of the community, and schools should accommodate any member of the community who wishes to take advantage of the educational system.

Adequate sex education should be provided that would include 'information on the physical, psychological and spiritual aspects of human sexuality. Young people should be informed about different forms of sexual behaviour, including heterosexuality, homosexuality and chastity, and should be free to make their own moral choices. They should be brought up to understand that they may experience heterosexual or homosexual feelings or both, and taught not to discriminate against others because of their sexuality' (*MFSS*, ED 319). In March 1988 the Green Party Conference passed a motion condemning the Clause 28 (now 29) Bill and urging all local parties to fight for equal rights for all, regardless of sexual orientation. We were advised at the time that the Green Party's 1987 general election manifesto might not be stocked by libraries because it breached the Act by advocating equal rights for all, regardless of sexual orientation, and insisted that whatever sexual preference young people choose it could enrich their own lives and the lives of people around them.

Throughout this book we have emphasized the worsening global situation. It is imperative that schools be aware of the environmental crisis that humanity faces. We cannot stress forcefully enough that a detailed description of the Earth's biosphere must be included in any school curriculum. Only by explaining how humanity interacts with its natural environment will we equip the next generation to deal with the problems that will be encountered in the next century. This is central to the green perspective on education. Every student should pursue an extended practical project that would have beneficial consequences for the environment and that would form an important part of each annual school record of achievement. In this way an entire generation would be brought up with a heightened awareness of its ability to intervene directly on behalf of the planet.

Governments tend to shy away from allowing political education in schools for fear of bias. General ignorance about how the political system works is evident to anybody who has stood in elections and canvassed households. It disenfranchises whole sectors of the population and is a national disgrace. Political education is a necessity.

Animal rights should also be taught in schools, and all experiments on animals, as well as the use of all products that necessitate animal suffering, should cease immediately. Schools nationally could use their collective institutional weight to challenge the abuse of animals. We must nurture reverence for the rich diversity of life on Earth.

Development education should be taught as part of the curriculum, starting at nursery level and leading later to an understanding of the needs of people in all parts of the globe. Inequalities of wealth and opportunity should be discussed from an early age, and students should be made aware both of the effects of colonialism and imperialism and of their continuing relevance today. The behaviour of transnationals and the importance of debt to less developed countries should form an important part of the curriculum. Each student should be familiar with the United Nations declaration on the rights of the child, and a copy of the declaration should be available for inspection in every educational establishment.

The priority of schools should be to impart self-reliance, initiative, kindness, spontaneity, courage, creativity, responsibility and joy. The damage done to many youngsters by the examination system is incalculable. Yet we sustain the myth that without a system of examinations most children would not bother to learn. Established wisdom suggests that public examination is the fairest method for judging the competition for places at university, for jobs or even for which school one attends at the age of eleven. The questioning of the value of the examination system is not new. Arthur James Balfour, speaking as Chancellor of the University of Edinburgh, said in May 1907:

> I do think it of importance that we should have present to our minds the inevitable evils which examinations carry in their train, or the system of competitive examinations as it has been developed of recent years in our universities. The truth is that a book which is read for examination purposes is a book which has been read wrongly. Every student ought to read a book, not to answer questions to somebody else, but to answer his own questions. The modern plan, under which it would almost seem

as if the highest work of our universities consisted in a perennial contest between the examiner on the one side and the coach on the other, over the passive body of the examinee, is really a dereliction and a falling away from all that is highest in the idea of study and investigation.

Recent research into the value of examinations as a method of obtaining knowledge has revealed that many pupils, after receiving a good grade in maths O-Level, have quite forgotten the techniques only months after sitting the exam. The conclusion must be that in the rush to pass the exam the concepts are not mastered, the necessity for passing the examination far outweighing the necessity for proper understanding. Other research shows that examination results rarely predict subsequent performance, and examples abound of individuals who failed at school but excelled in later life.

Although Greens welcome the recent moves towards 'profiling', they deplore the new emphasis placed on rigid testing by the Thatcher government. Surely a better method would be to abolish the present examination system altogether and replace it by profiling, which would include students' assessment of knowledge gained. This combined system would be a better way to chart personal development and provide the necessary pointers to future activity. It would also be a help to teachers, as students would have a chance to assess their teaching and make positive comments. All reports would be countersigned by students, and frequent discussions would be held about the best way forward for the individual.

The way we train our teachers has to be radicalized. People who wish to become tutors, at whatever level, need to be able to stimulate, coordinate the work of, understand and have a keen interest in the needs of their pupils and to be sensitive to them at all times. At present those who wish to transform education are thwarted by their peers, by administrators and by parents. Teachers should not see their aim as to control their pupils but should regard themselves as enablers, providing the correct atmosphere in which to enhance learning. Rigid, dominating behaviour should not be necessary in today's school.

The green way would be to break down the barriers between school, home and the community. Community education would go a long way to make such rigid domination a thing of the past. Students would emerge feeling that education is a life-long process, not a fifteen-year indoctrination. The child who has a free spirit and refuses to be cannon fodder is often labelled 'difficult' by today's educators and is thus marked for life. We need to recognize that there are many ways to educate and transform. We need to cater for each one of our students. We adults will be able to initiate change only when we recognize that our own impoverished expectations and frustrations spring, in part, from our schooling. The wasted potential in our schools is a national scandal.

Operation Babysnatch illustrates that wasted potential. In the 1960s an experiment at the University of Wisconsin demonstrated that special attention given to babies born to women who were socially disadvantaged could turn those children into what is commonly known as 'gifted'. Forty babies were 'snatched' from their mothers, taken to the university centre, played and sung to and generally stimulated. Later, tuition was given in small groups. By the age of 4 the children were scoring a mean IQ of 128 on one test, 132 on another. They were brighter than the average child from a traditional middle-class home. Forty children who had not received special attention scored IQs of 85 by the age of 4. Human interaction had provided the magical difference. No wonder so many of us long for the radical transformation of the education process.

Instead of the present emphasis on the acquisition of 'right' information once and for all, the emphasis should be on learning how to learn. Students should be taught how to ask questions, pay attention to the right things, be open to and evaluate new concepts, have access to new information.

Learning at present is a product, a destination. Learning should be a process, a journey throughout life. Education at present is hierarchical and authoritarian. It rewards conformity and discourages experiment. Egalitarianism, candour and dissent should be encouraged.

Greens realize that the changes advocated in this chapter would revolutionize education but believe them to be necessary in a society based on sustainable principles, in which individuals are encouraged to use education as a means of providing a useful and satisfying life. Learning is open-ended, and Greens would wish people to be able to opt in and out of the education system throughout their lives.

To this purpose green schools would be located in community education centres with gardens, cinemas, libraries, advice centres, nurseries, senior citizens' day centres, mother-and-toddler clubs and other facilities in which the community as a whole would be involved. These centres would offer a comprehensive cultural, recreational and educational experience for all. Students and educators would see each other as people, not as role players, and priority would be given to self-image as the generator of performance. Such 'learning and enabling' centres would be run by locally elected people.

Students with disabilities must be part of the community and their needs must be catered for. Adequate provision for those with learning difficulties and special needs would be provided and their representation on governing bodies ensured. Wherever possible, all members of the community would play their role in helping those with special needs, although this should not become a substitute for professional help.

Any new educational paradigm must lead to new ways based on life-long learning, the encouragement of self-discipline and the awakening of curiosity. More important, these skills must be applicable to people of all ages, nurturing and promoting the creative in us all.

Britain, supposedly the mother of democracy, is ruled not by democrats but by bureaucrats. The power we all nominally hold as voters is concentrated in the hands of a Parliament that is run in turn by a Cabinet, itself dominated by a powerful Prime Minister. To a great degree, what she says goes. Prime Ministers control Cabinets and Cabinets, via whips, whip MPs into line. As Lord Hailsham once put it, we live in an elective dictatorship. Between elections governments ignore the views of the opposition, overriding argument by weight of numbers. Parties are returned to power with only minority support, and many people who should be able to vote cannot do so because they are not on the electoral roll. Britain has no Bill of Rights, and we are seeing civil liberties legislated away irrespective of public opinion. 'A democracy is freedom under the rule of law' is a favourite statement of Mrs Thatcher, though she never explains exactly what she means by it.

A British government, if it so wished, could use an enabling Act to maintain its power on a permanent dictatorial basis, close down newspapers that criticized such action and imprison dissenters. The fact that no party has done so, or is likely to, should not blind us to the need for safeguards. As it is, Westminster rule is the rule of many by the few. Greens fear that increasingly sophisticated methods of marketing will ensure that elections will be won by parties and individuals with the most money and the most up-to-date computer. It has been widely reported that the American presidential election was won not by the oratorial skill of Bush but by the ability of the Republicans' computer to target every household in the United States with *Reader's Digest*-style mailings tailor-made for each nuclear family. Reagan's Mormon marketing man has been snatched up by Margaret Thatcher to help her stay in power throughout the 1990s, whatever shifts there may be in public opinion.

Democracy is in danger of becoming just another commodity to be bought by those willing to pay. The present Conservative government spends more on advertising than any previous administration and is one of the industry's biggest clients. The poll tax, privatization plans, water quality, the delights of nuclear power and the enterprise training scheme have all been the subjects of massive marketing campaigns that have married the selling of government policies to support for the party of government. Despite the banning of 'overtly' political advertising on behalf of local authorities like the former GLC (another victim of a decade of Mrs Thatcher's democracy), central government advertising budgets soar. Rather than being influenced by public opinion, the Cabinet assumes that the unpopularity of policies like water privatization and the misnamed community charge stems from poor marketing instead of poor policy making.

While we are seduced by the Saatchi brothers and their successors, our elected representatives have little to say on our behalf. Much of the time the debating chamber is empty. The authors recollect visiting the Palace of Westminster to watch a vitally important debate on the Local Government Bill (a Bill, incidentally, aimed at removing the power of local authorities by undermining their financial clout and enforcing privatization) only to find a mere 2 per cent of MPs (twelve of them) in attendance. MPs seem almost redundant. Certainly many of them behave as if they were in the House of Lords rather than making law through the process of informed discussion on behalf of millions of voters. The recent list of Members' Interests may help to explain why so few of our elected representatives appear in the chamber. A salary of £26,000 per annum (over twice the national average working wage) appears to need to be supplemented by a wide range of financial inducements.

Cabinets make the major decisions, and dissenting members of a party in government, or even of the most robust Opposition, are rarely acknowledged. More than any Prime Minister in recent history, Mrs Thatcher runs her Cabinet on the principle of 'I know best and if you don't agree, go'. Probably nothing illustrates this better than the comedy TV series *Spitting Image*, where we have seen her change from a cigar-smoking businessman to a laurel-adorned Caesar figure – and we all know what happened to Caesar! The resignation of Nigel Lawson (an elected MP) was provoked by the fact that he dared to question the validity of an adviser (unelected) of Mrs Thatcher. She is rapidly running out of senior members of the Conservative Party who are prepared to fill vacated Cabinet posts. Even her enthusiasm for promoting from the unelected House of Lords cannot maintain a full and compliant front bench. Mrs Thacher's decade at the helm has seen many assaults on our already far from perfect democracy.

While supporting the safeguards proposed by groups such as Charter 88, Greens argue that the system needs not just reform but radical change. Good intentions are not enough. All parties believe in greater democracy, at least on paper, but there is a chasm between rhetoric and reality. All parties succumb to what the political philosopher Roberto Michels described as the 'iron law of oligarchy': they become increasingly conservative and authoritarian and end up being run by small groups of unrepresentative leaders. Socialism, in both its soviet and its social democratic form, has come a long way from grassroots participation. Despite Mrs Thatcher's use of the rhetoric of freedom and liberty, she has acted in a far from libertarian way as far as striking miners, ambulance workers, gays and lesbians or even middle-class protesters against nuclear waste dumping are concerned.

A first step would be to make political parties more democratic, truly open to members instead of being run by cliques or closed committees. Parliamentary candidates should be selected by all supporters on a local basis, as is done in the American primaries, rather than by a minority, as in the .case of the Conservative Party, or imposed from above, Labour's method when controversial candidates seem likely to be picked. Candidates ought to represent the whole community. At present Westminster is largely irrelevant to those of us who are neither public-school-educated nor middle-aged men. Parties should work hard to remedy the male orientation of Parliament, providing crèches for meetings and making it possible for women to become involved in national politics. There is a need for more MPs from ethnic minorities and, above all, for younger MPs. Greens think that it is crazy that while citizens are able to marry at 16 and vote at 18, they cannot take a seat in Parliament until the age of 21. The Green Party's most successful by-election campaign before the breakthrough at the Euro-election in June 1989 was when a candidate of only 18 stood to challenge this rule, upping the green vote in the process. Greens are concerned that young people should have more say, both so that they can retain a faith in democracy and so that they can affect the decisions that will shape their future. The average age

of MPs elected in 1987 was 47, and only six MPs out of 650 are
under 30. The average age of the Prime Minister and her front-
benchers is near that of normal retirement (MPs' salaries are
somewhat higher than the publicly funded pension, so they have an
incentive to work for the good of our nation for as long as possible).
While minority groups deserve a greater say, majorities like women,
the young and those of us without the benefit of an Oxbridge
education should also be allowed to take the burden of rule off our
elderly citizens' shoulders.

For democracy to function we all need to be able to make informed
criticisms of government action. Knowledge is power, and such power
is not as accessible as it should be. We need a Freedom of Information
Act rather than government secrecy that stops civil servants exposing
publicly the worst abuses of ministers (as in the Ponting affair). The
new Official Secrets Act states that civil servants have a first duty not
to Parliament but to the government: the judge would have had to
recommend conviction to the jury if this law had been in force at the
time of Ponting's trial.

We also need a truly free press. At present those with large amounts
of money have the freedom to publish and get their message printed at
Wapping or elsewhere. Britain's press is renowned neither for its
incisive comment nor its independence of thought. The tabloids have
kept us informed of the private lives of the great and the good; at the
turn of this decade readers of the *Sun* were told far more about MP
Ron Brown's love life than about his politics or his ability to work for
constituents. The lives of Sunday newspaper editors and their liaisons
with parliamentary research assistants have taken up more column
inches than stories about the dissolution of the Soviet bloc, the US
invasion of Panama or government plans that will affect all of our
futures.

As well as more intellectually stimulating newspapers we need a
fairer voting system. In the European elections 15 per cent of voters
supported the Greens and were disenfranchised when the party
received no seats despite gaining the highest vote of any green party in
Europe. Seven per cent of voters who voted for the Social Democrats,
Plaid Cymru and the Social and Liberal Democrats were also robbed
of any say. Britain is virtually the only Western democracy without
some form of proportional representation (PR) and the only country
not to use PR for the European elections. Minority interests have no

voice as a consequence, and in practice a party with as much as a quarter of the vote could fail to get any MPs elected to Westminster. Greens favour what is known as the Additional Members System, which has operated successfully in West Germany since the last war. This best-of-both-worlds system elects half of Parliaments' members on a strictly democratic basis, with a 5 per cent threshold to eliminate extremists, and constituency representatives comprise the other 50 per cent. Thus everybody who votes for a party that gains over 5 per cent of the vote has some say but still has access to a locally elected constituency MP.

Lack of proportionality is not the only thing wrong with our present electoral system, however. It is heavily weighted in favour of parties and individuals who have access to wealth. Merely to stand in an election requires a £500 deposit, which effectively rules out poor independents who might wish to stand in order to draw attention to unemployment or poverty but encourages rich eccentrics. Before delivering a single leaflet or shooting a second of electoral broadcast, the Green Party had to put up £79,000 to contest the European elections, something that no other green grouping in the Community had to do. (One of the authors paid his 1987 general election deposit in the form of 1,000 50-pence pieces, much to the dismay of the returning officer, who had to count every one. Such is the nature of jumble-sale democracy.) Increases in the deposit have done nothing to cut the number of fringe or Fascist candidates standing at by-elections. Greens would abolish the deposit and replace it with a minimum of 100 signatures.

There needs to be a far stricter limit on the amount of money that a party can spend at election time. The spending limits on individual candidates within a constituency are abused in a number of imaginative ways that favour richer candidates, while at national level a political party can spend as much as it likes. Thus at the last general election the Conservatives spent £9 million, Labour £4 million and the Greens a minuscule £15,000 on national campaigning. Parties can spend millions only if they are given millions. The Labour Party is still bankrolled by the unions and the Conservatives by big business. When we buy a packet of biscuits or book tickets with a particular travel agent or go to the pub we pay a tax of a few pence each time to Mrs Thatcher and Conservative Central Office. Much of the Conservatives' annual income of £15 million is shrouded in secrecy, but £3 million is known to come from major industrial firms. In 1988 such companies gave their next favourite, the Owenite SDP, £2,000 and the Liberal Democrats just £1,000. Other right-wing pressure groups, such as the Economic League (which maintains security files on those it deems to be subversive), the Centre for Policy Studies and British United Industrialists received £250,000. Another £10 million donated to the Conservatives each year comes from unknown sources. A situation described by Labour's Frank Dobson as particularly dangerous: 'This is bad for democracy because these companies are trying to buy influence and it should be above-board.' Greens reject his contention that 'no one objects to people being allowed to buy influence but we do object to them doing it in secret', as the independence of political parties from economic interests can be guaranteed only by making such contributions to campaign coffers illegal. Moscow gold maybe a right-wing myth; chocolate money from United Biscuits isn't. How can a government commit itself to controlling industrial pollution if it is partly funded by ICI or Unilever? Other suppliers of Conservative Party funds include the insurance firm Commercial Union, which has interests in South Africa, arms companies, those involved with animal experiments and participants in other unsavoury trades. Many of the same fears apply to union domination of the Labour Party. The largest company donation received by the Liberal Party came from the British School of Motoring, but happily the Liberals retained their plans for boosting public transport. David Sainsbury has almost single-handedly kept the ailing SDP afloat, a point we should remember when we go shopping. Greens believe that company donations and union funding should end and that party political funding should be restricted to what can be recouped from a standard membership rate and modest state funding. Such state funding works in West Germany.

However fair a reformed electoral system might be, rule from Westminster will never be enough. Power needs to be taken from Parliament and put into more hands. Greens believe that power should be exercised as directly as possible at the lowest possible level: a local councillor is far more likely to be accountable than an MP. Party politics has no monopoly at local government level – independently minded Conservative candidates can be elected in Labour areas and vice versa. Local representatives are likely to be known personally to many of the electorate and can be contacted easily. Access to local councillors ensures that they will consider, and act on, local opinion. When it comes to the crunch Members of Parliament are far more likely to be influenced by party dogma, the party leader and party whips. District councils need to be given direct powers to administer much of the money presently spent by central government and to take decisions about local education, social services, environmental protection and economic planning. 'Think globally, act locally' is the slogan for local governments.

Decentralization can never be total, however, nor is it the solution to all our problems. It would make no sense to let Britain's poorest borough, Hackney, go it alone, shivering in the chill wind of recession, while super-rich Kensington and Chelsea retained its local wealth for local use. Any scheme for decentralization needs to redistribute tax income to overcome poverty. Roads, hospitals with specialist facilities, proper postal arrangements and a number of other tasks need to be coordinated at a higher tier. Critics of decentralization argue that tight national control and strong central powers are needed in case local communities decide to dump PCBs in their drinking water or build nuclear power stations, but a far more real danger is that strong central government, supported by big business, distant from its electorate and protected by laws of official secrecy, will create pollution on a national scale. The people of Billingham and other proposed sites for low-level nuclear waste had to fight long and hard to prevent Westminster from imposing poisons on them. The ecological dangers of centralization are proven and dangerous; the positive contribution that decentralization could make to a cleaner environment and a better democracy are clear.

Greens are regionalists, not nationalists, believing that where decisions cannot be made at a local level they should be tackled at a level below that of the nation state. Greens believe that it is wrong for Scotland and Wales to be governed by Westminster, the composition of which is totally different from the electoral preferences of those countries. This was the case throughout the 1980s and is set to continue into the 1990s. Equally, the north feels distant from a legislature established on one bank of the Thames. The south-west also has a strong regional identity. A partial solution to the problems of Northern Ireland would be to disunite the United Kingdom and to create a regional state in Ulster. Ireland has been devastated by centuries of English oppression, from the arrival of Henry II's army in

1169 to the activities of British paratroopers on the Creggan Estate during the Bloody Sunday massacre in 1972. Resentment can only ever be partially overcome, and it is understandable that among the Catholic population in the North the Brits are, and will continue to be, hated. But a regional or un-united kingdom would restore some confidence. Ireland has a long tradition of regional kingdoms, and as Republicans are unlikely to argue for a Celtic monarch, the restoration of Ulster, Connaught, Munster and Leinster as regional units would allay more Protestant fears than rule by Dublin.

The Green Party distrust the notion of a European super-power. After decades of watching the interventionist activity of both the USA and the Soviet Union, Greens would be loath to support a new super-power armed with nuclear weapons, exploiting the Third World and dominating a huge territory extending from the extreme west of Ireland to Kiev. Greens fear that all the good achieved by promoting local self-government and creating regional solutions to knotty national problems would be undone by a highly centralized Euro-government. If Westminster is distant, Strasbourg is farther away still. If MPs are unrepresentative, how much more unrepresentative will be Euro MPs with real powers? If, as Jacques Delors hints, democracy will reside in a new European capital of Strasbourg or Munich, how much say will we or the Basques or the Irish, Welsh or Portuguese have? Not very much, one suspects. Small is beautiful both in economics and constitutionally. European laws for all of Europe would not only give rise to a vast bureaucracy but would also be unfair to millions of people who disagree with such laws. Scots object to the poll tax because all but a handful of the MPs they elected in 1987 were from parties that opposed it as undemocratic and unfair. How would the whole of the UK react to laws enacted by Europe that British MPs were elected to oppose? European 'democracy' could defeat real democracy. Greens fear that a European bank, a single European currency and continent-wide economic management will lead both to financial instability and to economic expansion (to keep up with the other military–economic super-power of Japan and the Pacific). Europeanism has so far been propelled not by a concern for peace, democracy and the environment but by large multinationals seeking to gain economies of scale, remove unpredictable floating exchange rates and to allow the restructuring they need to indulge in ever more destructive bouts of economic expansion. While friends of

Europe argue that the Community has done much for the environment – for example, by making Britain remove nitrates from its water – the more astute point out that nitrates have seeped into our rivers only as a result of the EEC's Common Agricultural Policy, which has encouraged over-farming.

Yet Greens are pro-European, although they criticize the existing structure of the EEC just as much as they criticize domestic institutions. Ecological, economic and constitutional problems cannot be solved at the level of the nation state. They demand international cooperation, for which the first step is closer links between existing European countries and regions. A supranational tier is also vital to the creation of local democracy. A European tier of administration could, paradoxically, be used to help, rather than hinder, local democracy. First Greens would like to see a Europe of regions rather than nation states or one Euro-state. Secondly, Europe has to be based on commitment to people, not transnationals, and must work not for higher economic growth but for environmental protection, better social conditions and real prosperity for all peoples throughout the world. Finally, rather than legislating on everything, a European Parliament should act as a referee in regional disputes, protect minorities and generally act as a court of appeal and watchdog, just as the European Court of Justice is a counter-weight to national judiciaries and a means of safeguarding the rights of individuals within a state. Europe could protect the environment and local democracies from decentralized forms of abuse without itself having to indulge in continuous and all-enveloping law making. With such safeguards a European constitutional settlement for the next century could be made that would satisfy the Basques and other minorities, end the war in Northern Ireland and salve tensions in Belgium between French and Flemish-speaking citizens.

A green Scotland and Wales and a regional Britain within a green Europe are a long way off. Although most politicians purport to be green, few argue for the decentralization and direct democracy that would reduce their power. Rather than recognizing that all taxes should be raised and spent in the first instance at a local level, Mrs Thatcher has used rate capping and the community charge to restrict the ability of local democracy to remain democratic. The Conservatives abolished the GLC because it pursued policies that were different from the government's and were popular, believing that there could be no alternative. (The alternatives that emerged were legislated out of existence.) It is difficult to see a Labour government undoing the undemocratic and centralist work of its predecessor because central control obliges voters to accept the decisions of central government.

This decade, more than any other, has seen the concentration of more and more power (and wealth) in fewer hands. The National Council for Civil Liberties has noted that civil rights are under threat. Britain clearly needs a statutory Bill of Rights. At present the law is a law unto itself. This needs to change, and civil liberties need to be restored. A decentralized Britain will need guaranteed rights to ensure even local democracy. The Data Protection Act has done nothing to prevent private companies from buying electoral registers and assembling data files on virtually every voter in the country. For example, the United Association for the Protection of Trade (UAPT), operating from Croydon, merges the registers with official census data to come up with an exact social profile of 40 million people, together with their ages and addresses (complete with postcodes). Few UK readers of this page will have escaped their attention. Subscribing firms (which include shopping chains with 'discount' or other forms of credit card) feed in further information so as to get cut-price services in return. Court judgements are included. CCN, a parallel system, specializes in debt collection and direct-mail operations. There is no check on this information. Only a tiny minority of the population is aware that names are kept on private files. Neither company is enthusiastic about private inspection; thus false information can get on to a file and never be deleted. One person may acquire another's criminal record or bad credit rating, blocking his or her ability to negotiate a mortgage or buy a new TV with the aid of plastic card. Direct mailing is an invasion of privacy. If we are within a certain social grouping and have responded to one mail-order offer, we will be bombarded with hundreds more. The electoral implications are staggering. Computers could be used to identify social groupings that might be sold a particular political ideology. Political power and electoral success could reside in the organization with the biggest data banks. Mail-order Fascism could be on the agenda. The ability of security services to use such files – especially as they include information on criminal convictions and ethnic status – to harass whole sectors of the population is alarming. (Armed with such information in the 1930s, Hitler might have interned the whole Jewish population within weeks of coming to power and spotted political opponents through magazine subscriptions or through suspect socio-economic-racial grouping).

The National Front and other far-right groups instruct their members to keep 'security' files on opponents. The Economic League has a more professional approach: many people who have publicly demonstrated their concern for individual rights never receive a reply to job applications because the Economic League has blacklisted them on its index of supposed subversives, which escapes the Data Protection Act but is circulated to thousands of employers. Members of CND, the anti-apartheid and animal rights movements and sup- porters of radical political parties have all been denied employment on such a basis. There is scope for extremist groups to buy information (which may be false) about perceived opponents by masquerading as legitimate investigators. It is clearly wrong that the desire to take part in democratic procedures by registering to vote should be used to build up largely secret files for commercial purposes, which might be used in the future by anti-democratic forces, and this would be stopped immediately by the Green Party. A BBC survey in 1986 found that 89 per cent of the 1,000-strong sample thought that the selling of electoral registers to national data banks should be made illegal.

Official publicly held security records need to be brought under democratic control. Justification for phone tapping or keeping files on suspect terrorists and criminals may easily turn into justification for monitoring the whole population. Credit-card-style bars on passports and National Insurance cards could be used to store information about individuals without their knowledge. Erroneously recorded criminal convictions might be read off by police officials at airports or if someone were stopped for a spot-check. Files should be open to all and should be amended if they contain false information. Elected representatives should be able to inspect special files on criminals. If necessary, closed files should be established within statutory guidelines. It is clear that information about suspected republican terrorists has been leaked by loyalist sympathizers in the Northern Irish security forces to paramilitary groups who have used such information to carry out sectarian murders. It is illegal for police officers to give away such information, but it still happens. MI5, MI6 and the myriad similar organizations that exist, although we are largely ignorant of their shadowy presence, supposedly serve democracy but place themselves above Parliament and even Prime Ministers. (Security forces in the mid-1970s believed that Prime Minister Harold Wilson was a Soviet agent!) Peter Wright's claim in *Spycatcher* that he and his colleagues bugged and burgled their way across London while 'pompous, bowler-hatted' civil servants turned a blind eye is particularly worrying, given his allegation that the security services had tried strenuously to discredit Harold Wilson and force him out of office as Prime Minister. The assertion of Colin Wallace, a former army information officer, that MI5 opened false bank accounts in an attempt to discredit Ulster politicians as varied as Ian Paisley, Edward Heath and John Hume demands serious investigation. The Stalker affair, together with Wallace's claim concerning Clockwork Orange – 'a British intelligence undercover operation named Clockwork Orange was intended to prevent the re-election of the Labour Party, then led by Harold Wilson, in the second British election of 1974; to prevent a coalition between the Liberal and Labour parties; and to replace Edward Heath as leader of the Tory Party with someone more "ideologically sound" – strikes a chill in the heart of the authors. The suspicion that the security forces are above democratic control and act as a law unto themselves must be allayed. Assaults by MI5 and MI6 on the civil liberties of legitimate and legal organizations such as CND and trade unions are also extremely worrying.

The investigators need to be investigated if we are to have any faith in their impartiality and good conduct. The activities of the judiciary, police force and security services need to be checked independently. Using the police to investigate allegations of misconduct committed by the police is as ludicrous as requesting one chemicals manufacturer to investigate the pollution caused by another. The Somerset and Avon constabularies' inquiry into the Surrey force's handling of the Guildford Four affair failed to uncover anything untoward and left innocent men and women in prison with life-long terms. The pressure to maintain solidarity and defend the reputation of the force inevitably influences police investigations into their own alleged misconduct.

Even without the risk of corruption and the bending of rules by ambitious officers eager to make progress, policing in Britain would still be in need of reform. The success of Britain's police is measured not by the stability of our society, the peace of our communities or the well-being of citizens protected from crime but by the number of convictions and of cases 'cleared up'. Naturally, the force is under pressure to get results, but this often necessitates policing methods that increase rather than resolve conflict. Greens argue that prevention is a lot better than cure (or at least criminal convictions) and that some methods of policing can cause crime, just as some drugs have side-effects as devastating as the illness they aim to cure. Many see strip-searching, for example, as a way of intimidating women (and men) rather than as a security measure. Police racism is a source of tension. Relations between the vast majority of law-abiding black and Asian people and the police are very, very bad. If our police are to do their job properly and gain general trust, racism in the force must be eradicated, and the police must be seen by people of all races to act impartially.

All the evidence shows that the 1980s saw a move away from community care and towards full-scale militarization of the force. The 1984 Police and Criminal Evidence Act extended the powers of arrest and detention. The miners' strike of the mid-1980s was broken by repressive policing methods, which involved horseback charges and the restriction of the movements of those intent on picketing. Mrs Thatcher's concept of the 'enemy within' has extended the Falklands spirit to modern policing with the crushing of the Peace Convoy, the repression of trade-union rights and the killing of suspects in Northern Ireland and Gibraltar. Middle-class students demonstrating against government policy relating to loans, gays and lesbians protesting against Section 29 of the Local Government Act, which curtails their rights, and anti-nuclear activists have all felt the wrath that is meted out to such enemies of the state. A report by Manchester City Council into the policing of a student demonstration against the visit to the university of the then Home Secretary Leon Brittan concluded that it involved 'the unacceptable use of force and abusive language by police officers well trained in public-order policing against innocent civilians participating in a peaceful demonstration'. Sidney Clayton, the principal lecturer in law at Manchester Polytechnic, is reported as saying, 'I pleaded with two senior officers to control their men because they were behaving like animals. It was a perfectly peaceful demonstration until the police moved in.' Dossiers of allegations against the Manchester police were stolen from the students' union, and a bizarre series of events, including physical assault and the harassment of witnesses Sarah Hollis and Steven Shaw, caused widespread concern. The police force risks becoming a political army. Policing should be made to operate within a framework of consensus rather than armed violence.

Direct intervention by the police in violent and tense situations in today's far from green society may on occasion remain necessary, but inner-city riots – to take one example – are not just the work of criminals intent on destruction – they are fuelled by racism, poverty, unemployment, homelessness and appalling environmental conditions. People with a stake in healthy communities are unlikely to want to destroy them. Peace can be brought to our inner cities only through social change, and part of this change must involve changes in police recruitment (officers should be drawn from a wider segment of society), training and strategy. Policing must be restored to a community role.

Fair policing can exist only within a system of real justice. Recent events have shown that the judiciary is in crisis. Responding to the release of the Guildford Four, Lord Denning said, 'British justice is in ruins.' The Four were released only after the accidental discovery of papers showing that police officers had falsified information to get them convicted. But for such an accident Paul Hill, Gerald Conlon and the others would still be in prison. The Birmingham Six, who were convicted after confessing to a similar pub bombing in 1974 and at their trial looked as if they had been beaten, remain under lock and key despite widespread calls for their release. Although the forensic evidence is doubtful and the West Midlands police force, which obtained the confessions, shown to be riddled with corruption, Home Secretaries Douglas Hurd and David Waddington have refused to re-open the Birmingham case. 'Since then,' the *Economist* notes bitterly, 'ministers have done their best to carry on business in the usual British way, treating questions of civil liberty with much the same urgency as debates on the tariff on imported nasturtiums' (28 October 1989). That Lord Denning, the *Economist* and the *Sunday Telegraph* are worried about the state of British civil liberties tells its own story: establishment forces, rather than the left, the National Council for Civil Liberties or, indeed, the Green Party, are the ones who are kicking up a fuss. Civil liberties were eroded by both Labour and Conservative governments throughout the 1970s and 1980s. The hardly left-wing or green-orientated *Economist* has described the civil liberties record of the Thatcher government as 'the worst in modern times'.

Charter 88, which campaigns for a written constitution and the safeguard of such liberties and to whose manifesto the authors of this book are signatories, puts the case for change concisely:

> We have been brought up in Britain to believe that we are free: that our Parliament is the mother of democracy; that our liberty is the envy of the world; that our system of justice is always fair; that the guardians of our safety, the police and security services, are subject to legal control; that our Civil Service is impartial; that our cities and communities maintain a proud identity; that our press is brave and honest. Today such beliefs are increasingly implausible. The gap between reality and the received ideas of Britain's 'unwritten constitution' has widened to a degree that many find hard to endure.

In June 1988 the Green Party launched a green Magna Carta as its own charter for British democracy. Party Council members assembled at Runnymede on the 773rd anniversary of the signing of Magna Carta by King John. Such a Bill of Rights could safeguard liberties in a regional Britain and might include provisions for reforming the Civil Service and widening access to the legal profession. Wealth, or the lack of it, should not debar those seeking to become judges, barristers or solicitors. It could extend the view of Scottish law that uncorroborated confession cannot on its own be used to achieve conviction. If courts refused to accept confessions unsupported by other evidence, police officers would no longer be under pressure to gain confessions at any cost, and wrongful imprisonment would be far less likely.

It is not enough for the Green Party or any other political grouping to present a shopping list of measures designed to make Britain more democratic. Political parties themselves need to become more democratic. Greens believe that all power tends to corrupt and that even Greens elected to positions of power would do well to guard against its malign influence. The traditional radical cry of 'Vote for us and we will give you power' is a contradiction in terms. At the end of the day, representative democracy is a way of retaining the personal power and control of the politicians. Democracy must be about people's power: the people of this country need to be empowered to run their own lives and their own communities. Greens promote the rotation of elected officials and their capacity to be recalled, citizens' initiatives and other truly democratic structures.

Some environmentalists have argued that to solve the ecological crisis we need not more democracy but less; they call for eco-friendly benevolent dictatorship. Because the environmental crisis entails difficult decisions, they claim, a green future is impossible without some form of eco-Fascism. They are wrong. Greens demand change – and difficult change – but they have so far been elected with popular support. If they are to be turned into practical policy, green politics has to be introduced gradually and democratically if it is to succeed at all. Green politics cannot be imposed; on the contrary, it demands active support and participation. We all need to take action if the ecological crisis is to be overcome. We cannot be bullied to do so from above. Equally, Britain's political health demands a far more effective democracy than we have at present.

Power structures all over the globe, which are based on patriarchy and hierarchy, especially in the Third World, ensure that on a planetary scale few people have control over their own lives and their own communities. Green parties the world over believe that peace between humanity and nature, and between different human beings, can be achieved only by giving everyone a political say. Greens seek social, cultural and economic liberation and look to a radical restructuring of society that promotes self-reliant communities that can exist harmoniously within a framework of larger national and international units. Gandhi wrote in 'Enlightened Anarchy: a Political Ideal' (1939):

> Political power, in my opinion, cannot be our ultimate aim. It is one of the means used by men for their all-round advancement. The power to control national life through national representatives is called political power. Representatives will become unnecessary if the national life becomes so perfect as to be self-controlled. It will then be a state of enlightened anarchy in which each person becomes his own ruler. He will conduct himself in such a way that his behaviour will not hamper the well-being of his neighbours. In an ideal state there will be no political institutions and therefore no political power.

Power, whether in the form of wealth or of control over political decisions, needs to be distributed as widely as possible. Britain needs to revive and revitalize its democracy and to let all of its citizens play their proper role in it.

13 CONCLUSION

As we enter the 1990s and anticipate the world beyond the year 2,000, we need to find new ways of doing things. The post-war consensus politics that has worked, at least in a limited sense, since 1945, is ill equipped to deal with the new realities. Quite simply, a changing world demands a change in politics.

In an era of social, economic and intellectual transformation, one factor stands out above all the rest – that of the environment. We are standing on the abyss. As we write this book hurricanes are sweeping Britain, oil spills are threatening the coasts of Alaska and Morocco, mad cows are roaming the countryside and scandals over British food are breaking out almost daily. Whereas socialists once claimed that the working class had a world to win, we argue that all of us now have a world to save. As early as 1974 adherents of the environmentalist cause argued that nuclear power was uneconomic and dangerous, that carbon dioxide emissions should be reduced urgently, that CFCs should be banned and that the expenditure on weapons of mass destruction should be devoted instead to repairing the damage done to people and planet. If only others had acted on our advice then, the world would be a very much safer place today. Green politics is in a unique position to bring about the transformation needed to repair the planet.

The international green movement, with its common commitment to change from rampant industrial growth to sustainable management of the Earth's resources, has a job to do. There is no doubt that green politics will be an increasing force as the global environment worsens. Global ecocide is no longer questioned. Report after report, whether it be by scientists or by politicians, warns us that our present way of life is clearly unsustainable and that time is running out for change. We can no longer rampage across the Earth like indulged children, threaten each other with guns and bombs and leave three quarters of the world's population in abject poverty. We have to learn again how to interact with each other and how to build social structures based on need, not greed. We have to assume personal responsibility for the welfare of each other and the planet.

Green politics is a response to other forms of change. The old ideas no longer work, and we need new ways of looking at things. We need very different policies if we are to survive and prosper in the coming century – indeed, in the new decade. For example, we have shown that neither monetarist constraints nor Keynesian expansion works any more, if they ever did. Instead of burning up scarce resources to create short-term jobs at the expense of long-term sustainability, we need to encourage job sharing and introduce new patterns of work. To maintain standards of living we have to cut waste instead of pushing for growth. It is not enough to spend more money on health or, conversely, place caring on the market: we have discussed the need to tackle ill health at its roots. In the run-up to the 1979 general election, when unemployment was nearing the apocalyptic level of 1 million, the Saatchi brothers produced giant hoardings showing lengthening dole queues and the double-edged slogan 'Labour isn't working' for the then Conservative opposition. Ironically, given her economic record of not just 1 million but over 3 million unemployed, this marketing device, more than anything else, won Mrs Thatcher her position as Prime Minister. Greens would argue that not only Labour but all the old political traditions are obsolete. The world needs an alternative form of politics that will resist the storms inevitably to be whipped up by the greenhouse effect, not just to survive ecologically but also to navigate us through stormy social, cultural and economic change.

At the heart of the Green response to this challenge is the idea of interconnectedness, the understanding that all things are interrelated. Far from being single-issue, green politics is more sophisticated than the ideologies that have served us to date. Health, wealth and happiness cannot be reduced to purely monetary considerations. Politics in the 1980s was a crude, quantitative examination of costs. We argue that *qualitative* change is a precondition for getting things right. Good economic accounting, while necessary, is not an adequate answer to complex human dilemmas. Greens have a new and more advanced world view.

Green politics is different in the sense that it rejects conventional economics as the primary guide to the well-being of the nation.

Non-material values such as health, the welfare of the community and our relationships with each other must be part of the equation. Human progress, as measured by the amount of money in the exchequer, is an indicator of spiritual and creative poverty. The thing that makes our vision quite revolutionary is that we see economics as a tool for human progress, and the restoration of harmony with nature, and not as an end in itself. We totally reject the post-war conception of politics as the realization of greed and look to other goals.

Visions are all very well, but without concrete strategies to implement them they remain just visions. If we are to banish the nightmares of ecocide, exploitation and poverty, our dreams need to become reality. Without a means of getting politically from A to B, the green manifesto will remain little more than a manifesto for virtue, a collection of idealistic whims rather than a programme for achieving necessary change. Paradoxically, the task of restoring harmony will require struggle. It would be wrong of us, while seeking to end conflicts of class and culture, to pretend that such conflicts do not exist. Class antagonisms have to be overcome even when it might be easier, or at least electorally more expedient, to ignore them. We can protect the environment in ways that hurt the poor or in ways that protect the weak; we can conserve resources by introducing taxes that price the old into hypothermia, or we can work for nature while introducing greater equality. Green politics enhances the economic dilemmas of choice and scarcity rather than denying them. Whereas Marxism postulated a wealthy class of capitalists that lived off the backs of an impoverished reserve army of workers, Greens point out that we all live off each other's wealth. Through unfair terms of trade we take food out of the mouths of the hungry in South America and Africa, giving the Third World hardly anything in return for the cash crops and minerals we remove from their land. By squandering resources meant for the next generation and disrupting nature's capacity to sustain life, we take from our children and our children's children wealth that should be conserved for tomorrow. The decisions being made now affect not only us but all future generations. Above all, we steal from the natural world and from other species, enslaving and destroying, when we should be conserving and cooperating. Green politics demands that we side with the oppressed and not the oppressors. Green politics is about liberation.

The challenges are not minor. Politicians, bureaucrats and, perhaps most of all, advertising executives will try to take the radicalism out of green politics and salve public fears without initiating necessary change. We hope that we have shown you throughout this book the new priorities that must be established if we are to lead lives that are in harmony with the planet, priorities that require us to reach out for startlingly new ways of approaching politics and economics.

The new green consciousness has to emerge from the people themselves. Green politics is about grass-roots democracy and community involvement that allow people to make the decisions that affect their own lives, the lives of others all over the world and the health of the planet. If we are to learn to live with nature, we must first learn to live with each other. Green politics demands the overturn of patriarchal structures of power that rely on force to exist. It brings with it a new kind of power, the power of non-violence, which Greens believe is common to us all, to be used by all and for all. Only when we have discovered our own strengths rather than passively accepting power exercised by others will we be free to lead lives that are consistent with the ethics of green politics. When speaking to the International Green Congress in Stockholm, a founder of the German Greens, Petra Kelly, said:

> I believe we have so much power already today and I also believe we have much responsibility without joining any governments ... [We aim for] decentralism, global responsibility, developing at the grass-roots level, new soft technologies and soft energies scaled to comprehensible human dimension, developing a truly free and truly non-violent society in our own communities, showing solidarity across all national boundaries and ideologies with people who are repressed and discriminated against, practising civil disobedience against the nuclear and military state. All this can be done very effectively without having to send a lone Green minister into a Social Democratic cabinet – then making compromises all along the way to the point of no return.

Electoral success is vital, but it will not be enough. While we need Greens at Westminster so as to be in a position to legislate for change, legislation can at best only be part of a strategy of transformation.

The media constantly urge the party to cut corners and make its message more 'acceptable'. Some would argue that the situation is so urgent that the Greens must seize electoral power as swiftly as possible, whatever the cost. This approach, the one pursued by green 'pragmatists' in West Germany, has, in fact, been far from successful, as it has led to division and loss of support. Greens in Hesse ended up cutting teachers' pay and failing to oppose nuclear power while in coalition with the SPD. Indeed, Otto Schilley, former Green MP, has now joined the SPD.

All this is not to say that Greens should not play an active role in the electoral process, but they must not allow the pursuit of parliamentary power to cloud their vision. An electoral role allows the green message to reach the public. Legislative change is essential: at present, however green we act as individuals, we are prevented from living in balance with nature by the actions of successive governments. With over 100 councillors elected, the Greens have already shown that they can get things done on a local level across the country. While Greens have concrete policies of government, however, we would argue that the task of building a democratic, egalitarian and ecological society is one that demands the energy, enthusiasm and imagination of all of us.

SELECT BIBLIOGRAPHY

Green politics is a big subject. While we have criticized those who would reduce it to environmentalism and remove its political content, we in turn deserve criticism for not dealing with every area of importance. The following books fill in some of the gaps and look at spirituality and other green roots in greater detail than we have been able to do. They have guided us; we hope you find them useful as well.

Manifesto for a Sustainable Society, the Green Party. Available from Ecotrade Ltd, 2 Elbow Cottages, Hawton, Newark-on-Trent, NG24 3RW. Tel: 0636-700232. This is *the* Green Manifesto. Refined and redrafted by thousands of members of the party from the original document published in 1974, it is well worth studying in detail, though occasionally lacking in literary merit.

Remaking Society, Murray Bookchin, Black Rose Books, 1989.
The latest in a long line of vitriolic masterpieces from the grandfather of social ecology and East-coast anarchy. Highly recommended.

Green Pages, John Button, Optima, 1989.
The definitive guide to books, resources, ideas and organizations.

The Unsinkable Aircraft Carrier, Duncan Campbell, Paladin, 1986.
Britain as a giant missile platform.

The Eco Wars, David Day, Harrap, 1989.
'A concise encyclopedia of ecological activism'. Written in memory of Chico Mendes, Diane Fossey, Fernando Pereira and Hilda Murrell, it commemorates those murdered in defence of the planet, destroying for ever the myth that Green politics is a soft, middle-class option.

The Aquarian Conspiracy, Marilyn Ferguson, Paladin, 1982.
Not necessarily considered a traditional green book, but definitely a

powerful one, on the need for personal transformation and a new paradigm of power and politics.

To Have or To Be?, Erich Fromm, Abacus, 1984.
The Art of Loving, Erich Fromm, Unwin, 1987.
In these two books Fromm does it all, marrying ecology, socialism and spirituality to show how we can reject barren materialism and re-awaken our humanity.

A Fate Worse than Debt, Susan George, Penguin, 1988.
Susan George is an acclaimed expert on the problems of debt and the less-developed countries. She writes in a highly articulate and readable way and offers positive solutions to the world debt crisis. Highly recommended.

The Fate of the Forest, Suzanna Hecht and Alexander Cockburn, Verso, 1989/Penguin, 1990.
An examination of why the Amazon is burning and a clear guide to the politics of rainforest rescue.

The Coercive State, Paddy Hillyard and Janie Percy-Smith, Fontana, 1988.
A study of our declining democracy and eroding rights. Startling.

Fighting for Hope, Petra Kelly, Chatto and Windus, 1984.
This book by a founder of the German Greens is a collection of essays that take the reader through the principles of green politics. An insight into the need for personal empowerment as well as political action.

Towards an Ecological, Socialist Feminism, Mary Mellor, Virago, forthcoming.
A synthesis well worth waiting for!

What is Ecology?, David Owen, OPUS, 1989.
A valuable primer.

Seeing Green. Jonathon Porritt, Blackwell, 1984.
This volume by one of the pioneers who worked for the Green Party in its leanest years, while in need of an update, remains a classic.

The Self-managing Environment, Alan Roberts, Allison and Busby, 1979.

Roberts gets behind the doomsday scenario to explain the politics of ecology and the links between planetary salvation and human liberation. A book that has influenced the authors more than any other.

The Race for Riches, Jeremy Seabrook, Green Print, 1988.
As usual, the author argues sensitively for the combination of social justice and ecology.

The Politics of Hope, Jeremy Seabrook and Trevor Blackwell, Faber and Faber, 1988.
This is a highly personal, courageous and honest book based on the authors' experiences.

Animal Liberation, Peter Singer, Thorson, 1983.
Looks at one of the intellectual roots of greenery and shows that one cannot respect nature and abuse animals at the same time.

Economics and the Crisis of Ecology, N. Singh, Oxford University Press, 1989.
A pungent analysis of why greed and green don't mix.

The Battle for Bermondsey, Peter Tatchell, Heretic, 1983.
Shows the obstacles that are likely to be put in front of any radical alternative, whatever its colour.

Abandon Affluence!, Ted Trainer, Zed Press, 1989.
Quite simply this is the most detailed and best argued explanation of why we have to abandon greed and go green. If you don't read anything else, read this.

Getting There, Derek Wall with Penny Kemp, Peter Tatchell, Mary Mellor and Ted Trainer, Greenprint, 1990.
This is the first book to look at how we can achieve a green society, taking a tough look at how Greens can meet the realities of the political system within which we live and gain the power to bring about necessary change without being corrupted by it.

INDEX